The 1937
Newark
Bears

The 1937 Newark Bears

A Baseball Legend

Ronald A. Mayer

Rutgers University Press
New Brunswick, New Jersey

First published by Vintage Press, East Hanover, New Jersey, 1980

Reprinted by Rutgers University Press, New Brunswick, New Jersey, 1994

Copyright © 1980, 1985 by Ronald A. Mayer
All rights reserved
Manufactured in the United States of America

Library of Congress Cataloging–in–Publication Data
Mayer, Ronald A., 1934–
     The 1937 Newark Bears : a baseball legend / Ronald A. Mayer.
     p.   cm.
     Originally published: Wise Pub., 1980.
     Includes bibliographical references and index.
     ISBN 0-8135-2153-X (pbk.)
     1. Newark Bears (Baseball team)--History.   I. Title.
GV875.N47M39   1980   94-25334
796.357 ' 64 ' 0974932--dc20   CIP

To my wife Arlene,
my daughter Jacqueline,
and my son Glenn, who have
learned to live with a baseball nut

Contents

Acknowledgments   vii

Preface   ix

Team Roster   xv

1. A Year To Remember — 1937   3
2. Ruppert Buys the Bears   9
3. Weiss Joins The Team   19
4. The Championship — 1932   27
5. The Frustrating Years — 1933 and 1934   39
6. The Downhill Years — 1935 and 1936   57
7. Spring Training — 1937   73
8. Opening Day — 1937   101
9. On The Road   115
10. Out In Front By Eight   129
11. Twelve Days At Home   141
12. Atley Donald Sets Record   155
13. The Big Road Slump   169
14. Home Sweet Home   187
15. Clinched!   201
16. Batting Title Comes To Newark   215
17. Semifinal Play-Offs — Syracuse Chiefs   233
18. Final Play-Offs — Baltimore Orioles   247
19. Little World Series — At Newark   259
20. On To Columbus   275
21. The Parade   287

Postscript   289

Bibliography   293

Index   295

Acknowledgments

I WOULD LIKE TO EXPRESS MY GRATITUDE TO THE FOLLOWING for their valuable assistance: John Redding of the National Baseball Library in Cooperstown, Lowell Reidenbaugh, Managing Editor of the *Sporting News,* Willie Klein, Sports Editor of the *Newark Star Ledger,* Barbara Irwin of the New Jersey Historical Society, the Newark Public Library staff, Leslie Blasi, Sr., and Robert Waski.

In particular, I would like to thank the following ballplayers: Jack Fallon, for generously sharing his memories and allowing me to use photographs from his personal album, Jimmy Gleeson, for his comments and use of photographs, Spud Chandler, for his self-effacing reflections, as well as Joe Beggs, Atley Donald, and Marius Russo, for their kind thoughts. I would also like to thank the Newark Public Library for allowing me to use photographs from their files.

Above all, I would like to express my heartfelt thanks to two special people who helped make this book a reality: Barbara Burczynski, for her untiring assistance, and Ray Fagan, for his understanding and advice.

Ronald A. Mayer
East Hanover, New Jersey

Preface

FROM 1932 TO 1950, THE NEWARK BEARS BASEBALL TEAM OF THE International League was the top club in the New York Yankee farm system. The Bears, headed by Vice President George Weiss, developed and supplied hundreds of outstanding ballplayers to the parent club, helping to establish over the years the great Yankee dynasty.

During the span of eighteen years, the Newark Bears finished in the first division sixteen times, won seven pennants, and three Little World Series — a phenomenal achievement. It was not surprising that over that eighteen years, Newark built some mighty teams. According to most experts, however, the 1937 club ranks as their greatest.

This was the club that sewed up the pennant as early as August 24, boasting a 94-37 record with 23 games yet to play. And when the season finally ended, the Bears' record stood at 109-43, putting them 25½ games ahead of the second place Montreal Royals. During the post-season play-offs, Newark swept the Syracuse Chiefs four straight in the semifinals and the Baltimore Orioles four straight in the finals.

In the Little World Series, the Bears stunned the baseball world by losing their first 3 games at home to the Columbus Red Birds, the American Association pennant winner. Then in dramatic, story-book fashion, they came back to whip Columbus four straight for the Little World Series Championship. This performance convinced many knowledgeable baseball people that the Newark Bears of 1937 were the greatest minor league team in the history of professional baseball. Why did the experts consider them the ''wonder'' team? The answer was talent — a wealth of talent.

Every member of the team, including the Manager, Oscar Vitt, enjoyed major league careers beyond 1937 (the one exception was Jack Fallon). None made the Hall of Fame, but many had long and outstanding careers, leaving their lasting mark on the summer game. Others, although not achieving greatness, did enjoy distinguished careers. And then there were a few who could only boast they made the major leagues.

The 1937 Newark Bears possessed an extraordinary amount of ability. They could hit the long ball as well as for average. Their defense was solid; their pitching was strong and deep. In short, their lineup was a tower of strength.

The infield consisted of George McQuinn, a slick-fielding, solid hitting first baseman who would eventually help lead the St. Louis Browns to their only American League pennant in 1944. It would also take the better part of nine years for the Yankees to get Mc-Quinn back into the organization and on first base at Yankee Stadium.

At second was a brash, cocky, outspoken, self-confident young kid by the name of Joe Gordon. As a lead-off hitter, he led the Bears in home runs with 26. In 1938, he replaced the Yankee's popular Tony "push 'em up" Lazzeri and would star with the Bronx Bombers for seven years (MVP in 1942) before he told off Yankee owner Larry MacPhail and was shipped to Cleveland. At Cleveland, Gordon hooked up with shortstop Lou Boudreau to form one of the prettiest double play combinations in baseball.

"Good field, no hit" was the tag that followed shortstop Nolen Richardson throughout his professional baseball career. As fate would have it, however, the veteran Richardson was placed between two rookies and acted as the stabilizing and guiding influence for Gordon on his left and the 25-year-old third baseman, Babe Dahlgren, on his right.

Dahlgren, an excellent first baseman, was converted to the hot corner for two reasons — McQuinn's glove and his own bat. To prove the latter point, Dahlgren finished the '37 season with a .340 average. He would star in the major leagues for twelve years.

Behind the plate were two of the International League's outstanding catchers — Buddy Rosar and Willard Hershberger. Rosar would play one more year with the Bears, batting a lofty .387, before the Yankees would call him up for the '39 season. Unfortunately, the stocky catcher had to play in the shadows of the great Bill Dickey. His unpredictable disappearance for three days in July, 1941 — to take a police candidate's exam — sealed his fate and Rosar was eventually traded to Cleveland. With the Philadelphia Athletics in 1946, Buddy turned in his best year — catching in 121 games, batting a solid .283, and leading all catchers with 73 assists and a perfect 1.000 fielding average. It was an incredible defensive performance.

Hershberger, unlike Rosar, was sold to the Cincinnati Reds following the 1937 season. After limited playing time in 1938 and 1939, Hershberger was batting over .300 through July of 1940. On August 3, however, the moody and depressed catcher was found in the bathroom of his Boston hotel room — his jugular vein cut with a razor blade — a suicide victim at the early age of 29.

The outfield consisted of Jimmy Gleeson in left, Bob Seeds in center, and Charlie "King Kong" Keller in right field. Gleeson, after returning to the Bears in 1938, where he almost set a new record for two-base hits, was sold to the Chicago Cubs in August. Although Gleeson only enjoyed a .263 lifetime batting average, his second year with the Cubs was his finest. He batted a nifty .313 in 129 games, drove in 61 runs, and scored another 76. The rangy outfielder would eventually wind up in Cincinnati where he ended his short five-year major league career.

The much travelled Bob Seeds played center field and for obvious reasons was tagged with the nickname, "Suitcase Bob." In 1937, Seeds batted .303 with 20 home runs and led the Bears with 112 RBI's. The following year, on the strength of a .335 batting average, 28 home runs, and an amazing 95 RBI's after only 59 games, he was peddled by Weiss to the New York Giants for $40,000. Ironically enough, in his nine-year career in the major leagues, Seeds would only hit a total of 28 home runs, with 9 the most in any one season.

In right field was the class of the International League — a

21-year-old college kid named Charlie "King Kong" Keller. The muscular Maryland farm boy would lead the Bears to two consecutive championships — 1937 and 1938 — winning the batting title each year with averages of .353 and .365, respectively. In 1939, Keller would join the Yankees, Joe DiMaggio, and Tommy Henrich to form one of the greatest outfields in baseball history.

The Newark Bears story would not be complete without mention of utility infielder-outfielder, Francis Kelleher. The 21-year-old Kelleher played a key role throughout 1937, filling in for injured players and batting .305 in 93 games. Constantly blocked from cracking the famed outfield of DiMaggio, Henrich, and Keller, he was finally sold to the Cincinnati Reds in 1942.

On the mound, the Bears were unbeatable! The top four pitchers — Atley Donald, Joe Beggs, Steve Sundra, and Vito Tamulis — won 73 games and lost only 16 for a phenomenal .820 percentage. Donald, a determined young man with exceptional talent, won 19 games and lost only 2 during the season. At one point, he won 14 games in a row. Two years later in 1939, while pitching for the Yankees, Donald would chalk up 12 consecutive victories, a record at the time for a rookie in the American League. He would also help lead the Yankees to two pennants during his eight-year career.

The big right-hander, Joe Beggs, posted a superb 21-4 record during the regular season, also winning two play-off games and one Little World Series game. After a mediocre year with the Yankees, the sinker ball specialist was traded to Cincinnati and led the Reds in 1940 to an easy National League pennant and ultimately the World Championship.

The third right-hander, Steve "Smokey" Sundra, won 15 games and lost 4 before he was hospitalized in September for the removal of his appendix. He would miss both the play-offs and the Little World Series. The affable fastballer with the gargantuan appetite joined the Yankees in 1938, but he turned in his most outstanding season as a major league pitcher the following year. The Luxor, Pennsylvania native led the Yankees to their fourth straight pennant with an 11-1 record.

Vito Tamulis, who in the winter of 1935 almost ended his career with a serious case of pleurisy, posted an outstanding 18-6 record. One of the few southpaws on the club, Vito won his last 10 consecutive games. Playing in both the American and National Leagues, the diminutive lefty who possessed unusual confidence at an early age prompted Yankee Manager Joe McCarthy to comment, "He doesn't care whether the batter is Jimmy Foxx or Al Simmons. Some pitchers take years to acquire that poise."

There are other players who in part-time roles contributed significantly to this great Newark team. Pitcher Kemp Wicker, for example, joined the Bears in late May and won 7 games before returning to the Yankees in July. Outfielder Tommy Henrich stayed with the Bears for an even shorter period — seven days in early May — before McCarthy called "Old Reliable" back. In that brief period, however, he managed to hit a lofty .440 (11 for 25) and drive in seven runs.

A sore-armed Spurgeon "Spud" Chandler was also sent down by the Yankees late in the season to make room for a healthy pitcher in the Yankee pennant drive. Hampered by the sore arm, Chandler didn't pitch well for the remainder of the regular season. However, the right-hander made a major contribution by beating Columbus in the sixth game of the Little World Series.

Every great team has its share of unsung heroes and the Bears were no different. Journeyman pitcher Phil Page, reliefer Jack Fallon, knuckleballer John Niggeling, and Marius Russo, the rookie left-hander who would later become a Yankee great, all fit this unheralded class.

The man who orchestrated the entire team to perfection was the likeable and extroverted Oscar Vitt. "Ol Os," as he was affectionately called, managed ten years in the Pacific Coast League before joining the Bears. After his outstanding managerial job in 1937, Vitt was rewarded with the head job at Cleveland. Three years later, Vitt would be back on the West Coast, trying to figure out why a group of unhappy Cleveland players demanded that President Alva Bradley fire him. The players' revolt marked one of the strangest episodes in the history of major league baseball and earned them the nickname, "the Cleveland Crybabies."

It has been over forty years since the great 1937 Newark Bears played at Ruppert Stadium. During those years, the number of teams in the minor and major leagues has changed dramatically. The minor league ball clubs have dwindled to a little over 100 teams from a high of 464 in 1949. Jerry Izenberg vividly described it as ". . .a dying minor league system whose bare bones now bleach in half-dismembered minor league ball parks."

The major leagues have expanded from the traditional 16 teams to 26 (it's not over yet) and they continue to devour raw talent from the minors quicker than a Tom Seaver fastball. To field a team as versatile as the 1937 Bears would now take a minor miracle. It's as likely as someone breaking Joe DiMaggio's 56-game hitting streak or playing in more consecutive games than Lou Gehrig's 2,130. It just isn't done!

The 1937 Newark Bears are a once in a lifetime baseball legend. Hopefully this book will bring back memories for the hundreds of thousands of Newark fans who were part of that Legend. For those too young to have been there, maybe it will bring a bit of enjoyment and an appreciation for a team and a baseball era that has long since faded and will never return.

Ronald A. Mayer

Team Roster

THE TEAM ROSTER FOR THE 1937 NEWARK BEARS CHANGED drastically throughout the season. In an effort to build and maintain the strongest team possible, many players were either traded, sold, or sent to another club, while others were added. Yet despite all these changes, there were a number of steady players who appeared in major roles, contributing significantly to the successful 1937 season. For the most part, the Bears' roster consisted of the following (in alphabetical order):

JOSEPH STANLEY BEGGS

Pitched in the major leagues for nine years (1938-44, 1946-48) with the New York Yankees, Cincinnati Reds, and New York Giants. Finished with a 48-35 record and a 2.96 ERA. Best year was with the Reds in 1940: 12-3 record with 2.00 ERA, all in relief.

SPURGEON FERDINAND CHANDLER *(Spud)*

Pitched for eleven consecutive years (1937-47) with the New York Yankees and was interrupted only once when he joined the Newark Bears in August, 1937. Posted a lifetime record of 109 wins and 43 losses for a .717 percentage. Best year was 1943: led the league with 20 total victories, .833 win-loss percentage, 1.64 ERA, and 20 complete games. Also led the league in 1947 with a 2.46 ERA. Pitched in four World Series.

RICHARD ATLEY DONALD *(Swampy)*

Pitched for eight consecutive years (1938-45) with the New York Yankees, posting 65 victories against 33 losses for a .663 percentage. Best year was 1939: 13-3 record with 3.71 ERA. Pitched in two World Series.

ELLSWORTH TENNEY DAHLGREN *(Babe)*
Played first base for twelve years with nine different teams in both the American and National leagues. Finished with a lifetime batting average of .261. Best year was 1944 with the Pittsburgh Pirates: batted .289 and drove in 101 runs in 158 games. Played in one World Series.

JACK FALLON
Had an outstanding minor league career.

JAMES JOSEPH GLEESON *(Gee Gee)*
Played the outfield in the major leagues for five years with the Cleveland Indians, Chicago Cubs, and Cincinnati Reds. Had a lifetime batting average of .263. Best year was 1940 with the Cubs: batted .313 in 129 games.

JOSEPH LOWELL GORDON *(Flash)*
Played second base in the major leagues for eleven years with the New York Yankees and Cleveland Indians. Lifetime batting average was .268 with 253 home runs. Hit 25 or more home runs five times, drove in over 100 runs four times, and scored over 100 runs twice. Played in six World Series. Managed five years: Cleveland Indians (1958-60), Detroit Tigers (1960), and Kansas City Athletics (1961 and 1969).

WILLARD McKEE HERSHBERGER
Caught for three years (1938-40) with the Cincinnati Reds, batting .276, .345, and .309, respectively. Played in one World Series. Committed suicide at early age of 29.

FRANCIS EUGENE KELLEHER *(Frankie)*
Played in 47 games over two seasons (1942-43) with the Cincinnati Reds.

CHARLES ERNEST KELLER *(King Kong)*
Played the outfield in the major leagues for thirteen years with the

New York Yankees (1939-43, 1945-49, and 1952) and Detroit Tigers (1950-51). Had two outstanding back to back years: 1941 batted .298 with 122 RBI's and 102 runs scored, 1942 batted .292 with 108 RBI's and 106 runs scored. Played in four World Series.

GEORGE HARTLEY McQUINN

Played first base in the major leagues for twelve years with the Cincinnati Reds, St. Louis Browns, Philadelphia Athletics, and New York Yankees. Lifetime batting average was .276. Batted over .300 three times, scored 100 or more runs twice, and drove in 80 or more runs five times. Played in two World Series.

JOHN ARNOLD NIGGELING *(Johnny)*

Pitched in the major leagues for nine years with the Boston Braves, Cincinnati Reds, St. Louis Browns, and Washington Senators. Posted a lifetime record of 64-69 with a 3.22 ERA. Best year was 1942 with the Browns; 15-11 record with 2.66 ERA.

PHILIP RAUSAC PAGE *(Phil)*

Pitched in the majors for only four years with the Detroit Tigers and Brooklyn Dodgers, posting a 3-3 record. At the time Page was pitching with the Newark Bears, his major league career was over.

NOLEN CLIFFORD RICHARDSON

Played third base and shortstop for six years with the Detroit Tigers, New York Yankees, and Cincinnati Reds. Lifetime batting average was .247.

WARREN VINCENT ROSAR *(Buddy)*

Caught in the major leagues for thirteen years with the New York Yankees, Cleveland Indians, Philadelphia Athletics, and Boston Red Sox. Had a lifetime batting average of .261. Best year was 1946 with the A's: batted .283 in 121 games. Played in two World Series.

MARIUS UGO RUSSO *(Lefty)*

Pitched six years with the New York Yankees (1939-43 and 1946).

Posted a lifetime record of 45 wins and 34 losses with a 3.13 ERA. Best year was 1940: 14-8 record with 3.28 ERA. Pitched in two World Series.

ROBERT IRA SEEDS *(Suitcase Bob)*

Played the outfield in the major leagues for nine years with the Cleveland Indians, Chicago White Sox, Boston Red Sox, New York Yankees, and New York Giants. Had a lifetime batting average of .277. Played in one World Series.

STEPHEN RICHARD SUNDRA *(Smokey)*

Pitched nine years in the major leagues with the New York Yankees, Washington Senators, and St. Louis Browns. Best year was 1939 with Yankees: 11-1 record with 2.76 ERA. Posted a lifetime record of 56-41. Pitched in one World Series.

VITAUTIS CASIMIRUS TAMULIS *(Vito)*

Pitched six years in both the American and National leagues with the New York Yankees, St. Louis Browns, Brooklyn Dodgers, and Philadelphia Phillies. Had a lifetime record of 40 wins and 28 losses. Best year was with the Yankees in 1935: 10-5 record with 4.09 ERA.

OSCAR JOSEPH VITT *(Ossie)*

Played ten years in the major leagues at every position except pitcher and catcher. Split career between the Detroit Tigers and Boston Red Sox. Had a lifetime batting average of .238. Managed the Cleveland Indians for three years (1938-40), finishing in third place twice and in second place the last year.

KEMP CASWELL WICKER

Pitched in the major leagues for four years with the New York Yankees (1936-38) and one year with the Brooklyn Dodgers (1941). Finished his short career with 10 wins and 7 losses. Best year was 1937: promoted from the Bears to the Yankees during the season and posted a 7-3 record. Pitched in one World Series.

In addition to the names mentioned above, the following players appeared in minor roles for the Newark Bears during the 1937 season:

Lewis Blair	Jack LaRocca
Marvin Breuer	Bill Matheson
Walter Brown	Merrill May
Joe Gallagher	Pete Naktenis
Jack Glynn	Al Piechota
Pinky Hargrave	Cecil Spittler
Tommy Henrich	Bill Yocke

The 1937
Newark
Bears

1.

A Year To Remember 1937

I T WAS THE YEAR 1937. FRANKLIN DELANO Roosevelt, who several months earlier had trounced Alf Landon for the highest office in the land, delivered his inaugural address to begin his second consecutive term as President of the United States. Roosevelt again emphasized his objective of social justice. "The challenge to American Democracy," he said, is the "tens of millions of its citizens. . .who at this very moment are denied. . .the necessities of life. . .I see one-third of a nation ill-housed, ill-clad, ill-nourished."

Roosevelt was at the crest of his political fortune. But even in 1937, events moved swiftly. Only two weeks after his second inauguration, the President had to face problems which eventually led to shortening the life of the New Deal.

On February 5, Roosevelt unveiled his scheme of increasing the membership of the Supreme Court from nine to fifteen. Roosevelt's attempt to "pack" the Court met with strong congressional opposition and forced him to carry his fight to the people in his"fireside" radio chats.

On top of the Court blunder, Roosevelt was faced with still another problem — a wave of strikes which swept America. By early 1937, the "sit-down" strike reached epidemic proportions. Wives sat down against penny-pinching husbands; school children sat down against strict teachers; motorists sat down against apathetic street repair departments. It all came to a head on February 11, when General Motors capitulated and recognized the United Automobile Workers as the union instrument to represent labor.

In August, enthusiasm for Roosevelt was dealt an even more savage low. Just when the country appeared to be well on its way out of the Depression, there was a sudden economic setback. National income fell 13 percent, industrial production fell 33 percent, payrolls fell 35 percent, and profits, 78 percent. The result was coined in a new term "recession."

But not all events in 1937 were as gloomy as those in politics. After three years in production, Walt Disney introduced his first full-length animated film, *Snow White and the Seven Dwarfs.* Youngsters of all ages flocked to the movies to watch the lovable cavorting of Disney's dwarfs and to swoon over Prince Charming.

Snow White was an instant success, breaking all attendance records, grossing over $8 million, and translated into ten languages. It was called "the happiest thing. . .since the armistice." Critics were ecstatic not only about the brilliant animation, but also about the musical score. Such songs as *Heigh Ho, Whistle While You Work,* and *Some Day My Prince Will Come* were whistled or hummed by young and old alike. According to one legend, some of the sequences were so vivid that Radio City Music Hall had to reupholster all its seats after the movie's run. Apparently children were so terrified by Snow White's wicked stepmother that the seats were thoroughly drenched after each performance.

On the night of June 22, 1937 in Chicago's Comiskey Park, 60,000 screaming spectators were watching history being made in a fashion far different from *Snow White.* Joe Louis, the Brown Bomber from Detroit, knocked out James J. Braddock, the Irishman from New York's West Side, for the heavyweight title of the world.

Round after round, Braddock absorbed punishment, particularly around the head. Lacerations and bruises turned his pleasant Irish face into an unrecognizable mask. In the eighth round, after some polite sparring, Louis ripped a left hook to the body and brought another left hook to the jaw. Braddock wobbled on uncertain legs, his guard down. Louis followed with a pile-driving right that dropped Braddock to the canvas, battered, bruised, and bleeding, his title gone after one minute and ten seconds into the eighth round.

While the Louis fans were victory dancing in Chicago, the rest of the nation was doing the Big Apple. This national craze was described by *Variety*, the entertainment newspaper, in these words: "It requires a lot of floating power and fannying."

Also on the bright and happy side was *Variety's* pick of the Top Fifteen Tunes of 1937. High on the list and played by the great swing bands of the country were *Boo Hoo, Chapel in the Moonlight, So Rare, Harbor Lights,* and *That Old Feeling.*

The year 1937 had its share of tragedies also. Ironically, both were of the air. In 1932, pretty Amelia Earhart stole the hearts of America by flying across the Atlantic ocean alone, from Harbor Grace, Newfoundland to Ireland. She was the first woman to fly from Honolulu to the mainland of the United States, and the first solo pilot to fly across the United States in both directions.

But in the same year, all America mourned when Miss Earhart lost her life during a nearly successful attempt to fly around the world. Her airplane vanished at sea near Howland Island in the Pacific Ocean.

In 1937, the Hindenburg was the pride of Germany and the symbol of post-war German commercial expansiveness. The huge dirigible with sleeping accomodations for seventy had made the trip between Frankfurt, Germany and Lakehurst, New Jersey with the regularity of an ocean liner.

But at the end of a regular flight on May 6, the Hindenburg exploded in midair as it was attempting to land on the airfield in Lakehurst. Later it was found that a spark from static electricity ignited some leaking hydrogen. As it lay in glowing ruins, thirty-six of the ninety-seven passengers were lost. It was an event seen and heard by millions. In some uncanny way, the destruction of the Hindenburg came to symbolize the end of an era of innocence in which there was still hope of avoiding war.

There was no question that the major broadway productions of 1937 were inspired by the daily newspaper headlines. In addition to *Hooray for What!,* the year spotlighted three daringly topical musicals. June brought *The Cradle Will Rock,* a parable on the evils of capitalism and the virtues of labor. *Pins and Needles,* which arrived in the fall, touched on many topics of concern to members of the International Ladies Garment Workers Union. It drew rave reviews, ran for four years (a record at the time), and gave a command performance in the White House. However, the theatrical event of the year, and possibly of the decade, was *I'd Rather Be Right,* which became the first musical ever to deal directly with a living President of the United States and his administration. To top it off, George M. Cohan's portrayal of F.D.R. won the acting honors of the year.

And the comedy of the year was *You Can't Take it With You.* Critic Richard Lockridge aptly described the mad farce in these words: "There is not a fleck of satire in *You Can't Take it With You,* but only gargantuan absurdity, hilariously preposterous antics, and the rumble of friendly laughter with madly comic people." As it turned out, this was exactly what thousands of playgoers apparently hungered for in 1937.

Literature during the thirties, in the opinion of some critics, failed to fulfill the promise of the twenties. Specifically, Ernest Hemingway's *To Have and To Hold,* which dealt with the career of an American gangster, found less favor than his earlier books. However, *The Late George Apley* by John Marquand laid bare the sterility of the so-called cultured circles in New England. On the other hand, John Dos Passos gained his greatest success with the trilogy, *U.S.A.,* composed of *The 42nd Parallel, Nineteen Nineteen,* and *The Big Money.* Dos Passos surveyed American life from 1900 to 1930 in many varied aspects. What he portrayed was not pleasant; his more unscrupulous characters gained material success, while the few who aspired to improve the world were frustrated. Finally, in 1937, John Steinbeck's *Of Mice and Men* was published — the pathetic tale of the frustrated desire of two itinerant farm laborers for a small farm of their own.

This was the year 1937. A year in which a sense of uncertainty and uneasiness prevailed, interrupted occasionally by the tragic, the absurd, the shocking, the brilliant, and luckily, by some craziness.

In the world of baseball, the big news of 1937 was the Newark ball club of the International League — the greatest collection of minor league players in the history of baseball.

The Newark Bears, only five years in existence under the ownership of Colonel Jacob Ruppert and the New York Yankees, fielded a team of exceptionally talented ballplayers. Managed by the colorful and often demanding Oscar Vitt, they stormed through the International League to win the pennant by an unbelievable 25½ games. As a matter of fact, by early June there was little doubt, even by the most optimistic challengers, that the Bears were in a class by themselves.

If the Bears dominated regular season play, they steamrolled through the play-offs. Syracuse and Baltimore were destroyed in quick, precision-like fashion. The Little World Series, however, was a different matter. Off to a disastrous start, the Bears saw the series slipping away and their incredible season indelibly tarnished. Against unbelievable odds, they rallied and gallantly fought back to finally beat the Columbus Red Birds of the American Association. As destiny would have it, the Bears' victory in the Little World Series forced them to show the public the one quality that remained untested all season. Call it what you will — determination, courage, pride, heart, guts — it's a team trait that separates the near-great from the great. And the 1937 Newark Bears were unquestionably the greatest! This is their incredible story, which all began back in late 1931.

Courtesy National Baseball Library, Cooperstown, New York

Millionaire beer baron Jacob Ruppert, sole owner of the New York Yankees from 1923 to 1939, bought the Newark Bears in 1931. He liked to think of baseball as his hobby.

2.

Ruppert Buys The Bears

O N NOVEMBER 12, 1931, COLONEL JACOB RUPPERT, owner of the New York Yankees, purchased the Newark, New Jersey Baseball Club of the International League. Ruppert's business associate, Ed Barrow, announced to the press "that the Yankee owner had bought entire control of the club from Paul Block, newspaper publisher and sole owner of the Bears for the past four years."

Neither Ruppert nor Block would reveal the amount of money involved in the purchase, which included the league franchise, players, property holdings, and 100 percent controlling interest in stock. However, baseball insiders believed the price to be about $350,000. Some reports reached as high as $600,000.

Commenting on the purchase, the outgoing owner said, "I sold the Newark Baseball Club to my friend, Colonel Jacob Ruppert, owner of the New York Club known as the Yankees.

"I think the baseball fans of Newark will agree that I tried hard to give them winning baseball during the four years I owned the Bears, and although we were not very lucky at first, last season we came within two games of first place.

"Rochester, which has won the pennant in our league for three consecutive seasons, as everyone knows, is owned by the St. Louis Cardinals and naturally this ownership has been very helpful to the Rochester Club. I am confident that Colonel Ruppert, who is one of the finest gentlemen in sports in the country, will, because of his ownership of the New York Yankees, be able to do more for the Bears than I could. After all, I am only a newspaperman.

"I feel certain our baseball fans in greater Newark will be pleased at the news, as it will no doubt give Newark better baseball than it has ever had before."

Under Block's ownership from 1928 through the 1931 baseball season, his teams showed steady improvement but never won a pennant. In his first year, Block hired Walter Johnson, the immortal Hall of Fame pitcher, as his manager. But the "Big Train's" right arm couldn't help him in the dugout as the Bears finished a miserable seventh. In 1929, Block hired another Hall of Famer, outfielder Tris Speaker, with much the same results. The Bears finished a weak sixth. Speaker returned in 1930 and managed until the end of June, when he resigned under pressure from Block. The end for Speaker came swiftly when Block paid a visit to the stadium, didn't see his manager in left field, and then watched Montreal destroy the Bears before a slim, unenthusiastic crowd. Al Mamaux, one of the Bears' top pitchers at the time, replaced Speaker and brought the team from seventh to fifth, slightly better than the previous year.

Ironically, Block's best season was his last. In 1931, under a full season of Mamaux's popular leadership, the Bears finished second after waging a strong fight for the pennant down to the final week.

The sale and purchase of the Newark Bears was inevitable and both parties knew it. Block, as he admitted, was "only a newspaperman," but astute enough in business to realize that the Bears needed the financial resources of a major league organization, along with dedicated management from baseball professionals.

Ruppert knew full well, although he denied it repeatedly in public, that an extensive farm system was needed to succeed in major league baseball during the 1930's. Often he would be reminded of the continued success of the World Champion St. Louis Cardinals with their elaborate chain system totaling fourteen ball clubs.

The story has been told that in the fall of 1931, Yankee General Manager Ed Barrow, Field Manager Joe McCarthy, and scouts Paul Krichell and Gene McCann went to Ruppert's brewery with the idea of talking the Colonel out of starting a farm system. Ruppert had been reading about Branch Rickey's farm chain with the Cardinals and felt he might be missing something. After the meeting, all four visitors were secretly smiling to themselves because of the favor they had done the Colonel by talking him out of starting a farm system. On the way back from Ruppert's office, Barrow said, "Well, I guess we took care of that."

A few weeks went by before Barrow received an unexpected phone call. "I've just bought the Newark Club," Ruppert told him. Barrow was stunned in amazement. Max Steuer, the famous criminal lawyer who was also Paul Block's attorney, walked into Ruppert's office one morning at 8:30 and sold him the Newark team and the ball park.

Sitting behind the broad mahogany table in his office a few days after the purchase announcement, Ruppert made remarks that clearly indicated the farm system was on his mind. "We want the fans with us over in Newark. We want a winner. The happiest moment of my life will come next fall if the Yankees knock off the Cardinals in the World Series and the Bears beat out Rochester and trounce Columbus in the Little World Series." Turning to Barrow, he commented, "Goodness, Ed, I don't know what I'll do next fall; I can't see both teams play in the two series."

Colonel Jacob Ruppert was a New York aristocrat whose father had been a millionaire brewer. He owned race horses, was a member of the Jockey Club, and exhibited his St. Bernards at the Westminster Kennel Club show in Madison Square Garden. He was a fastidious dresser, who changed his clothes several times a day, wore custom-made shoes, and had a valet. He collected jades, porcelains, and first editions. He belonged to the Seventh Regiment of the New York National Guard — the "silk stocking" regiment — and at the age of twenty-two, was appointed a colonel on the staff of Governor Hill. His yacht, the Albatross, was one of the best known in its day. He served four terms in Congress, was considered one of the most eligible bachelors in town, and never quit being one. He claimed he enjoyed the company of women, but that men married only because they were lonely or needed a housewife. Ruppert attended the Columbia School of Mines but cared little for it. At nineteen, he went to work in his father's brewery at Ninety-First Street and Third Avenue. There he washed beer kegs twelve hours a day for ten dollars a week. After working at various jobs learning the business from the ground up, he was given a chance in the office. Immediately he showed executive talent and became general manager at twenty-three. At twenty-nine, he succeeded his retired father as President. By the time he was forty-eight, Ruppert was a wealthy man. He made millions in real estate and millions more in beer. But he was not happy until he became deeply involved in his hobby — baseball. He often said, ". . .any man goes to seed if he fails to have a real hobby."

On January 11, 1915, Ruppert plunged headlong into his hobby by purchasing the New York Yankees for $460,000 with Colonel Tillinghast L'Hommedieu Huston as half-owner. At the time, the ball club was a chronic second division team.

After the Yankees finished third in 1919, Manager Miller Huggins suggested to Ruppert that Babe Ruth could be purchased from the Boston Red Sox. It turned out to be the biggest deal in baseball. In addition to the purchase price of $125,000, the Yankees made a $350,000 loan to Harry Frazee, the perennially hard-pressed Red Sox owner. Frazee, a theatre buff, needed ready cash for the purpose of backing a new Broadway musical called *No, No, Nanette.* Frazee mortgaged his ball park as security.

Following the 1920 season, the Yankees were kicked out of the Polo Grounds by John McGraw. In May, 1921, Ruppert and Huston paid $600,000 to the Astor estate for a plot of land in the Bronx directly across the Harlem River from the Polo Grounds. A year later, the house that Ruth built was completed. Some thought it should be named Ruth Field, but Ruppert insisted on Yankee Stadium.

After years of bickering and disagreements, Huston finally sold his half of the club to Ruppert for $1,500,000 — six times what he paid for it a little more than eight years earlier. Ruppert, in turn, sold Barrow a small percentage, making the General Manager a part owner in a minor but profitable way.

During Ruppert's ownership and until his death in January, 1939, his Yankee teams won ten pennants, seven World Championships, and finished in second place six times. From 1921 through 1938, Ruppert's Yankees finished first or second every year except 1925 and 1930 — an outstanding achievement!

Although the purchase of the Newark Bears was gratifying to Ruppert, it was also a celebrated event in the greater Newark area where the fans were hungry for a winner. Ruppert received many letters and telegrams congratulating him and wishing him well on his purchase. The most celebrated message, however, came from Hollywood and was sent to the *Newark Evening News:*

Newark is a great city and Ruppert a great fellow. It's a fine thing for the Yankees to have their own ball club where they can direct the development of new men. Looks like Newark will have a winner now. I'll be seeing you all in Newark.

Signed
Babe Ruth

When the fanfare finally ended, what faced Ruppert and his close associates, especially Barrow, was a great deal of hard work. If any one could do the job, Barrow was the man. Ken Sobol, in his book, *Babe Ruth and the American Dream,* characterized Barrow as "a sturdy, bullet-headed, hard-faced storm trooper of a man; he demanded instant and slavish obedience from anyone working for him and was capable of cursing out the smallest mistake made by a subordinate."

Ruppert was planning a total reorganization of the Bears from top to bottom. At the executive level, he wanted experienced and astute baseball men, along with a widespread scouting system. On the field, he wanted top-notch players who would quickly bring a pennant to Newark. In the dugout, he wanted leadership. But as Ruppert was frank to admit, selecting a new manager posed a tougher job than signing Babe Ruth.

The selection of a manager for the Bears in 1931 resembled a hotly contested political race with every eligible candidate throwing his hat into the ring. The early list of hopefuls consisted of Eddie Holly, the unsigned manager of the Montreal Royals, and Cy Perkins, the Philadelphia Athletics' fifteen-year veteran catcher who had seen reserve duty for the Yankees in 1931. The 37-year-old Herb Pennock, a Yankee left-hander since 1933, was also under consideration, along with teammate star center fielder, Earl Combs. Some considered Combs an early favorite since he was close to Joe McCarthy and both were sticklers for discipline and clean living. Rounding out the Yankee player contingency was third baseman Joe Sewell, who played in 130 games in 1931, his first season with the Yankees. From 1920 to 1930, Sewell starred for the Cleveland Indians. If the Yankees wanted a playing manager, it was felt Sewell had plenty of active years left.

Another candidate was Art Fletcher, a thirteen-year veteran shortstop and a former manager in the major leagues. Fletcher managed the Philadelphia Phillies from 1923 to 1926 and led the Yankees to a second place finish in 1929. Also mentioned were Jack Onslow, the former coach of the Bears, his brother, Eddie, and finally, Bill Clymer, the former Newark manager. Applications kept pouring into Ruppert's office each day and it was rumored that the total at one point reached fifty. One of the more glamorous names considered was that of Charles Dillon Stengel. But it was reported that Casey was heading for Brooklyn as a coach.

After weeks of dominating the Newark press, the choice for manager narrowed to Al Mamaux and former Yankee pitcher Bob Shawkey. Shawkey, who had been obtained from the Philadelphia Athletics on waivers halfway through the 1915 season, starred for the Yankees from 1916 to 1927. In his fifteen years in the majors, he chalked up 198 victories against 150 losses. He also turned in four twenty-game years and pitched in eight World Series games.

After the death of Yankee Manager Miller Huggins in September, 1929, Barrow decided to choose the steady and dependable Shawkey, who seemed to be a wise choice. But Shawkey was burdened from the start with two hardships. One was that he succeeded Huggins; the other was that he had been "one of the boys" for a long time. His troubles began early. His first mistake was being too lenient with the players. They stayed out late at night, did as they pleased, and almost openly scoffed at him when he tried to discipline them. There were frequent rumbles in the clubhouse and dugout.

Nonetheless, Shawkey did a good job with the Bears and the team finished in third place behind the Athletics and the Senators. Despite the team's improvement, however, both Ruppert and Barrow had come to the conclusion that Shawkey was not the man they wanted. After all, the situation in Newark was different. Shawkey wasn't following a manager who had been a legend and he was continually faced with long-time teammates openly rebelling.

The biggest asset Al Mamaux had going for him was his immense popularity with the Newark fans. Without question, he was the most popular manager Newark had in years. There wasn't a day that passed without Ruppert hearing from the Newark fans urging the selection of Mamaux. Letters and petitions from organizations, public officials, and private citizens kept pouring into Ruppert's office. Three such letters were received by the Sports Editor of the *Newark News:*

At the last regular meeting of Newark Aerie No. 44 Fraternal Order of Eagles, a resolution was adopted by a unanimous vote to write to Colonel Jacob Ruppert endorsing Al Mamaux for appointment as manager of the Newark Bears.

The large membership of the Eagles feels that because of the altruistic service rendered during the past year by Al, he should continue as the leader of the Bears for the ensuing year.

Very sincerely yours,

Charles P. McCann,
Secretary

The following letter has been sent by me to Colonel Ruppert in the interest of Al Mamaux:

The people of Newark are very glad to know that you have taken over the Newark baseball team and we are all rooting for a pennant team in 1932.

As you probably know, during the past few years the team has made an uphill fight under great handicaps and the past year under the management of Al Mamaux, it made a wonderful showing.

Mamaux is a popular man with the people of Newark and he is a man who gets along well with players. He is a fine character, very reliable, and a perfect gentleman. I know that the people of Newark would be very glad if Mamaux were to be continued in his present position as manager of the team. He keeps good order on the field even when the umpires make mistakes, and I think you would find him an extremely fine representative in charge of your new team.

Personally, and I know him pretty well, I should be very glad indeed to know that your decision had been in favor of Mamaux as manager.

With best wishes for the season of 1932 in all your baseball activities, I am, very truly yours,

John P. Murray, Jr.,
Director of Public Works
City of Newark

One vote to keep Al Mamaux as the Bears' manager.

F.J. Braun
64 St. Paul Avenue
Newark

In addition to the letters, there were a number of petitions containing the names of the faithful Newark fans voicing their approval of Mamaux. The most impressive was submitted to Ruppert by John P. Rooney. It contained sixteen hundred names! The popularity contest finally got to Ruppert, who announced to the press that he would give Mamaux every possible consideration, but did not want to be "bludgeoned" into naming him if there was someone better.

On November 30, 1931, the *Newark Evening News* went on record by writing: "As to the Newark Bears, our guess is that Bob Shawkey will be Colonel Ruppert's choice, though Peple's [sic] choice may be Mamaux."

Three days later on December 3, the front page of the *News* carried the following headline:

MAMAUX NAMED BEARS' MANAGER
GETS ONE-YEAR CONTRACT AT OLD JOB
MIKE KELLY TO ASSIST HIM

The race was finally over. Ruppert, facing the press clearly and emphatically, stated that Mamaux would be in full charge of the Bears and would have the final word in selecting the players. To Newark fans, the Colonel made it perfectly clear that players sent to Newark would be there for at least one year, even if the Yankees' pennant chances were jeopardized for need of a star player in a close race. This was what the Newark fans wanted to hear and Ruppert knew it. In the years ahead, with only a few exceptions, he would stick to his word.

In addition to Mamaux as Manager, the Bears picked up Mike Kelly to take over their coaching duties. The peppery Kelly had been a former coach with the Chicago White Sox and had good experience with handling young ballplayers. He had also managed in the American Association for many years, winning pennants for St. Paul, the Yankee farm club under Miller Huggins. Topping off these executive appointments was Wilbur Crelin, the Bears' new Secretary.

Now that the race was over, Ruppert, Barrow, and Mamaux could settle down and turn their full attention to rebuilding the team. But this didn't last long. Scarcely two months went by before the shrewd Colonel announced a block buster appointment at the executive level. It would not only affect the near-term fortunes of the Bears, but more importantly, it would shape the future successes of the New York Yankees.

3.

Weiss Joins The Team

O N FEBRUARY 12, 1932, COLONEL JACOB RUPPERT NAMED George Weiss Vice President of the Bears and Vice President of all minor league enterprises operated by Ruppert. Weiss was also given the additional title of Assistant Secretary of the Yankees. Ruppert was obviously grooming Weiss to take over the Yankee position of his long-time friend and confidant, Ed Barrow, upon Barrow's retirement.

At the time Weiss accepted Ruppert's offer, he was serving as Vice President and General Manager of the Baltimore Orioles. For ten years before coming to Baltimore, he had owned and successfully operated the New Haven club in the Eastern League. He joined the Orioles in February, 1929, following the death of Jack Dunn. In his three-year period with the team, Weiss succeeded in doubling the attendance by introducing Boys' Day and Ladies' Day in Baltimore. Twice a week, the ladies were admitted free, while he had an organization of 8,000 boys registered to promote sportsmanship and interest in baseball. It is reported that his selling and trading of ballplayers brought more than $240,000 to the Orioles and that he left a surplus profit of $120,000. He showed sound judgment in choosing players and quickly built a reputation for square dealing.

Commenting on his new position with the Bears, Weiss said, "I have faith in Newark. It has always been a wonderful baseball city as well as a leading industrial center and noted for its civic enterprise."

George Martin Weiss began his executive career in baseball as early as high school when he became business manager of the New Haven High School team. It was this team that was destined to play a vital role in his life.

After graduation in 1915, the high school players stayed together and formed an independent semiprofessional team called the New Haven Colonials. Weiss naturally became their manager and director. At the time, he was a junior at Yale. His brilliant business mind and flair for promoting quickly had the Colonials outdrawing the established New Haven entry in the professional Eastern League.

Because he had to stay in New Haven due to his father's death, Weiss began in earnest to develop his team. It was not unusual for him to load the Colonials with top college athletes and big leaguers like Wally Pipp of the Yankees and Ty Cobb of the Tigers. In addition, the Federal League battle that was raging at the time forced the established New Haven club to quit organized ball, leaving the field wide open to the Colonials.

Weiss then began to book major league clubs for exhibitions. To meet this type of competition, he had to build a stronger, more competitive team. As the Colonials prospered, his reputation began to spread among major league circles.

Once the Federal League battle ended, it spelled trouble for Weiss. The New Haven club returned to the Eastern League and, with the backing of organized ball, stopped Weiss from booking exhibition games with major league clubs. Weiss countered by taking his Colonials to Waterbury, Connecticut. That move didn't last long. Weiss didn't like Waterbury and quickly returned to New Haven. There he proceeded to make arrangements to pay the local club for the right to book big leaguers at Lighthouse Point, just outside the city limits.

In the fall of 1916, Weiss booked the World Champion Boston Red Sox along with their star pitcher, Babe Ruth. Byron Bancroft Johnson, better known as "Ban," founder and President of the American League, got wind of the game and objected to it. In a bold move, he took the World Champion's medals away from the

Red Sox. Johnson also stopped Weiss and the Colonials from arranging any further games with major league teams.

In spite of this move, the New Haven club was going from bad to worse. By 1919, the owners of the New Haven franchise decided it was too difficult to compete with Weiss and offered to sell him the club for $5,000.

Weiss quickly jumped at the offer, commenting afterwards, "I had to borrow every bit of the $5,000, but I realized this was an opportunity that could not be passed up." Weiss shrewdly signed his own players and began selling them for large profits to major league teams.

In 1920, Weiss built a new ball park, appropriately naming it after himself, and began to develop players for the major league market. The New Haven club was entering a new era of prosperity. This was also the year Weiss entered his first business venture with Yankee General Manager Ed Barrow. Weiss booked the Yankees to play an exhibition game with his New Haven team. When the newly-acquired Babe Ruth didn't show up for the Yankees, Weiss refused to pay Barrow his guarantee. Barrow took his case to Commissioner Landis. But to the outrage of Barrow, the Commissioner supported Weiss. In later years, Barrow would recall this incident, realizing Weiss was the kind of hard-nosed, frugal, cunning business man he wanted running the Yankee's farm system.

Weiss operated the New Haven club until 1929, the year he joined Baltimore. During that time, he was always in the first division and he sold more players than all the other league clubs combined. His teams won three pennants and his fame continued to spread.

In December, 1931 at the minor league meeting in West Baden, Indiana, Weiss was chosen to run the Newark Club and begin the formation of a Yankee farm system.

"There he is," Barrow said to Ruppert in the lobby of the hotel the night they arrived for the meeting.

"There's who?" Ruppert asked, surprised.

"The man we want to run the Newark club."

"Who is he?"

"George Weiss."

Ruppert had never heard of him. "Who's Weiss?" he asked. "He knows as much about minor league baseball as anyone in the country," Barrow replied. "He knows the International League especially."

Weiss hadn't been in the Yankee organization very long before he began to preach the virtues of the farm system. He told Ruppert, "You have some small minor league connections now. Tie them in with Newark, get a couple more to fill in the spaces in between, and the first thing you know, you'll have a system that will be feeding players right up the line to the Yankees, with the Newark club as the proving ground."

And what a farm system Weiss developed! It was a marvel of organization. By the mid-1930's, he had fifteen teams either owned outright or sponsored on a working agreement basis, covering the entire gamut from Class D to AA. And because Weiss often shifted affiliations, he had new farm clubs springing up all over the country. Among others, there were teams at different times in Kansas City, Kansas; Joplin and Neosho, Missouri; Springfield, Massachusetts; Amsterdam, Binghamton, and Wellsville, New York; Snow Hill, North Carolina; Akron, Ohio; Butler and Easton, Pennsylvania; Beaumont and El Paso, Texas; Bassett and Norfolk, Virginia; and Fond du Lac, Wisconsin.

Several years after starting the farm system, Weiss would proudly comment, "Under chain government, a minor club takes financial set backs without quitting. We are developing players not only for replacement, but for making trades easier. You see, while we are building ballplayers, we always are ready to pay cash for them, too.

"We are doing our business for the best interests of baseball. Colonel Ruppert's policy is 'Never keep a man down.' If we cannot use him, he is given his chance with some other big league club."

Weiss remained with the Yankee organization for twenty-nine years, from 1932 to 1960, as Farm Director and then General Manager. During this period, he had a hand in signing virtually every player who saw action with the Yankees. The results were phenomenal. The Yankees won nineteen pennants and fifteen

World Championships. Weiss was given much of the credit because of his baseball genius and the highly productive farm system he developed.

Then in November, 1960, Weiss retired, issuing a one-sentence statement, "After forty-two years of operating clubs in organized baseball, twenty-nine with the Yankees, I have decided to avail myself of a clause in my contract, entered into in 1958, which will relieve me of full-time duty as General Manager of the Yankees as of December 31. . ."

His retirement was short-lived, however. In the winter of 1961, he was appointed the first President of the newly-organized New York Mets. His first move was to hire his old Yankee manager, Casey Stengel. This move helped to ensure the team's popularity and always kept Shea Stadium packed. Weiss held the Mets' presidency for more than five years, retiring in November, 1966 at the age of seventy-two.

Although retired, the architect of the Yankee dynasty left Met baseball fans with a solid foundation for the future. Most of the players on the Mets' 1969 World Championship team had been developed under Weiss. He had signed Tom Seaver, Jerry Koosman, Nolan Ryan, Tug McGraw, Cleon Jones, Ed Kranepool, and Bud Harrelson, among others.

In 1971, George Weiss won election to Baseball's Hall of Fame in Cooperstown, New York. The award marked the culmination of his long career of baseball excellence. In August of the following year, he died in Greenwich, Connecticut at the age of seventy-eight.

Despite his baseball genius, it was physically impossible for Weiss to cover every campus and sandlot throughout the country, searching to find young raw talent with a major league future. Fortunately, he inherited an outstanding team of scouts — baseball men with years of experience who could unerringly recognize and evaluate prospective major leaguers.

Dedicated men like Bill Essick, Gene McCann, Johnny Nee, and many more served as Weiss' arms and legs. This team of scouts was headed by none other than the super scout of them all, Paul

Krichell, the former St. Louis Browns' catcher with the slightly bowed frame. Back in the 1930's, it was often unclear which scout signed a particular ballplayer or who was instrumental in influencing a young kid to join the Yankee organization. One of the reasons for this was that more than one Yankee scout would often participate in the evaluation of a player's skills. On many occasions, Krichell would join the regional scout in convincing an eager boy and his proud parents of the advantages of a future with the New York Yankee organization. Regardless of who actually signed a ballplayer, the fact remains that the track record of the Yankee scouts was outstanding. It was the foundation on which the Yankee dynasty was built.

At one time, Krichell headed a twenty-man staff who scoured the country looking for young athletes. In the late 1950's, Casey Stengel said this about Krichell: "Maybe Krich has guessed wrong once in a while, although I can't point my finger at it. But for everyone he missed, Paul has come up with fifteen good ones. His record with the Yankees under different managers speaks for itself. He's never been fired."

Barrow considered Krichell "the best judge of ballplayers" he had ever seen, trusting implicitly in his scouting choices. As Krichell once recalled, "Barrow's three favorite words were 'proceed at once.' The way I used to get out of town, you'd think the cops were after me."

The list of ballplayers discovered by Krichell and his staff prior to and during Weiss' long involvement with the Yankee organization read like a *Who's Who* of baseball. Gehrig, Gordon, Rizzuto, Ford, DiMaggio, Dickey, Chandler, Donald, Keller, Murphy, Rolfe, Borowy, and Raschi were just some of the great names that Krichell had a hand in signing.

But scouting reports were not just limited to players. Krichell once told Barrow, "Keep that man McCarthy in mind. If anything should ever happen to Hug, he'd make a good manager for us."

The purchase of Joe DiMaggio was an excellent example of the total faith Weiss had in his scouts. Bill Essick was sent out to the West Coast to look at the sensational DiMaggio, who was then playing for the San Francisco Seals. Many other clubs were interested in him, but were frightened off by a report that he suffered a knee injury while playing shortstop. Essick, however, poking around on his own, found that DiMaggio had not hurt his knee while playing shortstop, but had injured it getting out of an automobile.

Essick was sold on DiMaggio. He convinced Weiss to make a deal for him, regardless of the cost. At the time, Barrow was still suspicious of DiMaggio's physical condition and tried to block the purchase. But Weiss, solely on Essick's recommendation, went over Barrow's head to owner Jacob Ruppert. The Colonel gave his approval and DiMaggio was bought for $25,000.

The greatest discovery of all was made by the top ivory hunter himself, Krichell. With a deep sigh, he recalled the events that led to the signing of Lou Gehrig. "In 1922, I saw Gehrig for the first time. It was in a game between Columbia and Rutgers at New Brunswick, New Jersey. He was a big, gawky, left-handed pitcher then. When he was not on the mound, Lou, because of his tremendous power, played the outfield or first base.

"That particular day, Gehrig was the pitcher, but during batting practice, I watched him clout a couple over the trees, about 375 feet away. I was excited. Three days later at South Field in New York, I saw him hit a ball onto the library steps in a game with Penn. That was a drive of more than 400 feet.

"Immediately, I called Barrow. I told him I had discovered the next Babe Ruth. Barrow told me not to get so excited, but ordered me to deliver Lou to the Yankee office on Monday morning. Gehrig, his college coach, Andy Coakley, and I appeared on time and Gehrig was signed." To obtain Gehrig's signature, Krichell had to shell out a $1,500 bonus.

The new Vice President of the Newark Bears, however, could not afford the luxury of dreaming of another Lou Gehrig. Weiss was too much the practical businessman. His immediate concern was signing good ballplayers and putting a respectable team on the field for the rapidly approaching 1932 season. It was important for the

Bears to get off to a fast start. It was also important for Newark baseball and the future of the Yankee chain.

Wilbur C. Crelin, the Bears' Secretary, was given the responsibility of getting the players to come to terms and sign contracts for the new season. Unlike today, the ballplayer of the 1930's had little say in the agreement. There were no player unions or free agent options, just the binding words of the reserve clause. If a player didn't sign, he didn't play! It was that simple. Of course, there were "holdouts," but these were more petty annoyances than serious threats. Noted among the holdouts were outfielder Dixie Walker, catcher Charlie Hargreaves, and pitcher Al Harvin. As spring training at Lakeland, Florida drew closer, the stampede to sign was on.

Under the new management, Newark turned in a creditable 1932 spring training and exhibition season. Early in the exhibition schedule, Ruppert showed a keen interest in his new team. He paid a personal visit to Lakeland and was delighted to see his young hopefuls win their fourth straight game from a major league club. Newark beat the Philadelphia Phillies, 7-5. After the game, Ruppert found Mamaux and congratulated the manager on a fine exhibition of baseball, particularly his well-conditioned athletes.

Other than Mamaux's bout with a "sinus ailment" and his refusal to follow doctor's orders, the only serious problem the Bears faced prior to Opening Day was a disabled pitching staff. But time and some help from the Yankees would solve that problem.

4.

The Championship 1932

THE 1932 BASEBALL SEASON FOR THE NEWARK BEARS — the first under Jacob Ruppert, Ed Barrow, George Weiss, and field boss Al Mamaux — was an overwhelming success and deservedly so. The new owner and his executive staff worked diligently to put together an exceptionally strong club. There were no less than fifteen new members on the 1932 team, twelve of whom were either Yankee property or were sent to the Bears by the New York club. Ruppert was making things happen. As a result, most experts picked the Bears to finish first. On the eve of the opener, however, Mamaux was cautiously optimistic. "I am not making any predictions. We have a good club, a hustling and loyal set of players. To say that we would do better than last season would mean that we expect a pennant. Let's hope we do as well. We have been handicapped by injuries, but then every club has a certain amount of hard luck. It may be that we are getting our's before the season starts. At least I hope so. Regardless what the outcome will be, I am sure the fans will have said we have tried our best."

Despite the bitter cold weather on Opening Day, over 13,000 Newark fans came out to windswept Ruppert Stadium to watch the Bears — resplendent in their new striped uniforms patterned after the Yankees — face the powerful Toronto Leafs as the temperature plummeted to 28 degrees. The starting lineup for Newark consisted of Johnny Neun leading off at first base; the number two hitter was catcher Norman Kies; batting third and playing second base was Andy Cohen; at cleanup was "The People's Cherce," Dixie

Walker; George Selkirk was hitting fifth and playing right field; Bob Barrett was at third base and hitting sixth; Jess Hill was the number seven batter in left field; Red Rolfe batted eighth and played shortstop; and the right-hander, George Miner, was on the mound.

Opposing Miner on the mound was another right-hander, Guy Cantrell. Newark drew first blood by scoring a run in the second inning on three consecutive singles by Hill, Rolfe, and Hargreaves. Hargreaves was playing for Neun, who had twisted his ankle taking a throw from Rolfe in the first play of the game and had to be helped off the field. Toronto tied the score in the fourth inning and the game remained that way until the top of the sixth when Miner was chased by three singles and two walks. That brought the Leafs three runs and a 4-1 lead. Toronto added an insurance run in the seventh on two hits and a walk off relief pitcher Milt Shoffner. In the meantime, Cantrell was standing the Bears on their ears.

As Newark entered the bottom half of the ninth inning, trailing, 5-1, a handfull of fans slowly began to exit. But many remained in their seats, either displaying their Opening Day loyalty or because they were too cold to move. Rolfe opened the ninth by singling inside the third base line. Hargreaves followed with another single to left field. There were now two men on base with no outs. The fans that were leaving stopped in the aisles. There was still some hope. Cantrell, feeling a little tingle of tension, lost his poise and hit Billy Zitzmann, batting for Shoffner. The bases were now loaded and the tying run was coming to the plate in the name of Andy Cohen. Toronto Manager Tom Daly, after much soul searching, decided to let Cantrell pitch. The Bears' second baseman and number three hitter promptly smacked a towering shot that headed for the left field bleachers. It looked like it had the distance, but the wind was curving the ball sharply towards the foul line. For a moment, there was silence. The runners halted. All eyes watched the flight of the ball as it dropped into the bleachers. And then the eyes shifted to the Umpire, Bill Summers, as he signaled the runners toward the plate. It was a grand slam home run and the game was tied! The frozen 13,000 fans exploded. An inning later, almost as an afterthought, Newark scored the tie-breaking run on relief pitcher Frank Nekola's single to win the inaugural game, 6-5.

The next day, the *Newark Evening News* printed the following account of Ruppert's day at the park:

HAVE FAITH, COLONEL!

For seven innings, Colonel Ruppert, owner of the Bears, sat and shivered in his box seat, resisting the temptation to enter the offices for a little warmth. Finally, when stretching time came in the last half of the seventh and the thousands of fans arose to get the kinks out of their cramped muscles, the Colonel made for the steam-heated quarters of Vice President George Weiss.

The score then was 5-1, Newark trailing.

The Colonel decided he'd stay right where he was. Then came that roar in the ninth and the Colonel decided to come out. He smiled even though he was too late to see Andy Cohen slam one into the left field stands for a home run with the bases full. The Colonel sat down and remained down until after the game.

Later that evening at an informal dinner for club officials and local baseball scribes, Ruppert enthusiastically commented on the victory. "I've had few happier days in my life. No World Series games the Yankees ever won gave me a greater thrill. And they call it minor league baseball. New York clubs would be lucky to draw as many people on such a day."

Off to a fast start, the Newark Bears won 13 of their first 17 games. By May 3, after taking 3 of 4 games from Buffalo, the Bears pulled two games out in front of the International League pennant race. In spite of this quick lead, Manager Mamaux made it quite clear that he needed additional strength from the Yankees, both on the mound and in the infield. Early spring injuries were still plaguing his pitching staff and his riddled infield defense left much to be desired.

Yankee Business Manager Ed Barrow, however, didn't agree with Mamaux. "Newark doesn't need strengthening now," he told

Mamaux. "You have one of the best minor league teams I've ever seen. We have a bigger problem in the Yanks than in Newark as I see it."

Over the short haul, Mamaux proved to be correct as the Bears started to get into a serious slump. By early June, after losing 9 of 11 games, Newark wound up in a fourth place tie with Rochester, 4½ games out of first place.

The pitching quality deteriorated to such a low point, in fact, that Mamaux reactivated himself in desperation. The 38-year-old right-hander and twelve-year major league veteran would help the Bears over the rough spots in the weeks to come.

Although Newark was losing, the fans were not discouraged as they continued to pack Ruppert Stadium. To further encourage maximum crowds, the Bears announced their new night baseball policy. As reported by the *Newark Evening News* on May 27:

> The Newark Baseball Club today announced its night baseball policy. An experiment game will be tried June 16 as part of the Montreal series. If things go well and it meets the favor of the fans, it will be a weekly Thursday night fixture.
>
> Under no circumstances will a more extensive schedule than one night a week be in effect in Newark.

On the night of June 16, over 4,000 fans paid their way into Ruppert Stadium to watch Newark play Montreal in this historic event. But the weather would have no part of it. As the bears took the field, it started to rain. One sports writer summed up the evening in these words: "The pounding of rain soon worked into the lighting equipment and the popping of 1,500 watt lamps gave a fireworks effect to the fascinating scene. One after the other, the lights blew out, the field gradually growing back into the shadows, and Newark's 1932 debut into lighted baseball was over."

Not to be deterred, the Bears gave it another try the following night and this time 7,000 fans turned out. The evening was splendid. The rain was gone. The lights stayed on. The Bears shut out Montreal, 5-0. And history was made.

Although Mamaux was correct in his constant cry for help, Barrow proved to be the long-term prophet. But it did take some additional personnel. Marvin Owen, considered the best defensive infielder in the league, was acquired from Toronto to help tighten the infield and Forrest Jensen was picked up from the Pittsburg Pirates to add batting punch. The Yankees also made their contribution by sending reliefer Johnny Murphy to bolster the pitching staff, which was finally starting to jell.

Over the Fourth of July weekend, Newark moved into first place again, opening a slim 1½ game lead before taking off on another road trip. The confident Mamaux in a flush of optimism was convinced the Bears could now win the pennant. "Just imagine how far in front we would be now if Jim Weaver and Johnnie Welch had pitched up to expectations earlier in the season." Commenting on his young shortstop, Mamaux continued, "I have never in all my years in baseball seen such a vast improvement in a ballplayer in half a season as that shown by Red Rolfe. His fielding and batting are much better than at the start of the season, and he can race back for pop flies as well as any shortstop I ever saw.

. . .when have you seen a peppier bunch in Newark uniforms? They act like pennant winners and play like champions, so there is no reason why we shouldn't be out in front when that final gong sounds."

By mid-July, Newark was still in first place, 3½ games ahead of second place Buffalo. By mid-August, the team widened the margin to 11½ games. The Bears were clearly on their way. Don Brennan, Jim Weaver, and Harry Holsclaw were all pitching well, with Murphy in relief. Forrest Jensen was leading the team in hits and Dixie Walker, Jess Hill, Red Rolfe, and Marvin Owen — all batting over .300 — were driving in runs by the bushel full.

During the remainder of August and halfway through September, Newark went on the rampage, finishing the season with a remarkable record of 109 wins and 59 losses for a .649 percentage. In the process, they won the pennant by 15½ games, Newark's first in nineteen years. The pennant earned the Bears the right to meet the Minneapolis Millers of the American Association in the Little World Series. Additionally, the Bears had set a "new league attendance record at home, 345,001!" It wasn't a bad performance for Ruppert's first season of ownership.

Brennan led the pitching staff — and the league — with 25 victories, achieving this mark on the last day of the season. Dixie Walker led the team in hitting with an outstanding .351 average, third best in the league.

But much of the credit deservedly went to the Bears' popular manager, the first in twenty years to finish two full seasons with Newark. On September 12 at Ruppert Stadium, 7,000 fans came out to celebrate "Al Mamaux Night." During the full hour of ceremonies, Al received a diamond ring, "a purse," and his favorite chocolate cake, baked by his mother-in-law. To show his appreciation, Al pitched six innings of shutout baseball before the old arm tired and he had to be replaced. All in all, it was a very fun evening.

Although Newark ran away with the International League pennant, facing the Minneapolis Millers of the American Association was another matter. The Millers possessed both power hitting and shrewd pitching. The short fences at their stadium, particularly in right field where the distance was only 260 feet from home plate, made the long ball a constant threat. Sluggers like Joe Hauser, who had 49 homers, Art Ruble with 29, Babe Ganzel with 22, Joe Mowry with 18, and Spencer Harris with 16 cracked the fences with regularity all season long. As one rival manager summed up the Millers' strength, "Any man in the lineup is apt to hit the ball out of the park, which means that a pitcher cannot afford to make a single mistake. The Minneapolis pitching isn't great, but it's smart. You get fellows like Rube Benton, Rosy Ryan, Carmen Hill, and Jess Petty and they pitch with their heads as well as with their arms, and that sort of hurling is always difficult to solve." It would prove to be an exciting series.

In game number one, a slim crowd of only 6,339 watched Don Brennan spin a magnificent four-hit shutout as the Bears clobbered the Millers, 11-0. The Bears collected 16 hits as they battered four Minneapolis pitchers — starter Rosy Ryan, Elam Van Gilder,

Rube Benton, and Carmen Hill. Charlie Hargreaves went four-for-five with four RBI's; Jess Hill went three-for-five with 3 RBI's; and Red Rolfe hit two-for-three with 2 RBI's. The trio accounted for nine hits and nine RBI's in the rout. But Ruppert and Minneapolis Manager Donie Bush both acknowledged it was Brennan's day.

Ruppert was outspoken in his praise of Brennan. "I think you could say right now that Brennan will be a star with the Yankees next season. Never have I seen a better pitching performance. He was simply superb."

Bush was equally generous in his praise of the Newark pitcher. "I heard a lot about Brennan, but I never believed he was the kind of pitcher he proved to be today. There's nothing like him in the American Association, and say, few pitchers in the big leagues have a better curve."

When asked directly about the embarassing loss, Bush explained, "We have no alibis to offer. Of course that long train ride didn't help us any, but Newark was the better team today. Tomorrow, it may be the other way around. We have real hitting power and it cannot be denied for long. Also we will get better pitching from Petty. It was just too unfortunate that Ryan had an off day."

Undaunted, the Millers made a sparkling comeback the next night, edging the Bears, 3-2, before 12,000 fans at Ruppert Stadium. Southpaw Jess Petty outpitched Harry Holsclaw and his famous screwball to gain the important second game victory that tied the series. Actually, Newark led, 2-1, going into the top of the sixth inning when the Millers scored two runs on three hits, helped by some sloppy defense on the Bears' part. Petty pitched outstanding ball, keeping his curve low throughout the game. He allowed only five hits and struck out eleven. After the game, the Miller's pint-size manager, who was seldom at a loss for words, was bubbling with confidence. "All we wanted was one game in Newark and we got it. As far as we are concerned, the Little World Series and what goes with it will go to Minneapolis. I'm not boasting when I say this. The Bears will not win a game in our park. No team in the American Association has been able to beat us regularly at home. All we need is half the pitching that Jess Petty served up last night when he turned Newark down and we'll breeze through.

"I'll send Henry after your Bears tomorrow and I'm confident that he will turn in another masterful job such as Petty did last night. Yes, it's all over but the division of the spoils."

As Bush had announced, the third game pitted the Miller's Lefty "Dutch" Henry against Pete "Polish Wizard" Jablonowski of the Bears in another threatening mound duel. It was a scoreless tie through the first six innings. In the top of the seventh, however, Joe Hauser blasted a home run that gave the Millers a 1-0 lead. In the bottom of the inning, the Bears came right back and tied the game as Charlie Hargreaves belted a round tripper. With Henry and Jablonowski matching each other pitch for pitch, the game went into extra innings. But in the top half of the tenth, Jablonowski made a mistake that cost him the game. He grooved a pitch and Babe Ganzel hit it out of the park. The Millers won by a final score of 2-1.

After three games at Ruppert Stadium, the Minneapolis Millers held an important 2-1 edge as the series headed for Nicollette Park in Minneapolis. The Newark Bears were now in deep trouble. Many felt the Millers were "invincible" in their own park because of the friendly short fences, ideal targets for their long ball hitters.

With each succeeding victory, Bush continued to shoot his mouth off. "I'll come back with Jess Petty Sunday and on Tuesday, I'll probably feed your Bruins Henry again. You know, I have half a mind to send Benton in again, but I guess the safest and best plan will be to pitch Petty and Henry.

"Although we won yesterday, I was greatly displeased with the way the Millers acted at the plate. Never before this season have we been in such a hitting slump as we were in this Little World Series. We got sixteen hits in three games. It's true that we were up against good pitching, but we should do better than that and I'm sure when the boys get home, they will make short work of this series.

"Another thing I want to let you in on. I only hope Mamaux slips Don Brennan after us in Minneapolis. If he leaves him in the box long enough, we'll get six runs off him or I'll buy you a new hat."

Mamaux, maintaining a low profile throughout the series, finally spoke out in a brief statement to the press which appeared to be aimed at Bush. "I'll have to send Brennan after the Millers Sunday. I have all the confidence in the world that Brennan will even up the series in the next game. We're not licked, you can tell the world that."

In game number four, true to his word, Mamaux returned with his ace and twenty-five-game winner, Don Brennan. Bush gambled and started the 48-year-old veteran, Rube Benton. After one scoreless inning, Benton complained of a sour shoulder. Pea Ridge Day opened the second inning and allowed two home runs on two consecutive pitches. Marvin Owen hit the first over the center field wall and then Jack Saltzgaver belted one over the left field wall. The Bears jumped off to an early 2-0 lead, picked up another run in the fourth and two more in the ninth. Inning after inning, Brennan pitched a courageous game. The big right-hander was roughed up for fourteen hits, but was tough in the clutch as the Millers managed only two runs. The Bears won, 5-2.

Once again, the series was knotted at 2-2. In retrospect, the fifth game turned out to be the crucial one and was loaded with excitement. It all happened in the wild, frantic top of the ninth inning. The score was tied, 8-8. There were two men out with Saltzgaver on third and Hargreaves on first. The next batter, Johnny Neun, slashed a line drive to center field and Harry Rice, the Millers' center fielder, tried to make a shoestring catch. It turned out to be the spark that ignited a hotly contested call. Rice claimed he caught the ball. The Bears claimed he trapped it. It was now up to the umpires. The only problem was that they added to the confusion by siding with the team that did the most arguing. This wild melee, which lasted forty minutes, was completely out of hand until Umpire in Chief Bill Summers put an end to the nonsense and forced a final decision in favor of the Bears. Neun was called safe and Slatzgaver scored the tie-breaking run. Minneapolis was outraged. Moments later, Red Rolfe added to the Millers' frustration by poking a home run that cleared the right field barrier, scoring Hargreaves and Neun ahead of him. The Bears now had a 12-8 lead. The Millers managed to push a run across in the bottom of the ninth, but still lost by a score of 12-9.

There was no stopping the super-charged Bears now. They came back the next day and beat the Millers, 8-7, in a game highlighted by another dramatic finish. This time, Newark was trailing, 7-5, in the top of the ninth inning and it looked like the series would go the full seven games. But Hill walked and scored moments later when Jensen's line shot to left skipped by the Millers' left fielder for a triple. The Bears were now trailing by only one run. The next batter, Marvin Owen, acquired earlier in the year to plug up the holes in the infield, blasted his third home run of the series. The Bears won, 8-7, claiming their first Little World Series Championship under Ruppert.

The two rival managers best summed up Newark's first season in these words. "You have the greatest minor league club I ever have seen, Al," said Bush. "I still think, however, that we were unlucky in having that questionable play called against us, but that's baseball. You beat us fairly.

"I thought we would win because of our experience, and the fact that you won is more credit to you and your young fellows. Maybe we'll meet again next year, but if we do, you will not have Brennan, Walker, Rolfe, and Jensen. They can't keep those fellows out of the big leagues."

Mamaux, flushed with victory, picked up the conversation. "What can I say? The base hits spoke for themselves. They're the gamest bunch of fellows I ever saw on a ball club.

"It has been a pleasure managing the Bears of 1932. At no time did we have the slightest trouble. No team ever had a better spirit or more will to win. Take the last two games. We were supposed to be weak against left-handers. But what did we do? Only hit Petty and Henry like they were never hit in their lives, and in both of those last two games, we were seemingly beaten, but did they quit? Why, they don't know what the word means. I will go down on record as saying we have one of the best ball clubs in the country and if the same club was in either big league, you could bet it would finish higher than last place."

There was joy in Newark once again, but the years ahead would be different. They would bring defeat and frustration — until the incredible year, 1937.

5.

The Frustrating Years 1933 and 1934

I F 1932 WAS A FINE YEAR FOR THE NEWARK BEARS, THEN THE next two years, 1933 and 1934, would have to be classified as sheer frustration. It wasn't that the Bears played poor baseball. As a matter of fact, most of the time they played exceptional baseball. They finished in first place both years! But what caused the grief and frustration for the team were the "Shaughnessy Play-offs," named after Frank "Shag" Shaughnessy, one of the great figures in minor league baseball history.

Shaughnessy's baseball career spanned some sixty years and covered virtually every aspect of the game; he was a player, a manager, and later, an executive. Shaughnessy played briefly in the American League with Washington in 1905 and with the Philadelphia Athletics in 1908. He both played and managed in the minors and had the distinction of winning six pennants in four different leagues. He also served as General Manager of the Montreal Royals and was eventually elected President of the International League in October, 1936, a post he held until his retirement in 1960.

It was while he was General Manager of Montreal in 1932 that Shaughnessy devised and sold his play-off plan to the minors. In 1933, the first year under the Shaughnessy plan, the first and second place teams met in one semifinal series while the third and fourth place teams met in another. The winners then squared off in a final best 3 out of 5 games to determine the International League's representative in the Little World Series. Weiss, who was a strong opponent to the Shaughnessy play-offs, fought hard from the outset to prevent its acceptance. He lost the battle, but did manage to reform the play-off scheme later in 1934. Instead of the first and second place teams meeting in one semifinal series and the third and fourth place teams in another, it was changed to the first and third place teams and the second and fourth. In addition, the best 4 out of 7 games replaced the traditional 3 out of 5. Probably the most important victory for Weiss was that the first place team during the regular season would be recognized as the "winner" of the pennant.

However, the winner of the play-offs would still represent the International League in the Little World Series. Although the play-off system was generally acknowledged to have helped save the minors from financial ruin during the depression-ridden 1930's, it was a constant source of embarrassment and frustration to the Newark Bears, haunting them for four long years.

The 1933 season for the Bears was characterized by the usual winning and losing streaks, occasional batting slumps, and the continued search for the long ball hitter, the fence buster. Al Mamaux and George Weiss greeted the season with mixed emotions. On the one hand, stars like Red Rolfe, Johnnie Neun, Jack Saltzgaver, Norman Kies, George Miner, Jim Weaver, and Johnny Murphy were all returning. But many of the great ballplayers were also leaving. From the 1932 championship team, outfielders Dixie Walker and Woody Jensen were elevated to the major leagues — Walker with the Yankees and Jensen with the Pittsburgh Pirates. In addition, Harry Holsclaw, the 32-year-old right-hander, was sold to the Minneapolis Millers in a straight cash deal. The biggest blow to the Bears, however, was the loss of Don Brennan to the Yankees. It would be a difficult task, to say the least, to replace a twenty-five-game winner. Evidently Weiss had a substantial rebuilding job to perform with the team.

In one of his first moves, Weiss managed to get the left-handed slugger, George Selkirk, back from Toronto to take up some of the slack left by Walker and Jensen. At the same time, the Yankees sent two outfielders to the Bears — right-handed hitting Myril Hoag and left-handed Dusty Cooke. Cooke not only added batting punch to the lineup, but he also had great speed on the bases. The Yankees also helped out in the pitching department by sending down two 23-year-old right-handers, Jimmie DeShong and Charlie Devens. DeShong, in particular, was an outstanding prospect, posting a 19-6 record with a 3.16 ERA at Sacramento in the Pacific Coast League. Devens was a strong right-hander with a puzzling side arm delivery.

As in 1932, the Bears jumped off to a fast start. By mid-May, they were in first place, led by the strong pitching of Weaver and the consistent hitting of Saltzgaver, Rolfe, Hoag, and Selkirk. Weaver, who took over from Brennan as the ace of the staff, won eight in a row without a loss and the young kid DeShong chipped in four more victories. As far as the offense went, Saltzgaver was hitting a sensational .373 (third best in the league); Rolfe was hitting .306; and Hoag was hitting .313 with 28 RBI's. Selkirk, although batting only .262, made his hits productive with 20 RBI's. Newark fans were delighted and it looked like an easy pennant for the Bears.

But Weiss was far from finished with his manipulating. In a surprise defensive move, he shipped the fleet-footed Cooke to the Boston Red Sox for outfielder Johnnie Westwood and infielder Marvin Olson. Westwood, the better of the two, had a reputation for being a brilliant ball hawk.

Their hold on first place didn't last long, however, as the Bears slipped into a serious batting slump. They lost 6 of 8 games and relinquished their lead to Toronto. For the next two and a half months, they played inconsistent baseball, winning a few, losing a few. The Bears were simply incapable of putting together a string of victories that would propel them into a solid first place lead. The consensus was that Newark needed a power hitter. This was the only thing that would assure them of another pennant.

Newark made two attempts to acquire the big home run hitter. In June, Vince Barton was picked up from Albany in a trade and cash deal for Jimmy Moore and another player. The Bears had great expectations that the left-handed slugger would hit the short right field bleachers for 30-40 homers. In July, another announcement was made, a real blockbuster of a deal. The Bears sent Selkirk to Rochester in an exchange of options for George Puccinelli, the "towering Italian." In 1932, Puccinelli batted a sensational league-leading .391, blasting 28 home runs and driving in 115 runs. The colorful Puccinelli was elated over the move, particularly since he was unhappy at Rochester, while the Bears felt "Pooch" would be a lucrative gate attraction since Italian fans made up a large part of the club's following. Conversely, Selkirk was unhappy; he was leaving many old friends and he had just leased a new apartment. Shrugging it off, Selkirk commented, "But that's baseball, and to be expected now and then." Shortly afterwards, the Yankees sent Don Brennan back to the Bears in exchange for young Charlie Devens. Brennan had posted a 5-1 record — not bad on the surface — but he had only completed three games. Devens, the Harvard boy with a 10-6 mark, was expected to help bolster the sagging Yankee attendance. A little later, the talent-loaded Yankees sent the 21-year-old Yale right-hander, Johnnie Broaca, to the Bears. The Yankee executives hoped that Mamaux could develop the husky fastballer as successfully as he had done with Devens. These changes, coupled with Neun's 22 for 46 hitting streak and Weaver's brilliant pitching, finally put the Bears back in first place. By the end of July, their lead rose to 2½ games. By early August, it increased to 4½. And on August 9, Weaver spun a beautiful four-hitter for his twentieth victory, extending the Bears lead to a full 10 games!

Then on August 29, the Bears clinched first place by sweeping both games of the double-header against Albany, 8-5 and 11-3. Myril Hoag, making his first appearance since he was rushed to the hospital a week before, turned in a spectacular day, particularly in the opener. Hoag blasted a grand slam home run to cap an eight-run inning. When asked about his health, Hoag replied, "Oh, all right, but I guess I'm weak. You know, if I was up to snuff, that ball I just hit [double] would have cleared the bleachers easily. I never hit a ball so squarely before."

When the Bears finished the season an easy 14½ games ahead of the second place Rochester Red Wings, talk naturally shifted to the upcoming play-offs. Newark would face Rochester while third place Baltimore would square off against fourth place Buffalo. This was the first time the Shaughnessy play-off system was in effect and it prompted much skepticism, particularly in Newark.

The local press, although showing some bias, picked Newark as the favorite on the strength of their victories in two "crucial" series during the season. The first one came in early July at Rochester when the Bears held a slim two-game lead. Newark went ahead and took 3 of 5 games to add to their margin. The second test came in August. This time, Newark had an eight-game lead and beat Rochester 4 out of 5 games, putting the pennant race away for good. In spite of this, the two teams still split the 24 games during the season. Based on the "crucial" series theory, which left much to be desired, the Bears were considered the "money club." It was also true that Don Brennan, the pitching star of 1932, had returned and Roy Schalk was in healthy condition. These players made Newark appear stronger than the team had ever been during the season. In addition to Brennan, Mamaux had assembled a formidable pitching staff — Jim Weaver, Johnnie Broaca, Jimmy DeShong, Pete Jablonowski, Marvin Duke, and Vito Tamulis. Mamaux also had Johnny Murphy, the brawny Irishman from Fordham, in relief. They were all ready and anxious to take on Rochester.

In the opening game, Mamaux selected his tall right-hander and 25-game winner, Jim Weaver, while Rochester player-manager Specs Toporcer gave the start to Sheriff Blake. For four innings, Weaver and Blake matched goose eggs. In the top of the fifth, however, Weaver suddenly found himself in deep trouble. With two out and two on, the dangerous Estel Crabtree stepped up to the plate. Weaver pitched carefully, but after getting two strikes on the left-handed batter, he let up and Crabtree belted one to deep left. Michael F. Gavin, covering the game for the *Newark Star-Eagle,* described the following scene: "Puccinelli was under it and as the ball cleared the fence, he stretched his glove hand into the bleachers and had the horsehide in his grasp when an excited young fan pulled the sphere out of the glove. It should have been the third out with no runs; instead, it was a homer and three big runs for Rochester.'' After the game, it was discovered that the ball snatcher was 16-year-old Frankie Tebulece from the iron-bound section of Newark. When Frankie was asked about the incident, he explained, "I didn't mean it. I've been going to the stadium several years and never got a ball. I just forgot everything when it came towards me. I didn't see Pooch, I was so anxious about the ball.''

In spite of the three-run gift, Newark managed to fight back and tie the game at 3-3. Then in the bottom of the eighth inning, the Bears came roaring back and scored three more runs, capped by Puccinelli's gigantic two-run homer over the 350-foot mark in left field. As characterized by a local scribe, it was "one of the most spectacular homers made in the park this season.'' So the Bears took the opener in this short three-of-five series by a score of 6-3.

In the second game, Don Brennan, last year's hero, faced the crafty and experienced right-hander, Tony Kaufman. Newark jumped on Kaufman in the first inning when Rolfe, Hoag, and Schalk all singled. Coupled with an error by Toporcer, they pushed across two runs. Rochester tied the score in the third on a two-run homer by Tom Carey and took the lead in the next inning when Roy Schalk booted Carey's ground ball with the bases loaded, allowing two unearned runs.

After his shaky start, Kaufman settled down and pitched a superb game, giving up only three hits the rest of the way — a Hargreaves single with two out in the fourth, a Barton home run in the seventh, and a Schalk double with two out in the eighth. Rochester won by a final score of 4-3.

The series now shifted to Rochester for game number three on Thursday. But the weather tossed its own curve and the game was postponed. It appeared that the delay favored the Red Wings since Dutch Henry was slated for Thursday and a second rate pitcher for Friday. Now Henry would be able to pitch on Friday and their pitching ace, Blake, could once again start on Saturday. In addition, Kaufman would have enough rest to oppose Weaver on Sunday if a fifth game was necessary. One could sense the balance of power slowly shifting in favor of Rochester. Toporcer thought so, too.

"We now hold the upper hand. Even should Henry fail to beat Broaca, and I for one don't think he will, we have Blake and Kaufman for the fourth and fifth games, and they both should win. With better support, they would have had shutouts in Newark."

Over 3,500 partisan fans, "who had little or no regard for their health," came out to watch the third game on this rainy cold day. Many were wrapped in blankets and overcoats. But they were rewarded for their loyalty as young Johnnie Broaca and Dutch Henry locked horns in a classic pitching duel. Through the first six and a half innings, the two matched each other pitch for pitch. The score was deadlocked at 2-2. In the bottom of the seventh — with two men out and the bases empty — it looked like an easy inning for Broaca and an endless game. But ex-Bear George Selkirk singled past first for his third hit of the game. Wally Gilbert followed with a single up the middle. Then when Broaca tried to pitch too carefully to Paul Florence, he wound up walking him and loaded the bases. What started as an easy inning quickly turned into serious trouble. Apparently Broaca was tiring, but Mamaux elected to stay with the kid because Toporcer, after much deliberation, allowed Henry to bat. Broaca ran the count to 1-1, but lost his concentration and grooved the next pitch. Henry lined a bullet right past Broaca's ear and scored Selkirk and Gilbert. Moments later, Carey singled and another run crossed the plate. The score was now 5-2 and Mamaux sent Jimmy DeShong into the game to relieve Broaca and get the final out of the inning. That was all the veteran Henry needed, however, as he bore down and allowed the Bears only one more run in the futile ninth. The Red Wings won the game, 5-3, and were now only one game away from eliminating the Bears from the play-offs.

In game number four, Mamaux sent his ace, Jim Weaver, to the mound for the second time. Newark's hopes in the play-offs now rested squarely on his shoulders. Toporcer was counting on his pitching star, Sheriff Blake, but the Sheriff just didn't have it that day. He was blasted from the mound in the first inning after Newark scored four runs. The Bears added another in the top of the third to give Weaver an early 5-0 lead. It looked like an easy win for the Bears, forcing the fifth and deciding game on Sunday. But the Red Wings had other ideas and came charging back in the bottom of the inning. They exploded for five runs on four singles and a pair of doubles before Weaver was relieved by Pete Jablonowski. Two innings later, Jablonowski found himself following Weaver to the showers as Rochester erupted for three more runs. But the real crusher came when Selkirk, who still belonged to Newark, stole home for Rochester's ninth run! Blowing a 5-0 lead and watching Selkirk steal from third was more than the Bears could take. They managed to squeak out two more runs, but their hearts weren't in the game. Rochester won by a final score of 9-7. It was the first in a long line of play-off eliminations that would haunt the Bears for years.

After the final game, both Toporcer and Mamaux expressed concern about the value of the play-off system and the future of baseball. Toporcer directed his comments to the Newark Manager. "It's a damn shame, Al, that your fellows should lose after proving beyond doubt that you had the best team in the league. And I fear for the future of baseball if our pennant races are to be meaningless."

Mamaux, stressing what elimination meant to the players, was bitter in his condemnation of the entire play-off system. "For fifty years, the team that finished first in the regular season was the pennant winner, and for the last seventeen years, the pennant winner shared in the Little World Series. It is most unfortunate that these boys who worked so hard should be the first victims.

"Tougher still, many of them needed that few hundred dollars they would have received from the Little World Series. Now they will be lucky if they get $100 each for the play-offs. If it weren't that even that sum means so much to them, I would suggest we give the paltry prize to a home for crippled children.

"But it was just in the cards for us to lose," continued Mamaux. "And perhaps our defeat was not in vain, for it will no doubt bring wiser baseball men to their senses and we will have no more of it."

Mamaux could sense this was no ordinary defeat. In spite of a pennant, a Little World Series, and first and second place finishes in three years, Newark's loss to Rochester sealed Mamaux's fate. In early October, the Bears announced they would not renew his contract. The position was available and the candidate rumors began popping faster than corks on New Year's Eve. Speculation became so widespread that Weiss saw fit to level with the press about the future manager of Newark. "Let's take No. 1 rumor. I believe that was Babe Ruth. Why, I'd jump out of my skin if Colonel Ruppert were to say we could have Ruth — and Ruth would come here to manage. That's definitely out.

"Herb Pennock? He has fine qualifications, but is unproven. We cannot gamble. You have my word — Pennock will not be the manager.

"Now take Bill Meyer. I am inclined to say that in light of the present events, Meyer has greater appeal than any other. The candidate that would be selected over Bill would, I assure you, have to be quite a man.

"Joe Sewell," continued Weiss, "has the earmarks, too, of a great manager. Mike Kelly? Fine! But we'll be swamped from now on with applications for the job."

Weiss' comments slowed the rumors and speculation until the *Newark Evening News* scooped the baseball world on November 23, 1933 with the headline that Babe Ruth was offered the job to manage the Bears in 1934. Ruppert "would not deny or affirm the story." Barrow "denied all knowledge of a move that would transfer baseball's greatest drawing card to Newark." Weiss called the move "far fetched" and added, "Ruth has not even been approached on the matter." Ruth, on a hunting trip near Middletown, New York, declined to comment.

Twenty-nine days and an ocean of ink later, Ruth finally admitted in an Associated Press interview that the job had been offered to him. "The Colonel (Colonel Ruppert) wanted me to go to Newark, but I couldn't see it," Ruth told the sportswriter. "He said it would be good experience for me, but I told him I've been in the major leagues getting experience for twenty years and this is a fine time to go back to the minors to get more. It's like learning all over again. They play an entirely different game in the minors."

The "Ruth-for-Manager" speculation was finally over. Now the Yankee brass could settle down and choose — from among the hundreds of possibilities — the best man for the important job. It didn't take them long, either. A week after Ruth declined, Weiss announced that the quiet and soft-spoken ex-Yankee star right-hander, Bob Shawkey, would be the new Newark Manager. The Yankees were looking for an experienced leader who could develop promising young players. Shawkey's fifteen years in the American League, his managing and coaching positions with New York, and his steady and even disposition all combined to make him the perfect choice. He fit the bill perfectly.

A smiling but serious Shawkey had this to say about his new job. "I never had any rules for my ball club, unless you take this one: Keep in condition. I don't believe in curfews and all that stuff. With the Yankees I asked only that every man do his best. It was Hug's way [referring to Miller Huggins].

"I know a lot about the ballplayers Newark has and some who will come here, but my arm is still good enough to go in there and work in batting practice and that's the point of vantage from which I intend to work, correcting faults or assisting men in their timing."

When asked about the possibility of pitching, Shawkey replied, "No, there is to be no pitching by the Manager. I did work a full game for Scranton against Wilkes-Barre last August and won it, 2-1.

"In another game, I went to work in the third and held Harrisburg to one run. My arm feels strong until about the fifth inning, when the muscles begin to tighten and I lose my stuff. I have no intention of placing myself on the eligible list as a relief pitcher."

Commenting on the overall team, Shawkey continued, "We have holes to fill in the Bears' outfield, infield, and pitching and catching staffs. I have been able to watch the Yankee youngsters working against them when Scranton played Binghamton. Of course, there was much night ball and that gives a false line on some men, but Jack LaRocca has a great fast ball."

As Shawkey so frankly stated, there were "holes" to fill on the Newark roster, and he and Weiss wasted little time in plugging up those holes. As a matter of fact, Weiss started rebuilding the team long before Shawkey was named manager. He sent Charlie Hargreaves, Marvin Olson, George Miner, and Pete Jablonowski to the Orioles in partial payment for a young second baseman the Yankees acquired back in August. Then in early 1934, the Yankees sent Don Brennan (he had returned to the Yankees for another try) and Jess Hill to the Bears on option as the building campaign continued. As Weiss had told the press, the Yankee organization wanted to "create a Newark Bears that simply must be bigger and better than ever." Shortly after Brennan and Hill, the Yankees also sent pitcher Walter "Jumbo" Brown and infielder Eddie "Doc" Farrell to the Bears. It was obvious the Yankees would spare nothing to launch Shawkey on the road to success. Both players had been with the Yankees the past two years — Brown as a starter and formidable reliever, and the 31-year-old Farrell as a utility infielder and occasional pinch hitter.

The changes in the Newark club were not restricted to the field. They extended to the front office, too. Ray L. Kennedy was appointed by Colonel Ruppert as the new Secretary, replacing Wilbur C. Crelin. Kennedy earned the position on the strength of his performance at Binghamton in 1933. The soft-spoken and amiable southern gentleman dazzled the Colonel by turning in a nifty profit while the frugal Yankee owner was expecting a slight loss. While Ruppert accepted a loss in the past as the necesary cost of developing players, the profit posted by Kennedy was a welcome surprise.

As Opening Day drew closer, rumors surfaced concerning potential holdout problems. Weiss firmly denied the accusations, but did admit that the players were slow in returning their contracts. "It is most ununsual," said Weiss. "In past years, we usually got all the contracts back within a week, some signed, some unsigned. But this year, they apparently are holding the papers just to think about them for a few days. However, they all received our best terms in their first contract and those returned will be sent back without any alterations being made on the salary figure. Our payroll is almost exactly the same as last year, and the league rules prevent us from going any higher."

In subsequent moves, the Bears picked up Dale Alexander, the heavy-hitting first baseman from Syracuse. He had won the American League batting title in 1932 with a .367 average while playing with the Boston Red Sox. The Yankees chipped in by sending two left-handed pitchers, Marvin Duke and Vito Tamulis, and two right-handers, Harvard's Charlie Devins and Floyd Newkirk, the latter following in the footsteps of the famous Mordecai Brown of another age. He had only three fingers on his pitching hand, having lost two in a childhood accident. The courageous Newkirk, gifted with an exceptional fastball and a sharp breaking curve, believed that his condition was more of a help than a hindrance. Catcher Norman Kies completed the Yankee transfers.[1] And Jim Weaver also returned to the Bears because the St. Louis Browns' pilot, Rogers Hornsby, said he couldn't fit him into his plans.

By Opening Day, the Bears fielded a brand new infield, except for Roy Schalk at second base. The only veterans in the outfield were George Selkirk, Vince Barton, and Jess Hill. As Shawkey said of his new team, "I am not given to making predictions, but do say we open the season with every player in splended condition, which is a big asset in this changeable spring weather.

"We still have a couple of question marks in our lineup, but that is not because of inferior material, but because of the presence of two or more talented youngsters fighting for the same berth. The Bears will hold their own."

The Bears did indeed hold their own. Through April and May, they played exceptional baseball. Although their team batting average was only seventh in the league with .266, their defense was very tight. They were third in club fielding with a .973 percentage and at one point led the league in double plays. The Bears also depended heavily on home runs and extra base hits. By early June, Barton was leading the league with 15 homers, hitting .305 with 43 RBI's. Alexander led the team in RBI's with 50, batting .318. And Selkirk and Hill were both swinging for high averages, hitting .353

---

1. It was common in the 1930's for ballplayers to move frequently from the minors to the majors and vice-versa during the season.

(with 30 RBI's) and .343 (with 26 RBI's), respectively.

The pitching was superb. Floyd Newkirk and Walter Brown each posted five victories with respective ERA's of 2.25 and 1.90. Vito Tamulis contributed four more wins and had a 3.37 ERA. But the big surprise was the outstanding relief pitching of rookie Frank Makosky from Boonton, New Jersey. The 22-year-old right-hander, who had previously been slated for Wheeling or Norfolk, was so exceptional in spring training that the Bears were forced to keep him.

In spite of these impressive statistics and a winning percentage above .600, the Bears still found themselves stalled in second place. The explanation was simple. The Rochester Red Wings were playing over .700 ball! Since it was impossible for the Red Wings to continue their phenomonal pace, it was only a matter of time before the Bears would overtake them.

Sure enough, on June 8, exactly fifty-two days after the start of the season, the Newark Bears moved into first place. Jack La Rocca, whom Shawkey touted as having "a great fast ball," got them there with a strong pitching performance. He allowed six hits, struck out ten and walked only one as the Bears smothered Albany, 9-1. Patience had its reward. The Bears were in first place and would remain out in front until they clinched their third straight pennant on September 6. They did it in dramatic fashion. Roy Schalk slammed a home run into the left field stands with two out and two on in the ninth inning to beat Syracuse, 4-1. After the game, as everyone cheered and hugged each other in the victory celebration, one of the players congratulated Shawkey. "Why congratulate me?" asked a modest Shawkey. "I had nothing to do with it. You fellows went out and won those ball games."

In some respects, Shawkey was correct in his assessment of why the Bears won the pennant. Brown was outstanding, finishing the season with 33 scoreless innings and a 20-6 record. The surprising Makosky was sensational in relief, winding up with 11 wins and 6 loses. And Marvin Duke posted a 10-7 mark and Tamulis finished at 14-8.

At the plate, Hill batted a cool .344 and led the league with 210 hits. Alexander was close behind with a .335 average, but more importantly, he led the team with 116 RBI's. Barton batted only .257, but shared the league's home run honors with Baltimore's Woodley Abernathy at 32. Barton also drove in an even 100 runs. Selkirk made an early contribution, but was recalled in August by the Yankees after he boasted a .360 average.

What the modest Mr. Shawkey failed to mention, however, was that he won with players who weren't expected to win. He won with performers who lacked experience in International League competition and with athletes who had been tested before in the big leagues and had failed. In addition, Shawkey was forced to suffer occasional disturbances from the Yankees. Nonetheless, the ex-Yankee star piloted the Bears to their third straight pennant. Equally important, the players were entering the play-offs in an entirely different frame of mind. In 1933, they were sullen and displayed the bitter front office attitude: so what if we won the pennant by 14½ games, why should we be in the play-offs? But with the passing of another season, the team had grown to accept the play-offs even though their management hadn't. They were confident, eager, and displayed quiet determination. The Bears were convinced they were the best baseball team in the International League and certainly superior to third place Toronto. They now wanted the chance to prove it.

The first game of the play-offs was a study in contrasts. Brown and Deven combined to pitch excellent ball, allowing only five hits over twelve innings, but they were victims of loose fielding. Gene Schott, the ace of the Toronto staff, allowed ten hits, but was blessed with brilliant support. A typical example occurred in the bottom half of the ninth inning. Joe Glenn was thrown out at home plate after tagging up from third on Schalk's fly. It would have been the winning run. Once again, Ruppert, Barrow, and Krichell — not to mention 3,000 fans — went away frustrated as Toronto won the opener, 3-2, in twelve innings.

The second game was also a disappointment to Newark fans as ex-Bear Don Brennan came back to haunt his old teammates. He fanned twelve batters and posted a 2-1 victory. Brennan, who had been "on loan" from the Cincinnati Reds since the end of the summer, was tough as usual with men on base. A typical example came in the third inning when the Bears loaded the bases with no one out. Brennan reached back for something extra and struck out both Hill and Alexander. He then forced Fred Muller to ground out. The Bears also received excellent pitching, as Vito Tamulis gave up three hits, struck out ten, and walked only four. But he allowed the Leafs to score two runs in the first inning without the benefit of a hit. That was his downfall. It now seemed the Bears were in deep play-off trouble. They had used up their two most dependable hurlers, lost both games at home, and were headed for Maple Leaf Stadium where the outfield was often likened to "a Texas prairie."

Shawkey was understandably discouraged with his team, but was not the kind to give up. As he observed, "There's nothing wrong with the lineup. And truthfully I can't understand what is wrong, unless the tension is too great for some of the boys. I am going to sink or swim with the regular lineup and go through with my original pitching plans.

"Jack LaRocca will pitch tonight and he should beat those fellows, particularly in this large ball park. But the pitchers can't win without runs. Brown and Tammy both pitched wonderful games and it was by no means their fault that we lost."

The change of scenery was apparently all the Bears needed in game number three. They got another outstanding mound performance from the redheaded rookie, Jack LaRocca, who gave up only three hits as he blanked the Leafs, 6-0. Additionally, the Newark bats finally came to life as they pounded out eleven hits, with Dale Alexander, Bob Gibson, and Joe Glenn leading the assault.

But in the fourth game, Newark's steady and dependable pitching staff collapsed. Marvin Duke, Charlie Devens, and Hank McDonald were roughed up for fifteen hits and seven runs as Toronto came back from a 4-1 deficit to win the game, 7-4. The end was now in sight. It would take a minor miracle for the Bears to win the play-offs.

Behind the courageous pitching of Walter Brown, Newark gallantly fought back to shut out Toronto in the fifth game. There were some anxious moments, however. The mighty right-hander, guarding a slim 1-0 lead, loaded the bases with no one out in the bottom of the eighth inning. But the Newark ace managed to meet the challenge by inducing Joe Morrissey to hit into a 5-2-3 double play and got George McQuinn out on an easy fly to center field. In the top of the ninth, Alexander smacked a two-run homer over the right field fence to pad the lead. The final score went to Newark, 3-0, and the team was now down by only one game in the play-offs.

Back at Ruppert Stadium, the Bears were still under a great deal of pressure. Shawkey called on Vito Tamulis in the sixth game and the little left-hander pitched his heart out. He gave up five hits and two runs, but struck out eight, walked none, and retired the last twelve in a row! The Bears won, 3-2, and Alexander drove in all three of their runs — an RBI single in the first and a two-run homer in the third. Don Brennan, the Bears' nemisis, started the game, but it wasn't his day. He lasted only three innings. He was wild, his fastball had no zip, and his usual sharp curve was hanging. It now appeared the Bears were about to pull off that minor miracle. With their latest victory, they had managed to come from behind and tie the series, forcing the play-offs to go the full seven games. In addition, the Bears now had the home game advantage at Ruppert Stadium.

Over 7,500 Newark fans came to watch the final game under the lights. Shawkey gave the nod to his rookie right-hander, Jack LaRocca. No doubt the Bears' manager vividly remembered game number three when Jack hurled a clutch three-hitter to blank Toronto, 6-0, and give the Bears their first play-off victory. In a bold and daring move, Manager Ike Boone selected Don Brennan to pitch for the Leafs. It was a gutsy decision on Boone's part, since Brennan had been knocked out of the box only the day before after pitching just three innings. It was the kind of decision that would bring Boone either instant success or severe criticism. Boone lucked out; his decison brought instant success. Brennan pitched a brilliant game, shutting out the Bears, 2-0, on three measly hits. He had a total of eleven strike outs, many of which snuffed out scoring opportunities for Newark. It was a magnificent, clutch-pitching performance which completely overshadowed LaRocca's fine showing. Once again, the Bears were eliminated from the play-offs in the first round, leaving behind a disappointed and frustrated group of players. Yankee management was clearly upset. Newark had seen two consecutive first place finishes and had nothing to show for it. The Bears had the right to be bitter, as Weiss indicated by his stinging comments. "It is eminently unfair to the players. The club that leads for most of the season during a 154-game campaign naturally is under the strain of protecting its position. It is too much to ask these same performers to go through two brief series where anything can happen.

"Then you get a club like Toronto, which acquired help during the last month of the season, quite obviously for use in the play-offs. Cincinnati would never have sent Don Brennan to the Leafs so late in the season if it weren't for these post-season games. If the Yankees ever did anything like that for the Bears, there would have been a tremendous howl around the league about chain store baseball."

Shawkey, packing in preparation for a hunting trip in the Canadian woods, echoed these strong statements in condemning the system. "In a seven game series," said Bob, "luck plays too great a part in the proceedings. The first two games which Toronto won are proof enough of that."

6.

The Downhill Years
1935 and 1936

URING THE NEXT TWO YEARS, 1935 AND 1936, THE BEARS would not have to concern themselves with what Weiss in 1934 had called "the strain of protecting its position." The position Weiss was referring to was first place and the Bears wouldn't come close. In 1935, they finished in fourth place. The following year, 1936, they didn't make much of an improvement, finishing third. Both seasons were big disappointments for both the Yankee management and the Newark fans.

Still smarting from the 1934 play-off defeat, Ruppert emphatically reiterated his position, making it perfectly clear that he bitterly opposed the play-off system. It was rumored that he felt so strongly about the eliminations that if they continued in 1935, he would dispose of the Newark Bears. During the winter major-minor league meeting in Louisville, Weiss fought hard, insisting that the pennant winner of 154 games should be able to represent the league in the Little World Series. But he was alone in his battle. Once again, Weiss and the Yankee management went down in defeat as the International League voted 7-1 to continue the play-offs. (It earned Weiss the nickname, "Seven-to-One-George.") The rumor about Ruppert's intentions to sell the Bears was just that — a rumor. Like it or not, the Newark Bears were going to play baseball in 1935 and the play-offs were going to be an integral part of the league schedule.

The International League's insistence on the play-offs, however, was not without cost. In a surprise move, the American Association decided to scrap its own post-season series between the leaders of its Western and Eastern divisions. It voted to award its pennant to the team with the highest winning percentage over the full 154-game schedule. The American Association then asked the International League to do likewise or to at least simplify the pennant race and have the "real champs" over the regular schedule meet the American Association champs. The International League refused and the American Association, in another surprise move, pulled out of the Little World Series. It was the first time since 1916 that the series wasn't played (except for the war year 1918).

Around the same time the play-offs were under scrutiny and the leagues were battling it out, Bob Shawkey quietly signed another one-year contract to manage the Bears. It was a fitting reward for the successful season, despite the play-off elimination. Shawkey was now looking ahead to 1935 and to a team that would win it all — both the pennant and the play-offs.

Never one to stand pat, George Weiss began a series of rapid-fire transactions that sent veteran ballplayers packing and young, inexperienced talent rushing to Newark for their big chance. Dale Alexander, Vince Barton, Eddie Farrell, Bob Gibson, Jess Hill, Fred Muller, and Walter Brown were some of the old timers who were either sold, traded, or signed with the Yankees. As a point of record, only three familiar faces from the 1934 team remained with Newark — second baseman Roy Schalk and pitchers Frank Makosky and Jack LaRocca.

Unlike prior Newark teams that consisted largely of surplus talent dropped by the Yankees, the 1935 Bears were comprised mainly from the Yankee farms of lower class ball. It was a youthful team with a dash of experience. A perfect example was Shawkey's pitching staff, considered to be Newark's major weakness. Bob Miller, Ray White, Cecil Spittler, Kemp Wicker, and Howard LaFlamme were all playing in the International League for the first time. As a result, the major responsibility for carrying the pitching staff would fall on the shoulders of three veterans, Makosky, LaRocca, and the newly-acquired Ted Kleinhaus, a southpaw from the Cincinnati Reds.

In spite of their youth and inexperience, players like George McQuinn, Nolen Richardson, Willard Hershberger, and Bill Baker, along with veteran Dick Porter, would turn in fine performances throughout the season.

Another noticeable change from the previous years was that most experts picked the Bears to finish fourth. Shawkey knew this, but he was banking on speed, hustle, and the natural enthusiasm of his young players to win ball games. Youth was the keynote, but a little help from the Yankees late in the season was a welcome asset.

The 1935 season for the Bears would not go down as one of their finest, but it did provide excitement and some memorable moments, one of which occurred shortly before Opening Day. On April 7 at Ruppert Stadium, Newark played their first exhibition game after returning from spring training in Clearwater. Over 10,000 fans packed the stadium to watch the Bears take on the Boston Braves, featuring the immortal Babe Ruth at first base. It was the Babe's first appearance in the East since joining the Braves. Many of the fans were anxious to see what effect the passage of another year had on the aging slugger. They didn't have to wait long. In the first inning, facing Frank Makosky with a count of two balls and no strikes, Ruth "selected a slow fork ball and slammed it into the right field stands at a point a modest 350 feet from home plate." In the sixth, against Bob Miller, Ruth hit a fast ball over the fence at the extreme right center field corner. It cleared the wall by about thirty feet and the press later reported, "The drive was generally estimated over 450 feet. Ruth himself believes it was close to 500 and he said after the game that he never hit a ball harder." As he had done so often in the past, Ruth stole the show and delighted the thousands of fans by leaving them with memories they would always cherish.

Surprisingly, the Bears started the season quickly, winning 10 of 14 at home and finding themselves sitting on top of the league. As the Bears left Newark for their first road trip, Weiss cautiously commented, "Our kindergarten class has astounded me by winning so many ball games at home. But I am afraid they'll crack up on foreign fields. If they maintain a .500 average on the road, they'll be doing mighty well and I'll be surprised.''

Weiss, the shrewd fortune-teller of baseball, was correct again. The Bears did poorly on the road. It was a combination of weak hitting and key injuries to Kleinhaus, Richardson, McQuinn, and Don Heffner (a Yankee gift on option). Consequently, the Bears tumbled all the way to fifth place. But the situation was not as gloomy as it appeared on the surface. Less than four games separated the first five clubs. It looked like it was going to be a dog fight down the stretch.

Shortly afterwards, in spite of some personnel changes, including the obtaining of Dixie Walker "for the remainder of the season," the Bears went into a severe tailspin. During a twenty-one-day road trip consisting of 25 games, they won 8 and lost 17. In addition, they had a losing streak of 13 games in a row, plummeting them to sixth place, 5½ games behind fifth place Syracuse. It was the lowest point of their season. After one game in which the Bears used four pitchers, it was sarcastically suggested that Shawkey use the young Bloomfield High School pitcher, Hank Borowy, who was touring with them at the time. He had been voted the Most Valuable Player in the Greater Newark Tournament.

On August 22, with only 19 games left to play, the Bears still found themselves mired in sixth place, six full games behind the fourth place Baltimore Orioles. They were down, but not yet out. Determined to make a fight of it, the Bears moved into Albany and swept the Senators for three straight games. They proceeded to win 3 out of 4 in Baltimore and then returned home to sweep the Syracuse Chiefs in four straight. Having won 10 of their last 11 games, the Bears were now tied for fourth place with only eight games remaining.

Ironically enough, three rainy days prevented the two games scheduled against Baltimore and left Newark deadlocked with only six games left. Still hot, the Bears won 4 of 6 from Albany, but it really didn't matter. The Orioles collapsed in their series with Syracuse. What seemed like a hopeless situation only a few weeks before had magically turned into an exciting and dramatic finish, culminating in a clinched play-off position for Newark. It was a total team effort on the Bear's part, but two names stood out above the others in this final stretch. One player was Steve Sundra, obtained earlier from Minneapolis, who had won three key games. The other was Dick Porter, who ran his batting average from .300 to .334, finishing the season as the team leader.

Shawkey had high praise for both players. He considered Sundra one of the best prospects in the league and thought that if he had been with the Bears from the start, they would have finished first instead of fourth. Commenting on Porter, Shawkey said, "Here is a fellow presumably past his peak, and generally when a man comes down from the major leagues into the minors, he figures he is simply playing out the string and performs accordingly. But Porter went to work without a murmur, set a fine example for the youngsters by hustling every minute, and wound up with the best batting average on the club."

A few days later, the Bears eagerly opened the play-offs against the second place Chiefs at Syracuse. Both teams were evenly matched despite the fact that the Chiefs had won 15 of 22 games from Newark during the regular season. The statisticians had noted that 9 of the Chiefs' 15 victories were by a slim one-run lead. In addition, the Bears had swept the four-game series the last time they faced the Chiefs. Each team had three .300 hitters, but the Bears had a slightly better team average of .275 to the Chiefs' .266. Newark had also led the league in fielding with a .977 percentage. It appeared to most observers that the series would be a close, hard-fought one and would probably go the full seven games.

In the first game, Steve Sundra hooked up with Joe Cascarella in a tough pitchers' duel. Both pitched magnificently, allowing only six hits apiece. But Sundra's control failed him in the fourth inning and the two men that he walked eventually scored, providing the Chiefs with a 3-2 victory. It was a heartbreaking game for the Bears to lose, especially since Cascarella's pinpoint control turned out to be the margin of victory.

In game number two, the Bears hoped to even up the series by starting their ace veteran, Ted Kleinhaus. After six and a half innings, the score was tied, 2-2. In the bottom of the seventh, however, the Chiefs loaded the bases and Shawkey sent Kleinhaus to the showers. Frank Makosky then came to the mound to pitch to Johnny Kroner. Kroner wasted no time and blasted one over the fence for a grand slam home run as over 6,000 partisan fans screamed in delight. The final score went to the Chiefs, 6-3.

The scene shifted to Ruppert Stadium for the third game. Although the Bears had their backs to the wall, down two games to none, the eternal optimists enthusiastically pointed out that Newark had boasted a .650 winning percentage at home during the season. In addition, Shawkey called on Jack LaRocca, who had pitched two previous shutouts against the Chiefs. It appeared the odds were finally with the Bears. Maybe the odds were, but the final score wasn't. The Chiefs won their third straight, 3-1, as over 9,600 fans witnessed the third exciting pitching duel. Once again, the Chiefs received a brilliant pitching performance from right-hander Reggie Grabowski, in spite of Shawkey's valiant attempt at juggling the lineup. Grabowski scattered four hits and allowed only one walk.

The next night, the Chiefs made it a clean sweep as Joe Mulligan pitched a three-hitter and the Bears went down, 5-2. Left fielder Nick Dallessandro was the batting hero of the evening with a perfect five-for-five, including two homers, a double, and three RBI's. Steve Sundra took the loss.

The short series turned out to be a dismal and embarrassing ending to the Bears' gallant drive to the play-offs.

Shawkey summed up his feelings when a well-wisher entered the clubhouse after the game and said, "Tough luck, Bob." "Tough luck, nothing," replied Shawkey. "The Syracuse boys simply gave us a good shellacking."

In addition to their "shellacking," the Bears also had the unenviable distinction of being the first team since the play-off system began to be eliminated in four straight games. Although not many people in Newark were interested at the time, the Syracuse Chiefs went on to defeat the Montreal Royals in seven games to capture the pennant in the International League. It was a small consolation for the Newark fans.

During the off season, the Bears' management announced that Sebring, Florida would be their new spring training camp for 1936. The final selection of Sebring was made after the Brooklyn Dodgers decided to move back to Clearwater. Apparently the Bears didn't want to compete with a major league team or even share their facilities. Sebring, nestled among the hills and lakes of central Florida, was 90 miles from Tampa, 220 miles from Miami, 275 from Jacksonville, and 100 from Orlando. It boasted a population of 2,500 — all eagerly awaiting the arrival of the Newark Bears. It marked the first time a "big minor league club" trained in Sebring.

About a month after the Sebring announcement, George Weiss calmly proclaimed in a terse statement to the press, "The Newark Baseball Club regrets to announce that Bob Shawkey will not return as its manager next season." After the buzzing died down, Weiss continued, "Shawkey's work here has been entirely satisfactory, but it is felt that interest outside of baseball will not permit his giving the 100 percent attention which is required in his position as manager of the club. He leaves with the respect, good will, and best wishes of every member of this organization."

The "interest outside of baseball" that Weiss was referring to was the Canadian gold mine that Shawkey owned. It was rapidly developing into a bonanza. Whether this was the true reason for Shawkey's dismissal or just a convenient excuse would be difficult to say. Shawkey did mention, however, that he would be willing to invest in a ball club "if the proposition was right."

Shortly after the firing, rumors of Shawkey's replacement began surfacing. Bill Meyer at Binghamton, Bill Skiff at Norfolk, and Johnny Neun at Akron were some of the contenders mentioned for the position. In an attempt to clarify the situation, Weiss was telephoned at Williamsport and asked for his comments. "Meyer is one of several men under consideration, but he isn't the No. 1 choice. As a matter of fact, I haven't been able to give the Newark vacancy as much thought as I want to because I didn't know that situation would come to a head so soon. The need of picking a manager to succeed Bob Shawkey became public sooner than I had hoped it would. If I knew now who the Bears' new pilot will be, I'd have no hesitancy in announcing it immediately. There are so many angles and so many things can happen during the next two weeks that even I have no idea right now who will get the job. There are so many deserving of consideration, including some that haven't even been mentioned by the newspaper guessers, that no individual can be said to have anything better than an outside chance at this time, and I say that without intending any disparagement of any of the men who have been suggested, including Meyer and Johnny Neun, each of whom has served our organization capably at Binghamton and Akron respectively.''

While all the speculation concerning the new manager was flying around, another surprise change almost went unnoticed. George Trautman, President of the American Association, decided to end the differences between his league and the International League by signing an agreement to resume the popular Little World Series. Once again, the rival leagues would square off in the fall classic and provide the fans with exciting post season baseball.

But the real surprise came when the Bears announced the selection of their new manager. It came as such a surprise mainly because his name had never been mentioned before. Rumors were so concentrated on local organizers — men like Meyer, Skiff, and Neun — that the appointment of Oscar Vitt, the high-spirited Oakland Manager, came as quite a shock to both Newark and Yankee fans alike. Eventually, Vitt proved to be an excellent choice.

The colorful Oscar Vitt starred at third base for the Detroit Tigers back in the days of Ty Cobb and Sam "Wahoo" Crawford. He played the hot corner for Boston when Ed Barrow managed the Red Sox to a pennant in 1928. Vitt also managed Salt Lake City, developed Tony Lazzeri, and had been the confidential adviser to Barrow on Pacific Coast baseball. He was with Hollywood for ten years, during which time he won three pennants and was so popular with the fans that they threatened to boycott the club when Oscar went to Oakland in 1934. Vitt, always a lively personality, piloted Oakland to second and third place finishes during the split season in the Pacific Coast League in 1935. Both Ruppert and Barrow were outspoken in their praise of Vitt's handling of young talent. It appeared Newark had found a highly capable manager, in addition to a witty, fast talking showman. It would also turn out to be a sportswriter's dream come true.

Vitt's arrival in Newark in February, 1936, however, was less than eventful. The sun-bronzed Manager was met at Pennsylvania Station by Secretary Ray Kennedy and only a handful of avid, shivering fans. Commenting on the weather, Vitt remarked, "This isn't so bad, we had some unusual weather in California the two weeks before I left. It was cold. Nothing like this, of course, but I really expected 'important' snow after seeing some of those mountain high drifts coming across Nebraska and some of those Midwestern states."

When asked about his immediate plans, Vitt flashed his broad, toothy grin and replied, "All I want to do now is look around, clear up whatever has to be cleared up, and get to Florida as soon as possible."

Kennedy whisked Vitt off to the Hotel Douglas, where he sat down with Weiss to discuss the future strategy of the Bears. Later that evening, Oscar was the guest speaker at a dinner that introduced the new Manager to the local scribes. In his customary speaking style — straight from the shoulder — Vitt quickly assessed the Newark situation. "How do I like Newark? Well, I never saw so much snow in all my life."

"Newark is an all-college ball club, eh? Okay, but I prefer sandlotters for raw material."

"The play-offs are all right if my team is in 'em'."

"Of course I expect to give Newark a winner — every manager is optimistic in February."

"The Bears will be okay if I haven't got too many base-on-balls pitchers."

Right from the beginning, Oscar Vitt displayed the kind of tough-minded leadership needed to bring a championship to Newark. The first day at Sebring, he set the tone for the rest of the spring training. "Only bad weather will prevent us from starting

After the Bears' incredible 1937 season, the colorful Oscar Vitt was named the new manager of the Cleveland Indians, replacing Steve O'Neill.

the season in top form. I believe in hard work and lots of it.''

When asked how long he planned to train and practice each day, Vitt shot back, "Well, when the boys' tongues begin to hang out, we might quit. That should take from two and a half to three hours.''

Vitt was always true to his word. He worked his athletes long and hard in the hot Florida sun. He insisted on physical fitness and believed it was the foundation of any good ballplayer's ability. He stressed calisthenics, running, long hikes, and was a stickler for strengthening a player's legs. He was often heard to say, "I'll take a half dozen .280 hitters in preference to a like number of .300 batters if only their legs are okay.''

In addition to physical fitness, Vitt concentrated his attention on perfecting the little things, the fundamentals that often go unnoticed by the average fan, but which can mean the difference between winning and losing. Hours were spent with pitchers perfecting their pick-off moves, with runners in the sliding pit, with outfielders hitting the cut-off man, and with infielders trapping runners between bases. Vitt was returning to the basics and he meant business. The situation became so intolerable that it prompted one youngster to comment, "I thought we came down here to play ball, I believe I'll go looking for a place where they exercise less and play more baseball.''

At one point during spring training, even the hard-driving Vitt became a little frustrated. During the team's trip to play the Philadelphia A's, the boys were treated to a scenic tour of Florida — West Haven, Palm Beach, and down the Tamiami Trail through the stately royal palms into the Gulf Coast town of Fort Meyers. It was a wonderful trip, but there was one major consequence. The following day, the A's humiliated the Bears by a score of 19-0! Vitt was incensed.

"Listen," he said sarcastically to no one in particular, "these athletes have been learning a whole lot about geography and it begins to look very much to me as if they have overlooked everything else. From now on, they're going to learn a little about hitting and perhaps pitching. Fortunately, we have no ball games today, so I'm going to take these boys into that Sebring ball park and try to teach them a few things. They're throwing to wrong bases and making other mistakes, and a little skull practice is very necessary. As for batting, they'll hit until it hurts today.''

While Vitt was busy establishing himself as a tough disciplinarian, the front office was slowly changing the complexion of the team. The Bears picked up right-hander Spud Chandler, who had pitched for both Oakland and Portland in the Pacific Coast League, and another right-hander, Al Piechota, who with Davenport had led the Western League with 157 strikeouts. However, the Bears lost two veteran pitchers at the same time. Right-hander Jack LaRocca was sent to strengthen the Oakland club under its new manager, Bill Meyer, and left-hander Ted Kleinhaus was sent up to the Yankees.

In the infield, first baseman George McQuinn received his long-awaited chance in the major leagues and was sold to the Cincinnati Reds, along with catcher Bill Raimondi. With first base open, the Bears went ahead and sold John Buddy Hassett to the Brooklyn Dodgers for 21-year-old first baseman John McCarthy and outfielder Ralph Boyle. McCarthy had played professional ball for only two years, but he displayed a good deal of potential. Boyle was a veteran who played for the Dodgers in 1934 and 1935, batting .305 and .267, respectively. Roy Schalk, who appeared in only 15 games for the Bears in 1935, had fully recovered from the torn ligaments in his right shoulder and would replace Don Heffner at second base. Heffner and Dixie Walker would join the Yankees.

On the eve of the opening game, Vitt was asked for his outlook on the 1936 International League pennant race. "I hesitate to predict a pennant for Newark," answered a cautious Vitt. "We'll give them a battle. We seem to have the perfect man for every position on the field, and whether we win or not will depend a great deal upon our pitching.

"Besides, I'm new in the league and don't know what the other clubs have. I'll be able to tell you more after the Bears make one swing around the circuit.''

Before a crowd of over 10,000 fans at Ruppert Stadium, the

Bears spoiled Oscar's debut by losing the opener to Toronto, 7-5. The Leafs won it in the ninth inning when they scored three runs with two men out. Not at all deterred, Newark came storming back and won their next 10 games in a row. By the end of May, after battling Montreal and Buffalo, the Bears wound up in first place, led by the timely hitting of Chief Koy, John McCarthy, Ralph Boyle, Roy Schalk, and Merrill May, as well as the clutch pitching of Al Piechota, Kemp Wicker, and Frank Makosky. Koy, at the time, was leading the league with eight home runs and at that pace would finish the year with 35-40.

Along the road to first place, Vitt received some good news and some bad news. The good news was the addition of two experienced pitchers from the Yankees, Vito Tamulis and Steve Sundra. Tamulis, who compiled a 10-5 record with the Yankees in 1935, was still recovering from a severe case of pleurisy. Sundra, who pitched the Bears into the 1935 play-offs, was already a familiar face on the team. The bad news was that catcher Willard Hershberger would go to Oakland to replace the injured Norman Kies, leaving Bill Baker as the team's full-time receiver.

The Bears continued to lead the league throughout the month of June — a credit to their fiery manager. Vitt, of course, didn't enjoy losing. He was determined to bring a winner to Newark. An excellent example of his high-spirited competitiveness was seen in late June during the second game of a double-header against the Syracuse Chiefs.

With the score tied in extra innings, the Chiefs' catcher, John Heving, caught a foul tip, split his finger, and had to be removed from the game. The Chiefs' other catcher, Doc Legett, had already pinch hit and was out of the game, leaving Syracuse without a catcher. Faced with this predicament, the Chiefs' Manager, Nemo Leibold, walked out to the third base coaching line and in full view of the spectators, beckoned Vitt to waive the rules and allow Legett to catch. Vitt shook his head in refusal, bringing down the wrath of the fans. As one reporter put it, "Everything from invectives to pop bottles swirled around his gray head..." Later, when Vitt was questioned about his decision, he declared, "My job is to win ball games. Permitting courtesy performers is all right in a one-sided game, but I will not do it when a game is tied." The Bears won in twelve innings, 9-7.

After the double-header with Syracuse, Newark went into its most serious slump of the year. It was a case of very little hitting and a lot of sloppy fielding. By July 7, Rochester took over first place and Newark was on a downward slide that was nearly impossible to stop. Some blamed it on the young players pressing too hard. The more they pressed, the less they hit. The less they hit, the more games they lost and the harder they pressed. It was a vicious cycle. By the end of July, the Bears were in third place and still falling.

A frustrated Vitt didn't know what to make of the problem. "What am I going to do?" he asked. "What can I do? It's getting so that I change the lineup more often than I change my shirt, and if you examine the haberdashery, you will note it is freshly laundered.

"If there were two or three men on the club who were hitting consistently, I might be able to switch them around until I found the spots where their hits would do the most good. But when nobody hits, the only thing one can do is sit back and wait until someone starts.

"As for obtaining help, there aren't any deals in sight at the moment, and even if we could get assistance somewhere, how would one know who to take out of the lineup? There's always that fear that the fellow who was benched might have broken out in a rash of base hits just when you took him out."

Although the Bears' pennant hopes were fading, a play-off berth was still within reach. In an unexplainable move, the Yankees sent Ted Kleinhaus back to the Bears and recalled Kemp Wicker. As reported by the press, it was "one of those unfathomed deals peculiar to baseball and particularly to chain systems..." By August 16, after a sweep of the Buffalo Bisons, the Bears finally managed to clinch a play-off spot, much to the relief of the loyal Newark fans. In addition, their pennant hopes were given a shot in the arm. "We're not quite out of this race," Vitt proclaimed. "I will admit that Buffalo's lead over us of 7½ games is practically a prohibitive advantage with only 26 games to play, but while Rochester and Buffalo are tearing at each other's throats this week, we'll be playing 5 games with Albany, and you can never tell. At any rate, we still have a very good chance to finish second, for the Red Wings are only 4½ games ahead of us now.''

In another player acquistion, the Bears picked up Francis Kelleher, a utility infielder who batted an outstanding .355 on the Akron farm club. The Bears were counting on the young and enthusiastic Californian from St. Mary's College to provide the spark in their quest for the pennant drive, but more importantly, to help with the play-offs. The best the Bears could do, however, was to finish in a dead heat with Rochester for second place. This required a single play-off game that turned out to be a disaster. Newark developed a bad case of the jitters, booted home three unearned runs for Rochester in the first inning, and lost the game, 5-2. They also lost the $2,000 purse and had to face the tough, pennant-winning Buffalo club in the first round of the play-offs.

Both Newark and Buffalo appeared to be evenly matched. During the regular season, they split the 22 games that they played against one another. Oddly enough, they each won 8 of 11 games at home. If there was any edge, it was that the first two games would be played in Buffalo, the next three in Newark, and the final two, if necessary, back in Buffalo. The Bisons therefore had the home field advantage.

In the first game, Spud Chandler pitched his heart out for seven straight innings. But in the eighth, the roof caved in and Buffalo scored six runs. On top of this, the Bears were punchless as southpaw Carl Fisher tossed a four-hit shutout. Buffalo easily took the opener, 6-0.

The next day, the Bisons made it two in a row as Ken Ash continued to baffle the Bears. The right-hander allowed seven hits and only one run. The combination of Marvin Duke and Ted Kleinhaus had trouble finding the plate and walked a total of nine Buffalo players, in addition to giving up eleven hits. The final score went to Buffalo, 7-1.

After two quick defeats, the Bears were happy to leave Buffalo and Offerman Stadium. Back in Newark before a scant crowd of 2,500 fans, the Bears picked up their first victory, 2-0, behind the exceptionally strong pitching of Vito Tamulis. Tamulis was never better. The lefty allowed only five hits, struck out seven, and had near perfect control. His most effective pitch was his change of pace "that drifted up to the plate like a butterfly and had the Bison swingers breaking their backs," as one sportswriter put it.

Prosperity was short lived, however, and Buffalo won the next game, 6-1. Bob Kline gave up six hits and one run as the Bears' bats continued to nap through the play-offs. It was a close game until the sixth inning, when Buffalo scored three runs off Steve Sundra on three singles and a double. The Bisons added two more in the eighth. After four games, Newark had managed to score only four runs. The batting slump that plagued them during July had returned to rear its ugly head in the play-offs.

Although the Bears chased starter Carl Fisher in the fifth game and scored four runs, it was nonetheless a case of "too little, too late." Buffalo won, 7-4, scoring five runs in the fourth inning off Ted Kleinhaus. Once again, play-off history repeated itself with monotonus regularity. Another season had brought another play-off disappointment.

A few day after the final loss to Buffalo, Vitt headed home to California and gave the press a temporary farewell. "It might not have been quite as successful a campaign as some of us hoped," declared Vitt as he boarded a midnight train. "But in ten years of managing ball clubs, I seldomed have enjoyed better treatment at the hands of the fans and my associates."

In the four years since the play-off system had begun, the Bears had managed to win only 5 games while losing 15. It was a dismal and embarrassing performance, to say the least. But it was destined to change. Ruppert and Company were running out of patience fast. They wanted a winner — a club that could take it all, both pennant and play-offs.

In 1937, their wish would be fulfilled. The Yankee management, the Bears, and their loyal Newark fans would finally see a winner. And what a season it would be, right from the start of spring training.

7.

Spring Training 1937

HERE WAS LITTLE DOUBT OSCAR VITT WOULD RETURN to manage the Newark Bears in 1937. Colonel Ruppert, Ed Barrow, George Weiss, and all of Newark were delighted with the job Ol' Os had done. It came as no surprise when Secretary Ray Kennedy announced that the personable field general had signed another one-year contract.

Buoyed by the Yankees' return to baseball dominance in 1936 with a team that trounced the Giants in the World Series, the Yankee management had high hopes for a similar performance in 1937 from the Bears. Obviously the Bears could not stand pat with their 1936 team. It had too many glaring weaknesses — one .300 hitter, little long-distance power, an irratic defense, inconsistent pitching, and a mixture of players who had either reached their peak or had never had the ability to make the major leagues. The challenge that faced Weiss and the Yankee scouting staff was a difficult one. They had to overhaul the entire team from top to bottom. The ever-efficient Weiss wasted no time. Long before spring training had rolled around, more than half of the '36 team had departed. The players were either sold outright, released, traded, or, more happily, moved up to the Yankees. They were replaced by a bunch of hopefuls who in the months to come would play their hearts out in an attempt to impress Manager Vitt. Aside from Nolen Richardson at shortstop, every other position was up for grabs. Vitt was therefore faced with the near impossible task of putting together a winning team from a roster mostly full of young, eager, and inexperienced ballplayers. And he had to accomplish this by mid-April. He did. The rest is history.

The training camp at Sebring was open less than a week when Vitt picked up a copy of the Jersey Giants' roster, glanced through the 51 players, and declared he had never before seen "...assembled on a single sheet of paper such a terrific and staggering collection of stumblebums and smudgepots."

Six hundred miles away in Gulfport, Mississippi where the Jersey Giants had just finished a three-and-a-half hour workout under the blazing Mississippi sun, Manager Travis Calvin Jackson murmured, "So that Vitt guy is blowing again, eh?"

Travis "Stonewall" Jackson, or "Stony" for short, started his professional baseball career in 1921 with Little Rock. The following year, he was purchased by the New York Giants and starred at shortstop for the next fifteen years. Stony played in four World Series for the Giants — 1923, 1924, 1933, and 1936. In 1930, he played in 115 games, batted a solid .339, and drove in 82 runs. His best RBI season, however, came in 1934 when he drove in 101 runs and belted 16 homers. Jackson called it quits after the 1936 season, ending his major league career with a respectable lifetime batting average of .291. But a few months later, he was right back in baseball. In January of 1937, before a battery of cameras in the New York Giants' office on West 42nd Street, Stony agreed to sign a three-year contract with President Horace Stoneham to manage the newly acquired Jersey Giants.

Vitt, who was never at a loss for words, apparently wanted to give the rookie manager a quick taste of what it was like to manage in the International League.

Jackson stepped out of his shower dripping wet to face Jack Cook, Secretary for the Jersey Giants, who continued to read Vitt's comments from the newspaper. "Now, isn't that a nice, smart, tactful, diplomatic thing for a guy like Vitt to be saying," whistled Jackson after Cook finished reading the article. "There's a guy putting himself right on the spot. He admits himself he's got a good ball club and declares we have an awful one. He'll have everything to lose and nothing to gain when he plays a bunch of hams like he says we are. After all, we're going into the league with a tail end club. Wouldn't it be awful to take a licking at the hands of such a club?

"Smudgepots and stumblebums he calls us, eh?" Jackson began to get into his street clothes and added, "I really thought Vitt had done enough blowing for one man when he blew the International League pennant last season, after having been far out in front through the greater part of the race, but I am afraid I underestimated little Ossie's volume."

The more Jackson talked, the hotter he became. "Putting the blast on our roster is he? Why, the man must be nuts. I looked through his roster the other day. All I could see on his club was a bunch of guys named Joe." Jackson smiled as he pulled out a Newark roster from his pocket. "Yes, sir, look at this, Joe Beggs, Joe Mitchell, Joe Gordon, Joe Gallagher — honest, I almost expected to see Joe Wall's name there too. ² And as for the other guys on the club, the so-called standouts, maybe you can tell me what forest fires fellows like McQuinn and Richardson and Seeds and May, for instance, set?" Jackson continued in his sarcastic vein, "McQuinn is so good they are moving heaven and earth to sell him. They'd sell May, too, tomorrow, if they could get an offer. Richardson was up there with the Yanks, but he didn't quite make the grade and they shipped him back."

Jackson paused to get his second wind. "So Vitt thinks I'm too old to play third and that LeRoy Anton should have been retired by this time under the Social Security Act, eh?" The Jersey pilot went on, "Well, well. Let's skip that part about myself, even though I happened to be the regular third baseman for the National League Champions only last year. We couldn't expect Vitt to know that. But it is funny to hear him talk about Anton. Why, as far as age is concerned, Anton is a mere babe in arms compared to Richardson. If, as Vitt claims, Anton should be retired under the Social Security

2. Joseph Francis Wall played a total of fifteen games in the major leagues as a atcher and outfielder — four with the New York Giants in 1901 and six in 1902. He lso played five games with the Brooklyn Dodgers in 1902. Wall died in 1936 at the ge of 63.

1937 · **SPRING TRAINING SCHEDULE** · 1937

Wednesday, March	10	First squad leaves
Thursday, "	11	Training session
Friday, "	12	Training session
Saturday, "	13	Training session
Sunday, "	14	Main squad leaves
Monday, "	15	Training session
Tuesday, "	16	Training session
Wednesday, "	17	Training session
Thursday, "	18	Training session
Friday, "	19	Training session
Saturday, "	20	Training session
Sunday, "	21	Louisville at Arcadia
Monday, "	22	Yankees at Sebring
Tuesday, "	23	Training session
Wednesday, "	24	Baltimore at Sebring
Thursday, "	25	Cincinnati at Sebring
Friday, "	26	Yankees at St. Petersburg
Saturday, "	27	Red Sox at Sarasota
Sunday, "	28	Phillies at Sebring
Monday, "	29	Brooklyn at Sebring
Tuesday, "	30	Baltimore at Winter Garden
Wednesday, "	31	Training session
Thursday, April	1	Phillies at Winter Haven
Friday, "	2	Toronto at Sebring
Saturday, "	3	Louisville at Sebring
Sunday, "	4	Brooklyn at Clearwater
Monday, "	5	Training session
Tuesday, "	6	Sebring Firemen
Wednesday, "	7	Red Sox at Sebring
Thursday, "	8	Training session
Friday, "	9	Toronto at Haines City
Saturday, "	10	Entrain for Macon
Sunday, "	11	Macon at Macon
Monday, "	12	Augusta at Augusta
Tuesday, "	13	Macon at Macon
Wednesday, "	14	Training session at Spartanburg
Thursday, "	15	Binghamton at Spartanburg
Friday, "	16	Binghamton at Spartanburg
Saturday, "	17	Norfolk at Norfolk
Sunday, "	18	Norfolk at Norfolk
Monday, "	19	Training session at Newark
Tuesday, "	20	Training session at Newark
Wednesday, "	21	Training session at Newark
Thursday, "	22	International League opening

HEADQUARTERS

HOTEL SEBRING   **SEBRING, FLA.**

March 11—April 11   54

NEWARK BEARS

1937

OSCAR (OS) VITT

•

PLAYER ROSTER
AND
SPRING TRAINING
SCHEDULE

1937 — NEWARK INTERNATIONAL BASEBALL CLUB, INC. — 1937

Jacob Ruppert, Pres.　　Geo. M. Weiss, Vice Pres.　　Ray L. Kennedy, Secy.　　R. J. Campbell, Bus. Mgr.

	Bats	Throws	Age	MANAGER		Home Address	Club—1936
				Wt.	Ht.		
Oscar (Os) Vitt	R	R	47	170	5' 9"	Oakland, Calif.	Newark Mgr.
PITCHERS							
Beggs, Joseph	R	R	22	172	6' 0"	Aliquippa, Penna.	Norfolk
Bithorn, Hiram	R	R	19	202	6' 1"	Puerto Rico	Norfolk
Branch, Norman	R	R	21	180	6' 2"	Montgomery, Texas	College
Donald, Atley	L	R	24	186	6' 1"	Downsville, La.	Binghamton
Fallon, John	R	R	24	185	6' 3½"	Quincy, Mass.	Binghamton
Mitchell, Joseph	R	R	21	186	6' 4"	Alexander City, Ala.	Norfolk
Naktenis, Peter	L	L	21	185	6' 1"	Hartford, Conn.	College
Piechota, Albert	R	R	22	190	5' 11½"	Chicago, Ill.	Newark
Russo, Marius	L	L	22	190	6' 1½"	Ozone Park, L. I.	College
Spittler, Cecil	R	R	24	175	6' 0"	Cranford, N. J.	Newark
Yocke, William	L	L	25	175	6' 2½"	Wheeling, Va.	Norfolk

CATCHERS						
Hershberger, Willard	R	25	165	5' 10"	Fullerton, Calif.	Oakland
Holm, William	R	23	165	5' 10"	Chicago, Ill.	Norfolk
Rosar, Warren	R	22	170	5' 10"	Buffalo, N.Y.	Binghamton
INFIELDERS						
Gordon, Joseph	R	21	175	5' 11"	Portland, Ore.	Oakland
Kelleher, Francis	R	20	186	6' 1"	Crockett, Calif.	Akron
Matheson, William	R	21	185	6' 0"	Oakland, Calif.	Binghamton
May, Merrill	R	25	180	5' 10½"	Laconia, Ind.	Newark
McQuinn, George	L	25	170	5' 11"	Ballston, Va.	Toronto
Richardson, Nolen	R	32	175	6' 1½"	Houston, Texas	Newark
Witek, Michael	R	21	165	5' 10"	Luzerne, Penna.	Norfolk
OUTFIELDERS						
Boyle, Ralph	L	27	170	5' 11½"	Cincinnati, Ohio	Newark
Gallagher, Joseph	R	23	210	6' 2"	Buffalo, N.Y.	Norfolk
Glynn, Jack	L	24	178	5' 11"	Franklin, N.J.	Oakland
Longacre, Edgar	R	24	175	6' 1"	Swedesboro, N.J.	Binghamton
Seeds, Robert	R	29	177	6' 0"	Texola, Okla.	Yankees

Jimmy Mack, *Trainer*

The 1937 roster at spring training changed drastically throughout the season. Many players were either traded, sold, or sent down, while new players were added.

Francis Kelleher, 21-year-old utility infielder-outfielder, played key role in 1937 filling in for injured players.

Act, then Vitt should be arrested for cruelty to the aged and in-firmed because he is using Richardson. After all, Richardson is five years *older* than Anton. And that Bob Seeds has long since forgot-ten when he got out of kindergarten, too.

"Sure we picked up a lot of free agents and brought them down here, but we did that so that DeBerry and Brazil, who run our Greenwood club, could look 'em over. If Vitt would have looked at our roster a bit closely, he would have realized that, but he didn't. After all, Newark has only twenty-six men listed on its roster to our forty, and we have still eleven other players in camp whose names don't appear on the roster.

"Yes, after Jolley and Sulik and Wilson and Anton and Lee and these other players he ridicules get through with him this summer, he'll have to spell his last name with an F instead of a V."

The gauntlet was dropped! Vitt, with his caustic comments, had set the stage for a rivalry the Jersey City and Newark fans could en-joy all summer. And it was one that Ruppert and Stoneham could profit from handsomely.

On Sunday, March 21, 1937, the Newark Bears opened their twenty-two-game exhibition schedule against the Louisville Col-onels at Arcadia, about forty miles from Sebring. The Bears won, 5-4. The bright spot of the game was the chunky 20-year-old third baseman, Francis Kelleher, who had joined the Bears at the tail end of the 1936 season to help in the pennant drive. Kelleher tripled with the bases loaded, driving in three of the five runs, and later he scored the fourth. However, the rap on the kid was that he was too slow for the infield. But two great defensive plays had the experts reconsidering. The first was a slow roller to Kelleher's left that he scooped up and rifled across the mound to nip the runner. The se-cond was a vicious grounder to his right that he backhanded and fired to first to get the out. Merrill May, the veteran third baseman, sat in the dugout and took some good-natured needling from Vitt as he watched Kelleher challenge his position.

The next day, the Bears opened at Firemen's Field in Sebring and beat the New York Yankees, 5-3, for two in a row. In spite of the heavy downpour before the game, a capacity crowd of over 1,000 came out to watch such Yankee greats as Frankie Crosetti, Joe DiMaggio, Lou Gehrig, Red Rolfe, and George Selkirk. Ruppert threw out the first ball with assistance from Mayor McBee of Sebring. "I don't care who wins," said the Colonel, "I can't lose."

In the very first inning, Gehrig delighted the local residents by blasting a three-run homer off Atley Donald, the young right-hander who had posted a 19-9 record at Binghamton in 1936. But that was it for the Yankees. Long Island southpaw Marius Russo and right-hander Al Piechota pitched shutout ball for the rest of the game. Piechota allowed only two hits in the last three innings. Russo, the kid who had just finished pitching for two Brooklyn semiprofessional teams — the Bushwicks and Bay Parkway — was the more impressive, retiring nine Yankees in a row. The young lefty, who commented after the game that his knees were knocking on the mound, struck out both Crosetti and Gehrig, with big Lou going down swinging at a sharp breaking curve. Bill Matheson, who stepped off the train from Oakland on Sunday night, was the batting hero of the afternoon. The 22-year-old infielder replaced Nolen Richardson at shortstop in the sixth inning. In the seventh, he came to bat with two on, the Bears trailing, 3-1, and belted a long home run.

Two days later, the Bears won their third straight exhibition game as they beat the Baltimore Orioles, 4-1. Richardson drove in three of the four runs with a double and a single. Billy Holm, the skinny 23-year-old catcher who batted .314 with the Norfolk Tars, collected three singles, a walk, and figured in all the scoring. Holm also made an acrobatic catch on a foul pop up, jumping over a pile of bats to make the grab. What impressed Vitt the most was his pitching. Joe Beggs, Bill Yocke, and Hiram Bithorn, who combined to win 52 games at Norfolk the previous year, stymied the long ball hitting Orioles. The trio allowed only seven hits.

Vitt was guarded in his praise, obviously protecting his young men from overconfidence. "Take that Baltimore club," said Ol' Os, "our boys played a creditable game and deserved to win, but I just don't want the young men to get thinking that these birds are going to be easy during the season...

"They are going to be much tougher with big Puccinelli, Powers, and young Heffner in there, and we didn't face their best pitching. Also consider they have been in camp only four days while some of our boys have been here two weeks. Naturally I am mighty proud of what the Bears have done to date, but we have had the breaks and I don't want the youngsters to get thinking this is going to be a breeze."

The Bears ended their winning streak the following day when the Cincinnati Reds managed to shut them out, 1-0. Once again, the Bears' pitching was brilliant. Piechota, Russo, and Donald allowed a total of only three hits and one unearned run. Vitt, however, showed little concern for the defeat. He was too preoccupied. Early in the day, he had accompanied a half dozen players, including outfielder Charlie Keller, to the stadium for some batting practice. Since no pitchers were present, Vitt took the mound and young Keller put on an exhibition of power that had the manager ecstatic. "That boy hit thirty balls in practice...," marveled Ol' Os, "and about eighteen of them would have been home runs in Newark."

Keller, considered one of the outstanding college prospects at the time, had arrived early in the week from the University of Maryland. The Yankee organization was high on Charlie, particularly after watching him play during the summers of 1935 and 1936. Keller played in a league that had the best college players in the area. In this fast company, he hit .385 and .466, respectively, playing in 90 games each year. During the twelve-game play-off series in the fall of 1936, Keller posted an incredible .500 average. Was it any wonder the scouts were buzzing? But the muscular 185-pound college senior chose to begin his professional baseball career at the start of the 1937 season rather than in June when school closed. Both Paul Krichell and Gene McCann had watched Keller for several seasons and were convinced he would eventually make the big leagues. At the same time, however, they felt he wouldn't make Double A in 1937! Even the experts miss one now and then.

The next day at St. Petersburg, the Yankees avenged their earlier

After two consecutive batting titles, Charlie Keller joined the Yankees in 1939. Keller teamed up with Joe DiMaggio and Tommy Henrich to form one of the greatest outfields in baseball.

loss to the Bears by defeating them, 4-2. Pete Naktenis, who had pitched in seven games for Connie Mack's A's in 1936, and Hiram Bithorn both pitched well, allowing only six hits. Bithorn was particularly effective. The Puerto Rican youngster, who before had said his greatest thrill would be to pitch against the Yankees, allowed only three hits in five innings. But in the fourth, the right-hander became the victim of two unearned runs. With two men out, George McQuinn fumbled a grounder hit by Gehrig. Bill Dickey followed with a single and put runners on first and second. George Selkirk then belted a long triple that bounced off the low rampart in right field and scored Gehrig and Dickey. The Yankees picked up two more runs in the sixth.

On Saturday, March 27, Joe Cronin brought his Boston Red Sox to Sebring and whipped the Bears, 6-4. Cronin must have had a lapse of memory and thought it was October. He used his two top pitchers, Lefty Grove and Wes Ferrell, who had posted records of 17-12 and 20-15 the season before. The combination was too much for the young Bears. Grove mowed them down over the first three innings and Ferrell took over in the fourth, fanning McQuinn, Bob Seeds, and Joe Gallagher. McQuinn, the slick-fielding first baseman, had returned to the Bears' roster after batting .328 with the rival Toronto team in 1936. Seeds, on the other hand, played most of the prior season with Montreal until he was purchased by the Yankees in late August. Young Gallagher, despite his .350 batting average at Norfolk, was fighting stiff competition and excessive weight, both of which offered him little hope of permanence with the Bears. Newark finally reached the tired Ferrell in the ninth inning, scoring two runs on two hits and three walks. The Red Sox sent rookie Dick Midkiff in for relief, but the Bears could manage only two more runs, putting a mild scare into Cronin.

On Sunday, the Philadelphia Phillies beat the Bears, 5-2, as the temperature in Sebring dropped from 90 to 70 degrees. It turned out to be the sloppiest game of the early exhibition schedule. While the Newark pitchers allowed only seven hits, they walked an unbelievable thirteen batters. They also booted three runs. And the base running was so poor that Vitt called for a "classroom session" after the game. Of all places, it was conducted in the ballroom of the Sebring Hotel. What prompted Vitt's late night session began in the first inning of the game. With no outs and runners on first and third, McQuinn bounced a ball to the first baseman, who threw to second for the forced out. McQuinn unexplainably stopped running between home and first and was easily doubled up for the next out, In the second inning, with Kelleher on third and Willard Hershberger on first, the young catcher from Oakland decided to steal second base without a signal. Seeing that Hershberger couldn't make it, Kelleher raced for home but was thrown out. But the topper came in the fifth. Seeds walked with two men out and Vitt decided to send Ralph Boyle in to pinch run. Seconds later, Boyle was picked off first base! It was an afternoon that Vitt wanted to quickly forget.

"You wouldn't think it possible for a fellow who has played as long as Ralph Boyle to be caught napping off first, or Willard Hershberger to try a double steal with a pitcher batting and two out, would you?" asked a frustrated Vitt. "Well, I am glad it happened that way," he continued. "These boys will never make those same mistakes again."

The next day, the Bears broke their four-game losing streak by whipping the perennial second division Brooklyn Dodgers, 5-3. Newark collected a total of ten hits, nine of them in four innings off Ray Henshaw, who had been picked up from the Cubs over the winter. Jack Glynn, George McQuinn, and Bob Seeds each had two hits, with McQuinn and Seeds accounting for four RBI's. Glynn, the former Oakland outfielder, was playing exceptionally strong ball and looked like a sure bet to make the team. Piechota and Russo allowed ten hits and three runs. Neither pitcher was exceptionally sharp, but they both had enough when it counted.

The following day, the game scheduled against the Baltimore Orioles at Winter Garden was rained out, giving everyone except the front office a day off. There were two player announcements made. The first involved Jimmy Gleeson, the 24-year-old switch-hitting outfielder from Kansas City of the American Association, who was acquired for Ralph Boyle, the final remnant of the 1936

Three years after his fine season with the Bears, Jimmy Gleeson batted .313 for the Chicago Cubs in 1940, driving in 61 runs in 129 games.

outfield. In the trade, the Bears picked up four years in age and an outfielder with great promise.

Vitt was delighted with the exchange, commenting on the newly-acquired Gleeson, "If nothing else, he has more power than Boyle, which is important in Ruppert Stadium. Only the visitors enjoyed our short fences last year. If Keller stays in there, Glynn and Seeds will have to hit that much harder to keep him out of the lineup. And say, a switch hitter who drives the ball like he does wouldn't make a bad pinch hitter.

"Yes sir, he has made the situation look very rosy for Ol' Os!"

Vitt, recognizing early the potential his young club possessed, continued his crystal gazing. "Last year Boyle was our only .300 hitter. I'll make the prediction now that all our outfielders will be in the select circle this year. Our infield is also improved. McQuinn and Gordon are going to better the .270 average of McCarthy and Schalk. Richardson should be just as good and we are going to have

"Utility" man Francis Kelleher (left) and second base star Joe Gordon. Kelleher batted .305 in 93 games, while Gordon led the team in home runs with 26.

more punch at third. May wasn't at his best last season and is bound to be better, and if Francis Kelleher wins the third base job, you are going to see the hardest hitting infielder in the minors.

"Hershberger and Rosar figure to hit better, collectively, than Baker and Kies, and we are going to have more aggressiveness and brains behind the plate."

It was also announced by Secretary Kennedy that outfielder Joe Gallagher would join Binghamton at Spartanburg, South Carolina. Earlier, Gallagher had complained that he wasn't receiving the proper attention in the Newark camp. Since he was slated to go to Binghamton anyway, Joe felt he might as well get an early start. He requested the move and Weiss and Kennedy approved. Gallagher hopped on the next train for Spartanburg, explaining, "Why should I be wasting my time trying to please Vitt when I can be up at Spartanburg winning my way into the heart of Bill Skiff, whom I am going to play for all season?"

A few days later, the Yankees made an announcement of their own. They were sending Vito Tamulis and Jim Tobin to Newark. The big surprise was Tamulis. The left-handed Lithuanian from Boston was considered by many to have an excellent chance of making the big club. In 1935, he spent a full season with the second place Yankees and posted a 10-5 record. Over the winter, however, Tamulis became ill, was slow to recover, and finished the season with Newark, pitching three consecutive shutouts.

One of the reasons Tamulis and Tobin were sent to Newark was that they were considered troublemakers. It was nothing serious; they just enjoyed having some harmless fun. But the stuffy Yankee management, particularly Joe McCarthy, didn't care for outspoken, practical jokers. They didn't like all the funny pranks — firecrackers, buzzers, shockers and the like. Baseball was a serious business as far as the New York Yankee organization was concerned. As a result, the two pitchers were sent down to Newark. However, McCarthy spread the story that the left-hander was not in condition. Tamulis felt differently and was quite frank in his comments. "Of course I clown around — throw firecrackers and hand out loaded cigars. But I do those things only off the ball field

Left-hander Vito Tamulis posted an 18-6 record for the Bears in 1937. He was sold to the St. Louis Browns after the season.

and it's my way of amusing myself.

"What difference should it make to them what I do after hours as long as I keep in condition and pitch good ball. True, I fool around with the ball in pepper games, but all that stuff keeps me bending and aids me in keeping in shape. Other fellows call it work. I call it play.

"No! I don't intend to reform. If I can't get some fun out of life with a ball club, I'm going some place where I can get it. My fooling around has never hurt anyone unless it's true that I was sent back here only because I was a clown. If that's the case, I've been given a terrific sock on the chin, for I've lost a major league salary, probable World Series share, plus a $1,000 bonus the Yankees promised if they kept me all season.

"That's no laughing matter. I lost $10,000 in salary and World Series money last season because I was sick and the doctors and hospitals took all I had saved. I thought I proved I was all right by winning my last five games, including three shutouts for Newark last fall, and during the winter McCarthy told me he was counting on me.

"I was singing like a bluebird when I went south, figuring that all my troubles were over and that I was finally established as a big leaguer. You know, it does a fellow good to go around wearing that New York on his chest.

"But what happened? I am not allowed to pitch a single inning. McCarthy said I wasn't in shape. Of course I took it easy. Didn't he tell me I was set, and more than two weeks ago, I told Art Fletcher I was ready to pitch. Why didn't I tell McCarthy myself? What do they have these stooges for anyway?

"Now I'm back with Newark and I guess there's nothing else for me to do but prove all over again that I am a major league pitcher. If I'm going good around the middle of the season and they need a pitcher to get them in the World Series, maybe they'll forget about my clowning and take me back. They may even laugh at my jokes."

Whatever the actual reason, Vitt was not overjoyed with his two additions, particularly the talkative Tobin. He had managed Tobin before and felt he was a thorn in his side. While explaining Tobin to

Secretary Kennedy, Vitt was overheard to say, "He's the kind of guy who will walk up to you and say, 'Look at the feet on Kennedy.'"

"Listen," retorted Kennedy, "We want no ballplayers around here who insult the Secretary. Besides, it's only a size nine."

On April 1 at Winter Haven, the Bears edged the Phillies, 6-4, thereby splitting their two games with the National League team. Charlie Keller led the victory and continued to show great promise. In the eighth inning, with McQuinn on third and the Bears trailing, 3-2, he belted a screaming line drive over the center fielder's head for an inside-the-park home run and a 4-3 lead. The Bears picked up two more runs later, but the key blow belonged to the young Keller. After the game, Yankee scout Gene McCann, who among others had dogged Keller for years, exclaimed, "I never scouted a ballplayer so thoroughly in my life and I never looked at a better one."

Vitt, however, exceeded McCann in his praise of the kid. "Only once before in my life have I seen a young player hit a ball as far as young Keller. It was back in 1919 when I was a coach of the Red Sox and we were training at Tampa. Our Manager, Ed Barrow, decides to make an outfielder out of a young pitcher named Ruth and he loses a ball over the distant race track.

"I am not predicting Keller will be another Ruth, but if God gives him good health, there is no reason why he shouldn't be. The boy simply can't miss. He is only 19 and can hit a ball every bit as good as Ruth could at that age. And he has those big shoulders, can throw and field, and more important, he loves to play baseball."

Back at Sebring two days later, the Bears demolished the Toronto Leafs by a score of 8-2. The two Toronto pitchers were rapped for twelve hits and eight runs. Ed Longacre, George McQuinn, Buddy Rosar, and Mickey Witek all had hot bats. As far as Vitt was concerned, it was simply a lovely day for playing baseball. Longacre, who played the outfield for Binghamton in 1936, and Witek, the second baseman at Norfolk, had little hope of making the team, nonetheless. But the catcher, Buddy Rosar, who had played with Binghamton the year before after failing with the Bears, was a totally different story.

On Saturday, the Bears beat the Louisville Colonels for the second time, 8-1, on some brilliant pitching by Pete Naktenis and Norm Branch. Naktenis held the Colonels hitless through the first six innings, but became the victim of an unearned run. Branch, the redheaded Texan, pitched shutout ball for the last three innings and gave up only three hits. Glynn, the young New Jersey outfielder, led the team at the plate with three hits and three RBI's.

Over at Clearwater, the Brooklyn Dodgers avenged their earlier loss by drubbing Marius Russo, 9-7. It was Russo's first bad day of the spring. In only five innings, he was roughed up for nine hits and nine runs. The aging Heinie Manush and rookie shortstop Johnny Hudson each hit two home runs over the short right field wall. The bright spot for the Bears was the continued power hitting of Charlie Keller. His tremendous triple in the third inning drove in two runs and was longer than any of the four Dodger homers.

On April 5, with no game scheduled, Vitt still called for a light workout in order to keep his youthful charges razor sharp. The practice paid off handsomely the next day as the Bears whipped the Sebring firemen in one of the more amusing games on the exhibition schedule. The local firemen consisted of three paid employees and about forty Sebring volunteers. In addition to their baseball prowess, they boasted fire fighting facilities not often found in a town of only 2,500 people. They claimed a modern box-alarm system, a $60,000 fire house with four pieces of motorized equipment, and a hydrant system second to none. The story was told that Secretary Kennedy shrewdly placed this game late on the schedule so that if the firemen ever beat the Bears, Kennedy and Vitt could leave town in a hurry.

Prior to their next game against the Boston Red Sox, three players departed from the Newark camp. Mickey Witek was shipped to Binghamton, while Chief Koy and Bill Baker, both of whom had seen little action so far, left for the West Coast to join the Oakland club.

Then behind the six-hit pitching of two rookies, the Boston Red Sox blanked the Bears, 3-0. Despite the shutout, Newark played a fine game. Nolen Richardson, the Bears' 33-year-old shortstop, fielded eight chances flawlessly, three of which robbed batters of sure base hits. Veteran Merrill May played equally well at third. But as is so often the case, one bad pitch can lose a game. Jack Fallon, the former Holy Cross star, grooved one to Jimmy Foxx and the old "Double X" parked it over the 425-foot left field wall, scoring Bobby Doerr and Roger Cramer ahead of him. That was the margin of victory.

The Bears' farewell to Florida was something akin to a twenty-one-gun salute as they buried the Toronto Leafs, 16-2, at Haines City. McQuinn continued to show the strength of his bat with a home run and a triple. Glynn, who at this point had already clinched the left field job, chipped in with two doubles and another triple. And Joe Gordon, the shortstop from Oakland who was now playing second base, banged out three singles to bring the Bears' hitting total to eighteen. Right from the start, young Gordon was impressive at his new position. "That boy looks like a born second baseman," said Yankee Manager Joe McCarthy. "They tell me he never played the position, but he looks like he has played it all his life." After the game, the team packed their gear and headed north, with stops planned at Macon, Augusta, Binghamton, and Norfolk. Along the way, some of the Newark hopefuls would be dropped from the roster.

The next day, the Bears shellacked their class A affiliate, the Macon Peaches, by a score of 13-5. Newark whacked out a total of twelve hits. Gordon and Hershberger each collected three, including tremendous triples, while McQuinn hit a stupendous homer over the center field wall. Not all the action was restricted to the playing field, however. Ol' Os put on a show of his own coaching third base. Vitt's antics all started when Charlie McAbee, Macon's 18-year-old third baseman, put on his hog calling act. McAbee, wearing what appeared to be a jockey's cap, had the voice of an auctioneer and the "actions of a centipede with St. Vitus dance." Always the showman, Vitt quickly picked up the routine and began to imitate the kid, much to the delight of the fans.

The following day, the Bears travelled 135 miles across Georgia to take on the Augusta Tigers, another Yankee farm team.[3] Newark beat Augusta, 12-8, but the pesky Tigers tied the score twice, sending the game into extra innings on both occasions. The first time, it took an outstanding throw by Keller to cut a runner down at the plate to save the game. The second time came in the tenth inning when the Bears went ahead, 8-7, and the Tigers came right back to tie the score again. But the Bears put the game away in the eleventh when they tagged a young pitcher named Dopey Dean for five hits and four runs. Buddy Rosar had a perfect day at the plate, going five-for-five. Gordon, Keller, and Seeds each had three hits, with Gordon and Keller both contributing home runs.

Immediately after the game, the Bears hopped on the bus for the trip back to Macon, where they played the Peaches the next day and edged them, 3-2. Pete Naktenis turned in another respectable pitching performance and Willard Hershberger picked up three hits and scored the winning run.

With Opening Day drawing near, the Central train of Georgia puffed through the night and headed for Spartanburg, South Carolina, the training camp of the Binghamton Bingos. Binghamton was still another great Yankee farm team and usually the first stop for a player dropped from the Newark roster. It was easy to understand why some players were becoming a little uneasy.

Two more personnel changes were announced. First, pitcher Jim Tobin, who a week earlier had said if he couldn't play in the major leagues, he would pitch only in the Pacific Coast League, was sold to Pittsburgh. No doubt Vitt breathed a sigh of relief to have one clown gone. Next, catcher Bill Holm was transferred to the New York-Pennsylvania League, leaving Hershberger and Rosar to share the catching duties. With these latest changes, the roster was

---

3. One of the veterans on the Augusta team was a 35-year-old shortstop named Pee Wee Wanninger. Pee Wee had that unique distinction of being the player that Lou Gehrig batted for back on June 1, 1925. Gehrig proceeded to set an individual performance record that will probably remain unsurpassed. He played in 2,130 consecutive games, spanning fourteen years.

nearing the twenty-player limit. There was no immediate concern, however, since Newark had until the May 10 deadline to further trim the roster.

On Friday, April 16, the Bears beat the Bingos by a score of 10-5. Tamulis, who was expected to be on the mound for Opening Day against the Montreal Royals, was hit hard. In the second inning, he was belted for six hits and all five runs. Vitt, who was understandably upset by the inning, told Tamulis, "You're not ready. I better warm up somebody else." "Aw, that was just an accident," remarked Tamulis, "I wasn't turning on the pressure." Against his better judgment, Vitt left the southpaw in the game. Over the next four innings, Tamulis gave up only one hit! Beggs finished the last three innings, allowing two hits and no runs.

On Saturday, Newark shutout the Norfolk Tars, 7-0, behind strong pitching from Joe Mitchell, the right-hander who pitched for Norfolk in 1936, and Marius Russo. Mitchell blanked the Tars for the first six innings and Russo for the last three, with the lefty fanning five. Keller, Gordon, and Seeds led the offense by collecting seven of the Bears' sixteen hits. The victory was dampened, however, by the news that Bill Matheson's father had died of a heart attack in Oakland.

In Norfolk, it was the same old story again. The Bears whipped the Tars, 12-3, on fourteen hits. Glynn, Gleeson, and McQuinn each homered with a man on base. Walter Johnson, Jr., son of the famous Hall of Famer, was hammered for seven hits and six runs in just three innings. It seemed the only thing the father and son had in common was that they both threw with their right arms. As the player pruning continued, pitchers Mitchell and Branch were left at Norfolk, while outfielder Longacre was optioned to the San Fransico Seals. The Newark roster now had only twenty-one players, just one over the limit. The Bears went on to win their final game of the exhibition season, edging Trenton of the New York-Pennsylvania League by a close score of 5-4 in ten innings.

As the curtain closed on the 1937 exhibition schedule, the Bears boasted an outstanding .714 winning percentage and a 15-6 record (not counting the victory over the Sebring Firemen). They had also won their last eight games in a row! On the eve of Opening Day, Oscar Vitt could sit back, relax, and reflect on a most gratifying spring. A glance at the Newark batting averages would bring envy to the eye of any other manager:

Buddy Rosar	.514
Jimmy Gleeson	.500
Willard Hershberger	.361
Jack Glynn	.356
George McQuinn	.325
Merrill May	.319
Joe Gordon	.317
Bill Matheson	.304
Charlie Keller	.290
Nolen Richardson	.229
Bob Seeds	.220
Francis Kelleher	.190

It now appeared the 1936 team had been completely rebuilt. Only Richardson, May, Kelleher, Tamulis, and Piechota were holdovers. The rest of the Bears were newcomers to Newark as well as Double A ball. As Vitt so accurately stated, ". . .we've got a faster club than we did last year. We've got more power at bat and a better club defensively. We are also going to have much better catching and far more hitting from our backstops. The pitching is a question mark, as usual. But that can't be helped. We've got some young pitching with good records where they came from. You can't tell how they measure up against Double A hitters until you try them." The test for these young players would come soon enough, as Opening Day at Ruppert Stadium was just around the corner.

Aerial view of Ruppert Stadium. Getting ready for Opening Day.

Joe Basile, "The Brass Band King," played on Opening Day at Ruppert Stadium.

A view of Ruppert Stadium from the right field bleachers. The stadium was packed on this cold April afternoon.

8.

Opening Day
1937

T HE NEWARK BEARS OPENED THE 1937 SEASON ON APRIL 22 before 5,400 loyal, shivering fans at Ruppert Stadium. Despite the light rain and cold chill, the pre-game festivities went off on schedule. Joe Basile's twenty-five-piece band grandly entertained the early arrivals in the bleachers and unreserved grandstand. Later, a detachment of regular Army soldiers led a parade of players to the flagpole to officially begin the Opening Day program. Since Newark's Mayor Meyer C. Ellenstein, was detained at the Court House on city business, he sent over Deputy Mayor William L. Fox to throw out the traditional first ball. Fox gingerly took the mound while Frank Shaughnessey, the International League's President, crouched behind the plate. The Deputy Mayor's accuracy left much to be desired, however, as his first pitch went wild. His second effort showed a big improvement. Fox delighted the fans by grooving one right over the middle of the plate.

With the conclusion of these Opening Day festivities, the game finally got underway. In true championship fashion, the Bears easily defeated the Montreal Royals, 8-5. As Manager Vitt commented afterwards, "Give me six runs in the first inning every game and I'll be satisfied."

Down 2-0 in the bottom of the first, Jack Glynn singled with one out. George McQuinn followed with a double, scoring Glynn. Bob Seeds then homered over the 348-foot marker in left field and the Bears led, 3-2. But the inning was far from over. Charlie Keller walked, Joe Gordon singled, and Willard Hershberger scored both

Bob Seeds touches home plate after walloping a 348-foot homer on Opening Day to help defeat Montreal, 8-5.

men with a long double. Vito Tamulis, helping his own cause, proceeded to send Hershberger home with a single for the sixth and final run of the inning.

Even though the Bears jumped off to an early lead, Tamulis had a rough time of it all day. He scattered fourteen hits, walked three, and gave up five runs. The young southpaw was constantly in trouble, but always managed to escape any serious damage, going the full distance for his first victory. He would record seventeen more by the end of the season.

The Bears swept the series from Montreal by winning the next two games, 7-6 and 6-4, with Atley Donald and Joe Beggs each contributing victories. The Bears' excellent showing and fast start, in addition to some front office player announcements, kept the personable Vitt in good humor. On the eve of the opener, the young Puerto Rican right-hander, Hiram Bithorn, was sent to Binghamton for some more seasoning. Although Bithorn was disappointed, it wouldn't be many years before he would be the first Puerto Rican to pitch in the major leagues.'

In two related moves, the Yankees sent Steve Sundra and Jack LaRocca to the Bears to strengthen the Newark pitching staff. Vitt was overjoyed, particularly with the addition of Sundra. The brawny Cleveland right-hander had pitched for Vitt in 1936, posting a 12-9 record and leading the International League with a 2.84 ERA.

The Rochester Red Wings were the team to next move into Ruppert Stadium for a three-game series. The Bears won the first game by a score of 9-3 behind the strong and dependable pitching of Al Piechota. This was the first game Piechota pitched without the help of his tonsils, which were removed in late spring training. When he was jokingly asked about the advantages of pitching without tonsils, Piechota replied, "Oh, it was a big difference. Why, last year, I had to breathe with my mouth wide open. Now I breathe through

---

4. In Puerto Rico today, Hiram Bithorn Stadium stands next to the new Roberto Clemente Coliseium, both proud monuments to these two players and their lasting impact on the game.

my nose.'' In the offensive department, Charlie Keller cracked his first home run of the season into the left field bleachers, despite the strong wind blowing in from that side. George McQuinn and Bob Seeds each picked up three hits, with Seeds knocking in four runs.

Ironically enough, McQuinn had mildly complained about the wind factor at Ruppert Stadium only a few weeks before the season began. As he put it, "Every day you come out of the tunnel to the dugout and the first thing you look at is that flag. Nineteen out of twenty days, it's blowing in, at least that's the way it seems to me, and you're licked before you start.

"Of course, when you hit the ball low and on the nose, no wind is going to hurt you, but still you operate under the mental hazard of fearing that every ball you hit in the air will be caught, regardless of how hard you hit it. Then they catch one on you and, boy, they get you down.

"The fellow who hits along the foul lines doesn't have so much to worry about, for very often the wind helps him, but it's always against a left-handed hitter like myself who hits toward deep left or left center. Last year, I don't think I got more than two or three hits in Newark, and when I played there before with the Bears, I had to do my best hitting on the road to go as high as .288.

"Maybe if they starched the flag and had it appear as if it was always blowing out, I would step up there and biff a few. I try not to look at it and will feel fine after hitting a few in batting practice when someone on the bench will say, 'Look how that damn wind blows in.'

"Otherwise I like to play in Newark and am trying to hit more to right field in order that I may get a little break from the wind myself and drop a few in the bleachers. Also, a few blows to right may bring those outfielders around a bit and give me more open space to hit in left field.''

Another perfectionist on the team was Charlie Keller. Although the heavy hitting outfielder was blasting up a storm for the Bears, he was still griping to the press because he didn't like the sound of his bat against the ball. "You just get the feel you are hitting the ball right when you hear that lovely sound,'' said Keller.

George McQuinn played first base and batted .329 with 21 home runs and 83 RBI's.

"Why that bird hits 'em farther with the handle than I used to hit 'em when I connected perfectly," retorted Vitt. "They sound all right to me on third base, too. Maybe the acoustics are bad around home plate."

As it turned out, however, Keller's bat wasn't the only thing Vitt listened to at Ruppert Stadium. Throughout the season, there were a good number of Jersey City fans who showed up to watch their biggest rival team and to taunt the Bears' feisty manager. They hadn't forgotten Vitt's earlier insults to the Jersey City players. "Stumblebums and smudgepots," he had called them during spring training. Their loyal fans could regularly be overheard heckling Vitt with such comments as: "You fathead, wait until we get you in Jersey City."

In the second game of their series with Rochester, Newark extended their winning streak to five games, beating the Red Wings, 9-7. The Bears made a quick rout of it, scoring all nine runs in the first four innings. Ol' Os, of course, was delighted with the team's performance and hoped they would continue to do the same. But the third and last game with Rochester was rained out and the Bears apparently lost their drive. In the meantime, the roster was further tightened as Bill Matheson was sent to Louisville in the American Association.

In a surprising turn of events, the Bears lost their next three out of four games to the Buffalo Bisons. One of the brighter moments of the series came in the second game, which the Bears won, 2-1. Atley Donald went the full distance, striking out eight, giving up five hits, and allowing one run — a homer by veteran slugger Ollie Carnegie. It was Donald's second victory. He would record twelve more before experiencing the bitter taste of defeat in late July.

Richard Atley Donald, a Mississippi native who preferred to be called by his middle name, entered baseball in 1934 in a somewhat unorthodox fashion. While attending college at Louisiana Tech., he was scouted briefly by Johnny Nee, the Yankees' chief bird dog in the South. Either Nee was unimpressed or he simply forgot about the kid. In any event, it was difficult to believe someone could overlook a gifted prospect like Atley.

But Donald, a young man with lots of courage and talent to match, was not about to let himself be overlooked. With a little prompting, his baseball coach at Louisiana decided to help the kid out and wrote a letter to Ed Barrow. Either Barrow never received the letter or he chose to ignore it. Whatever the reason, the tenacious Donald was still determined to play baseball. He simply packed his belongings and headed for the Yankees' training camp in St. Petersburg!

Donald arrived several months before the Yankees and because he had lots of time on his hands, decided to pay a visit to Nee — a winter resident of St. Petersburg. Nee gave Atley a quick brush off, suggesting he come back when the Yankees would be there. Donald

Atley Donald (left) and Spurgeon Chandler. Donald led pitchers with a .905 winning percentage (19-2) and chalked up 14 consecutive victories. Chandler, obtained late in the season from the Yankees, pitched brilliantly in game six of the Little World Series.

took his advice, rented a furnished room, and found a job in a local grocery store to earn his keep until the Yankees arrived.

When the Yankees finally reached St. Petersburg, Donald was there bright and early, rapping at the door of the clubhouse. Nee happily referred the bothersome pitcher to McCarthy, who willingly gave Donald a uniform. McCarthy, of course, had an ulterior motive. The Yankee Manager felt the best way to discourage volunteers from joining the team was to let them take a beating from hitters like Ruth, Gehrig, Lazzeri, Combs, and Dickey.

McCarthy was standing behind the batting cage when Donald took the mound to face the heavy Yankee barrage. Surprisingly enough, McCarthy was impressed by what he saw. "He looks like Lon Warneke out there," remarked the Yankee Manager. That was quite a compliment for Donald, since Warneke — known as the Arkansas "hummingbird" — had helped win the National League pennant for the Chicago Cubs in 1932 with a 22-6 record. Of course, Donald wasn't quite ready for the big leagues, but he did make enough of an impression on McCarthy to be sent to the Wheeling club in the Middle Atlantic League. Donald finished the season there with a 12-10 record and was on his way to the big leagues. At Norfolk in 1935, he posted a 13-13 record and led the league in strikeouts with 160.

In 1936, Donald blossomed into a superb pitcher. With Binghamton in the tough New York-Penn League, the 26-year-old right-hander won 19 and lost 9. He completed 19 games, led the league in strikeouts with 189 (a record at the time), and turned in a 3.12 ERA. At one point during the season, he ran off a string of 12 consecutive victories. It was no surprise, then, that Donald reached his peak in 1937 with the Bears and was given a tryout with the Yankees the following year.

But his stay with New York was brief and disappointing. He started two games, finished neither one, and pitched a total of only twelve innings. He also issued fourteen walks, probably the major reason the Yankees sent him back to Newark for more seasoning. With the Bears that year, Donald pitched 193 innings in 25 games, fanning 135 and posting a 16-7 record. It was good enough to earn him another shot at Yankee Stadium.

In 1939, Atley Donald finally became a permanent member of the Yankee pitching staff. And this time, the rookie didn't disappoint the Yankees or himself, posting a 13-3 record, completing 11 of 20 starts, and helping the team to another American League pennant. Donald's 13 victories (including 12 in a row — a record at the time for a rookie in the American League) were second only to team leader Red Ruffing's 21. Most of the credit had to be attributed to Atley's exceptional fastball, which was popping all season long. At Cleveland Stadium in late August, his fastball was clocked at 94.7 miles per hour, ". . .the fastest ever recorded by the Cleveland Indians. . . ," the local press reported.

Despite Donald's outstanding season, the Yankees didn't use him in the World Series that year because they needed only seven pitchers to sweep the Cincinnati Reds in four straight. It would be two years before he was given an opportunity to participate in the fall classic.

In 1941, after turning in a 9-5 record, a 3.57 ERA, and completing 10 of 20 starts, Donald got the nod to start the now famous fourth game of the World Series against the Brooklyn Dodgers. He was relieved in the fifth and escaped the loss when the Yankees scored four times in the ninth inning. It was the time Tommy Henrich swung and missed the third strike that would have ended the game. But catcher Mickey Owen missed the pitch, Henrich ran safely to first base, and the Yankees promptly blasted home four runs to win, 7-4.

The following year, Atley helped lead the Yankees to still another pennant as he posted an 11-3 mark, completed 10 of 19 games, and finished with a 3.11 ERA. Once again, he saw action in the fourth game of the World Series, this time against the young St. Louis Cardinals. But in the fourth inning, the Cards scored six runs and Atley was relieved by Hank Borowy. Unfortunately, the Yankees never recovered from the inning and St. Louis won by a score of 9-6. The Yankee starter was tagged with the loss.

During the next three years, Donald won 24 and lost 18 games for the Yankees, finally calling it quits after the 1945 season. During the eight years he wore a Yankee uniform, Atley Donald won 65 and lost 33, finishing in the majors with a .663 percentage and a 3.52 ERA. It wasn't a bad career for a kid who practically had to camp outside the clubhouse in St. Petersburg to get the attention of the Yankee management.

While the Bears were losing their four-game series to the Buffalo Bisons, the Toronto Leafs moved into undisputed possession of first place. Newark trailed by only a game, however, and this set up the first important series of the young season, beginning with a Sunday double-header against Toronto.

The Newark fans were anxious to arrive early that day. Whether they came wedged in busses, packed in cars, or simply on foot, they were all moving in one direction — down Wilson Avenue to Ruppert Stadium. The largest crowd in Newark's history piled through the portals, crowded the aisles, and eventually "spilled onto the field."

There were 20,569 fans that turned out for the games. Some were lined up in front of the grandstand and others were roped off in an area between the two bleacher sections in center field. One of the sections was filled to capacity almost an hour before the game even began. With fans scattered all over the playing field, it was necessary for the umpires to improvise and set up a new ground rule: any player that drove a ball into the roped off area was limited to two bases.

At the same time, across the meadows in Jersey City, 24,294 fans had packed Roosevelt Stadium to watch the Jersey Giants play. This prompted Secretary Kennedy to remark, "We'll have to borrow Yankee Stadium the first time Newark plays Jersey City."

The first game of the double-header dragged on for two hours and twenty minutes as the Bears humiliated the Leafs, 23-1! Local baseball buffs quickly raced to the record books to find out if the score had set a new record for Newark. It had, topping the 21-0 defeat of Harrisburg in 1884 and the 21-15 drubbing of the Orioles in 1934. Actually, the game ended in the eleven-run second inning when the Bears sent seventeen men to the plate for eight hits, four walks, and three errors. In the fourth, the game was temporarily halted as more fans crowded onto the field. The two managers conferred with the umpires on the placement of the overflowing spectators. Vitt asked Toronto Manager Dan Howley if he had any objection to putting fans on the field in front of the grandstand. Howley, whose team was already behind, 10-1, replied, "I don't care if you hang them on the grandstand roof." Al Piechota added to Howley's frustration by allowing Toronto only six hits and one run.

In the second game of the double-header, the Leafs managed to fight back and make up for their loss. They edged the Bears, 3-2, on three unearned runs in the second inning. Jack LaRocca was the losing pitcher.

At the end of the long, five-hour afternoon, the happiest bunch of all were the park concessionaires. Although their work was demanding, they now had a handsome bundle to show for it. The record crowd had consumed over 11,200 hot dogs, 3,200 bags of peanuts, 6,000 cartons of ice cream, 6,000 bottles of beer, 9,600 soft drinks, and 2,400 pieces of candy. Before the first game was even over, 1,200 seat cushions had been rented and all 9,000 score cards had been sold. Indeed, it was a pleasant Sunday afternoon at Ruppert Stadium.

One of the highlights of the day was an outfielder by the name of Tommy Henrich. Henrich had been obtained from the Yankees only the day before and was undoubtedly the best-known outfielder in the minor leagues at the time. During the Bears' eleven-run uprising in the first game, he went to bat twice and delivered on both occasions with a single and a double.

Born and raised in Massillon, Ohio, he signed his first professional contract with the Cleveland Indians in 1934. He played a total of three years in the Cleveland organization, hitting .326 in Class D ball, .337 in Class C, and .346 in Class AA. But at the end of 1936, he was sold to Milwaukee in the American Association. Strangely enough, Milwaukee was also a Cleveland farm team.

Even at the tender age of 24, Henrich was a bright young man who quickly discovered that he was being shifted around within the

Cleveland organization. In a bold move, Henrich wrote to Commissioner Kenesaw Mountain Landis and explained his situation. Judge Landis fired back a telegram asking Henrich to prove his charges. After further correspondence between the two, Landis called a meeting at the Roosevelt Hotel in New Orleans where the Cleveland club was training. Both Cleveland and Milwaukee executives attended the meeting, in addition to Landis and Henrich.

As Henrich would say years later, "Landis was familiar with the kind of shenanigans that were going on and he went after those guys." It should also be noted that Landis had no love for Cy Slapnicka, the Cleveland General Manager.

As a result of the meeting, Henrich was declared a free agent. Within two days after returning to Massillon, he was contacted by eight clubs, including the Yankees, who outbid everyone and signed Henrich for $25,000. Henrich joined the Yankees at the beginning of the 1937 season, stayed with the team for two weeks, and was then shipped to Newark. He played with the Bears for only seven games, long enough to bat a lofty .440 (11 for 25) with seven RBI's.

During this period, Joe McCarthy was plagued with problems in his Yankee outfield. He got fed up with Roy Johnson's attitude and knew that Jake Powell might require an operation for appendicitis. Coupled with Joe DiMaggio's nagging arm trouble, McCarthy had no choice but to tell General Manager Ed Barrow, "Bring up that kid at Newark." Back went Henrich to the Yankees, where he became a permanent fixture in right field for the next ten years, joining DiMaggio and Charlie Keller (his Newark team mate for seven games) to form one of the all-time classic outfields.

Mel Allen, the great Yankee broadcaster, nicknamed Henrich, "Old Reliable," because of his innate ability to consistently deliver the key hit in the clutch. It was this exceptional trait that always made Henrich stand out. His lifetime batting average for eleven years was .282, and Bob Feller considered him one of the toughest .282 hitters in baseball. Henrich's best year was 1948. He batted .308, drove in 100 runs, and led the league in runs-scored and triples with 138 and 14, respectively. Here was how Henrich summed up his love affair with baseball: "I had a lot of fun playing baseball. For me it was a dream come true. Playing the game I love for a living.''

The Bears finished their series with Toronto by taking the next two games, 5-1 and 8-1. Atley Donald struggled through the first one, giving up eleven hits, while Vito Tamulis scattered seven in the next game, posting his second victory of the young season. Ed Barrow was in the stands that day and was delighted with the performance of his future Yankee club, particularly in the seventh inning when the Bears exploded for five runs to break up a 1-1 tie. It was like watching the great 1927 Yankee team and what Earle Combs used to call "five o'clock lightening."

Besides Barrow, there was another distinguished guest who came out to see the game, a man who would later become one of the great Yankee managers — Charles Dillon Stengel. "Casey" heaped his own brand of praise on the Newark players, remarking, "The club I saw today seems to have much more stability. Your boys know more baseball than they did last year and there's something about the manner in which they do things that indicates they have confidence in themselves. Class simply sticks out all over them."

9.

On The Road

THE BEARS LEFT NEWARK AND RUPPERT STADIUM WITH A slim one-game lead to begin their first road trip of the season. Prior to departing, it was announced that Jack Glynn had been optioned to Milwaukee and Pete Naktenis to Binghamton. The Bears headed north with their first stop at Montreal, followed by Rochester, Buffalo, and Toronto. It was a trip of streaks. After losing their first two games, sandwiched between rain and unseasonably cold weather, the Bears ran off six straight wins. Following additional rain and a loss to Toronto, they added three more victories in a row. The Bears combined excellent hitting with superb pitching to win 9 out of 12, increasing their first place lead to 3½ games. It turned out to be an outstanding road trip. No one knew at the time — not Colonel Ruppert, Ed Barrow, George Weiss, Ray Kennedy, or Oscar Vitt — but the International League race was already over! The Bears would never surrender first place and the most popular sports event in town was watching just how high their lead would grow. Incredibly enough, it was only May 20.

The first two Montreal games were rained out and during this time, the Yankees announced two very important additions to the Newark roster. Ellsworth "Babe" Dahlgren and Walter "Jumbo" Brown would join the club in their series against Rochester. Babe Dahlgren, a natural first baseman, would be converted by Vitt to play third base. Along with George McQuinn, Joe Gordon, and Nolen Richardson, he would form the regular infield for the rest of the season.

In the case of Brown, it was a falling out with McCarthy and the rest of the Yankee management over his weight, which was estimated at between 260 and 280 pounds! Both players were welcome additions to the Newark lineup, particularly the proven Brown. Under Shawkey's managerial rein in 1934, the rotund right-hander had won 20 and lost 6. He had also led the league with his earned run average.

At the age of 23, prior to joining the Bears, Babe Dahlgren had already played one full season in the major leagues with the Boston Red Sox. Eddie Collins, the Red Sox General Manager, bought the first sacker for a cool $50,000 after he had only played in a handful of games with the Pacific Coast Missions in 1935. With the Red Sox the same year, Dahlgren played in 149 games, scored 77 runs, and batted .263 with 63 RBI's. By today's standards, this respectable performance would have made Dahlgren a top contender for Rookie of the Year honors. But Red Sox owner Tom Yawkey was hungry for a pennant and purchased the great first baseman, Jimmy Foxx, from Connie Mack and the Philadelphia A's. This purchase quickly ended the Babe's career with the Red Sox.

The following year, the Red Sox sent Dahlgren back to the minors with the Syracuse Chiefs. There, the sure handed first baseman had another outstanding year. He batted a lofty .318 with 180 hits, including 16 homers and 121 RBI's. It wasn't a bad season for a kid who was given a taste of the big leagues only to have it snatched away again. But the minors were not unfamiliar to Dahlgren, even though his apprenticeship had been relatively short-lived.

The Babe started his professional baseball career in 1931 with Tucson in the Arizona League, batting a sizzling .347. An all-around athlete in high school — basketball, football, soccer, swimming, and track — Dahlgren next moved to the Pacific Coast League. He played four years for the Missions, from 1932 to 1935, hitting .243, .287, .315, and .302, respectively. He was then purchased by the Red Sox in the early part of 1935.

Ruppert's purchase of Dahlgren after his fine season with the

Syracuse Chiefs in 1936 was somewhat unusual, since most of the players who came to Newark and the Yankees were home-grown products of their newly-established farm system. However, Ruppert had another idea in mind. Lou Gehrig was holding out for more money and the Colonel was considering Dahlgren as first base insurance in case Gehrig became too stubborn. But Lou signed and Dahlgren was sent to Newark, where Vitt was given instructions to "allow Babe to familiarize himself with other positions in the infield." That was how Dahlgren ended up at third base for the Bears in 1937.

In 1938, Dahlgren joined the Yankees but saw limited action, playing in only 29 games and batting a miserable .186. In explaining his weak performance, the Babe remarked, "I think part of my trouble was that full season on the bench. When I did get into the lineup ... my timing was way off. I was over-anxious and I wasn't studying the pitchers the way I did in the minors. I watched the other boys on this club and simply went up there swinging for a home run."

When Gehrig retired in early 1939 due to myotrophic lateral sclerosis, Dahlgren took over at first base. He played in 144 games and batted .235 with 15 home runs and 89 RBI's.

The following year, Dahlgren played in 155 games and raised his batting average to .264, hitting 12 homers and driving in 73 runs. But the Yankees lost the pennant and finished third behind second place Cleveland and number one Detroit. This spelled trouble for Dahlgren and in the spring of 1941, he was traded to the National League Boston Braves. As McCarthy explained, "His arms are too short. He makes a lot of fancy plays, but my other infielders aren't as bad as they looked on their throws to first base late in the season."

Dahlgren saw the situation differently, however, commenting, "Someone had to be blamed for losing the pennant and I was the fall guy."

Regardless of who was right, Dahlgren's move to the Braves marked the beginning of his travelling circus. After playing only 44 games with the Braves in 1941, the Babe was sold to the Chicago

Cubs. He continued with the Cubs in 1942, but also played for the Brooklyn Dodgers in the National League and the St. Louis Browns in the junior circuit. In 1943, it was the Philadelphia Phillies, and for the next two years, it was the Pittsburgh Pirates. But in 1944, Dahlgren turned in his best major league year. He played in 158 games for the Pirates and batted .289 with 101 RBI's. In 1946, Dahlgren closed out his twelve-year major league career, returning once again to the American League St. Louis Browns.

In a tribute to Babe Dahlgren's ability as a professional first baseman, John Lardner wrote in June, 1940, "Terry made no mistakes at first, but Dahlgren is twice as fast as Terry. Sisler was fast, but Dahlgren is more agile and resourceful. Lacking what is known as grace, he may impress you on first sight as a scrambler and an acrobat. So he is, but pretty soon you realize that he never misses. He is sure as death."

Lardner further wrote, "...if an old-timer were to swear to me on a stack of Testaments that there was ever a greater defensive first baseman than Ellsworth (Babe) Dahlgren of the Yankees, I wouldn't believe him."

After the rain subsided in Montreal, the Royals finally got their home opener underway in a most successful fashion. They routed the Bears by a score of 4-1. At one point, it seemed the game would never start because of the endless inaugural ceremonies. Over 5,000 fans sat under the ominous threat of rain, waiting impatiently as the band played not one, not two, but three national anthems, *God Save The King, The Star Spangled Banner,* and *O' Canada.* The songs were followed by a fifteen-minute speech in two languages by the Montreal Mayor, who finally declared "the baseball season open." But before the game could get underway, there was a ten-minute photo session on the mound. The frustrating delay was quickly forgotten, however, when Gus Dugas belted a three-run homer off Steve Sundra in the sixth inning, breaking a 1-1 tie.

The following day, the Bears took it on the chin from Rochester, 5-3, giving their first road trip the earmarks of an impending disaster. In the meantime, the team's roster continued to change.

Jack LaRocca, who had been with the Bears less than two weeks, was sent to Oakland. Merrill May, the veteran third baseman, was put on the inactive list, and Walter Brown was suffering from an injured knee. Newark now had only nineteen available players.

Nonetheless, the Bears finally got cracking on May 11 when they began a six-game winning streak by beating Rochester, 4-1, behind the six-hit pitching of Atley Donald. The young right-hander posted his fourth straight victory, striking out 8 for a total of 27 in thirty-five innings. At this pace, he would reach 200 by the end of the season. The Bears broke the game wide open in the fifth, beginning with Buddy Rosar's double. Donald then doubled Rosar home and Joe Gordon got on base with a single. The next batter was Jimmy Gleeson and he scored Donald with a single. Then the newly-acquired Babe Dahlgren doubled, chasing both Gordon and Gleeson home with the third and fourth runs of the inning.

James Joseph Gleeson, the switch-hitting outfielder from Kansas City, Missouri, had played in only 41 games with the Cleveland Indians in 1936. Apparently Gleeson's .259 batting average didn't impress the Cleveland management enough and he was sent back to New Orleans, where he batted .320 the year before, leading the Southern League with 105 RBI's. In the winter of 1936, Gleeson was sold to Kansas City. But when he held out during salary negotiations the following spring, Kansas City quickly traded him to Newark for outfielder Ralph Boyle. As a result, the young Mr. Gleeson became a key player on the Bears' 1937 Championship team.

It was ironic that Gleeson should have become a member of the Yankee organization, since he had passed up the opportunity to sign when he was a 20-year-old junior at Rockhurst College in Kansas City. Yankee scout Eddie Herr had offered him a contract, but Jimmy decided to finish his college education instead. Herr left his scouting job with the Yankees in the fall of 1932. When Jimmy got his sheepskin in the spring of 1933, he signed with Cleveland.

Despite his solid performance with the Bears in 1937, Gleeson found himself back in Ruppert Stadium the following year. After a brief holdout during spring training, Gleeson finally signed his new

Left fielder Jimmy Gleeson batted .299, drove in 81 runs, scored another 101, and belted 16 homers.

contract. Fortunately enough, the mild disagreement over his salary had no effect on Gleeson's performance. More than halfway through the season, he was having the best year of his career. The versatile outfielder was on his way to breaking Red Holt's 1924 record of 57 doubles when fate stepped in. On July 25 in Baltimore, Gleeson was hit by a pitch that badly bruised his thumb. At the time of his injury, he had 42 doubles and was batting a solid .315. Jimmy finished the season with 50 two-base hits, a mark reached by only five other players in the history of the International League.

Although the battered thumb ended Gleeson's chance for a new doubles record in the league, it didn't stop him from getting a second shot at the major leagues. Chicago scout Clarence Rowland trailed the young outfielder from Toronto to Rochester and liked what he saw. On August 23, 1938, the Chicago Cubs bought Gleeson from the Bears. The press reported the deal "involved an unstipulated number of coarse bank notes and one ballplayer, identity still undetermined. Gleeson will be delivered to Mr. Wrigley's ball club next spring."

Gleeson, of course, was delighted to hear of this sale. One of his colleagues, recalling how Jimmy held out with Kansas City and was traded to Newark in early 1937, jokingly asked, "Think you'll hold out next spring, Jimmy?" Gleeson laughed but didn't say a word.

Buoyed by his sale to the Cubs, Gleeson finished the 1938 season with Newark by turning in a solid performance. He played in 123 games, batting .312 with 16 home runs, 113 runs scored, and 82 RBI's. In the play-offs, the Bears defeated both Rochester and Buffalo. Although Gleeson batted only .229, he still managed to knock in 11 runs.

Jimmy starred in the Little World Series, but unfortunately in a losing cause. The Bears lost in seven games to the Kansas City Blues (also owned by Ruppert), the American Association pennant winner. Gleeson scored ten runs, drove in another six, and hit a respectable .333, second only to Les Scarsella's .370 average.

In 1939, Gleeson found himself replacing Augie Galan in left field for the Chicago Cubs, batting third in the lineup. He played in 111 games and hit a weak .223. He bounced back the following year, however, when he played in 129 games and raised his batting average 90 points to a nifty .313. He also drove in 61 runs and scored another 76, turning in a fine season in only his second year with the Cubs.

But apparently it wasn't good enough. In a surprise move that winter, the Cubs traded Gleeson to the Cincinnati Reds for short-stop Billy Myers. In 102 games with the Reds, the rangy outfielder slumped badly, hitting only .233 with 34 RBI's and 47 runs scored. It was a far cry from his previous year with the Cubs.

At the age of 30 in 1942, Gleeson finished his short five-year major league career in typical quiet fashion. At the end of the season, he enlisted in the Navy to become a chief petty officer, working in physical education under the direction of Commander Gene Tunney.

While at the reserve station in New London, Connecticut, Gleeson was in charge of sorting out athletes returning from overseas to make up teams for the local base. It was here that he met up with the future Hall of Fame catcher, Lawrence "Yogi" Berra.

"Everybody was looking for that kind of duty, so we had to check them out to see if they could really play ball like they said," Gleeson explained.

"One day, they say they're sending me over a boxer and a baseball player. Standing attention in front of me is this skinny 135-pounder and a roly-poly 190-pounder. Naturally, I thought Yogi was the boxer. He was a seaman deuce, the lowest you can get, and the funniest thing in a sailor's hat that you ever saw. There was two feet of snow outside so I couldn't try him out. I gave him a job in the gym and everybody fell in love with the guy."

When April finally rolled around, Gleeson stationed Yogi in the outfield since he had Joe Glenn (another future Yankee) catching behind the plate. The Navy base had a heavy playing schedule, including exhibition games with the New York Giants, the Boston Red Sox, the Washington Senators, and the Philadelphia Phillies.

The late Mel Ott was with the Giants then and inquired about baseball talent. "We have a youngster here who can really powder the ball,'' Gleeson told Ott. "You watch in batting practice.''

Yogi hit everything solidly and Ott tried his best to get his boss to purchase him for $50,000. But Yogi had already signed with the Yankees and they wouldn't part with him.

Years later in 1964, after Berra had been appointed Yankee Manager, one of his first coaching selections was none other than his old Navy boss. Gleeson had high praise for Berra. "Everybody liked Yogi at the base,'' Gleeson pointed out. "He made friends easily and he could really hit. I was his manager then and now I'll be working for him. It's a strange coincidence, but I'm happy about it.

"He may appear to be a happy-go-lucky guy,'' Gleeson continued, "but it goes farther than that. He handled pitchers perfectly and always gave the high sign to the bench as soon as a hurler started to lose his stuff. He makes the right moves by instinct and I'm positive that all players, youngsters and veterans alike, will have a great deal of respect for him. I believe he'll do a great job.

"The more you talk to Yogi and know him personally, as I do, you realize that he has the knack of getting to the bottom of a situation and coming up with the satisfactory solution.''

In addition to being Yogi's first base coach, Gleeson served as a major league scout and a minor league manager in the Yankee farm system. Over his long and illustrious baseball career, Gleeson had a hand in the development of such outstanding ballplayers as Jim Bouton, Al Downing, Phil Linz, Tom Tresh, and Joe Pepitone.

Gleeson's character was probably best summed up by Downing when the young pitcher was brought up in 1960 from the Binghamton farm team (managed by Gleeson). "If it weren't for him, I wouldn't be here right now,'' Downing said.

In the last game of their series with Rochester, Newark chalked up another victory as the Red Wings went down, 12-5. Vito Tamulis picked up his third win, but needed relief assistance from Joe Beggs. Gordon belted his first home run of the season, and Gleeson tripled with the bases loaded, helping the team to an easy triumph.

The Bears next headed for Buffalo to show off their three league-leading hitters — Charlie Keller, batting an even .500, Frank Kelleher with .452, and Buddy Rosar, hitting .438. The rain followed right along, cancelling one game and setting up back-to-back double-headers. Newark swept both ends of the first twin bill, 9-5 and 6-3. In the first game, Gordon and McQuinn each drove in four runs and Keller homered for the ninth. In the night cap, Bill Yocke gave up one scratch hit over the last four innings as Willard Hershberger hit his fourth homer.

The Sunday double-header drew 8,000 spectators and Atley Donald won his fifth game in a row, 7-4. Although Donald gave up three hits and three runs in the first inning, he managed to go the full game, allowing only five hits the rest of the way. Gordon made some spectacular plays at second base, fielding eleven chances without an error and giving notice to the aging Tony Lazzeri that he was ready to take over.

Although the second half of the double-header dragged into extra innings, it didn't change the final outcome of the game. The Bears won when Hershberger delivered a clutch single to score McQuinn in the ninth inning.[5] Keller, as usual, played outstanding ball. In addition to a long home run over the center field fence early in the game, he made a sensational one-handed catch in the seventh to send the game into extra innings. He then came through with a key single in the ninth. It was only a sample of what the kid from Maryland would do the rest of his career.

In Jersey City, the Giants managed to take three games from Toronto, helping to build Newark's first place lead. Already the rival managers throughout the league were moaning, "This isn't the Newark club, it's the Yankees."

The Bears ended their winning streak at six straight when they lost to the Toronto Leafs, 4-2. Joe Mulligan, the Toronto right-hander from Holy Cross, pitched a superb game, allowing only two hits for Newark — a double by Dahlgren in the seventh innning and

---

5. In the International League, the second game of a double-header was seven innings.

another by Keller in the ninth. King Kong extended his hitting streak to sixteen consecutive games, but he would be stopped the following day.

Newark took the next three from Toronto, sweeping the Wednesday double-header, 6-2 and 7-0, and beating the Leafs again on Thursday, 7-5. In the Wednesday opener, Steve Sundra pitched his first complete game and posted his second win of the season, scattering seven hits. The Bears managed to get only four, but combined them with six walks, four Toronto errors, and key punches by Gleeson and Hershberger.

Who, on this fine spring evening, could have imagined that Hershberger — confidently rounding the bases or pulling down a wild fastball — would commit suicide three years later in a Boston hotel room? It was a tragic ending for this gifted young player.

Willard Hershberger broke into professional baseball in 1930 with El Paso in the Arizona-Texas League. In those days, the nineteen-year-old kid from Lemon Cave, California played second base. Halfway through his second year with El Paso, however, the team's first-string catcher fractured his leg. Naturally, the second string catcher was pressed into immediate service. Through a strange turn of events, he became embroiled in a heated argument with a local sports writer, lost his temper, and flattened the writer with one punch. In the process, he broke his thumb and El Paso was suddenly without a catcher. Since Hershberger had done a little catching in high school, he was quickly repositioned to fill the team's void. With Hershberger behind the plate, El Paso went on to win not only the pennant, but the play-offs to boot. Bill Essick was so impressed with the young catcher's ability that he quickly brought him into the Yankee organization.

In 1932, Hershberger travelled all over the country for the Yankees, from Hollywood to Newark. He played most of the season, however, with the Central League Erie team, where he batted .348 and was named to the All Star team. Nonetheless, he wound up catching the last 15 games of the season for Newark.

Although Willard went to spring training with the Bears in 1933, he failed to make the club and was shipped to Binghamton. With the Bingos, Hershberger continued his fine hitting performance, ending the season with a .305 average and again named to the All Star team.

During the next three years, Hershberger was shuffled around from one team to another. He played at Hollywood, Oakland, and then Newark. In spite of all this jockeying, he still managed to hit above .300.

In 1937, he shared Newark's catching duties with Buddy Rosar and had an exceptional year. At the end of the season, the Bears traded him to the Cincinnati Reds in exchange for first baseman Les Scarsella (on option) and shortstop Eddie Miller. Some cash was also thrown into the deal. The acquisition of Hershberger was one of the first moves in the rebuilding of the Reds under their new Manager, Bill McKechnie.

For the next three years, with the great veteran receiver, Ernie Lombardi, playing behind the plate, Hershberger saw little action for Cincinnati. In 1938, he played in 49 games and hit .276. The following year, he played in 63 games and hit .345. Both were respectable seasons, especially for a part-time performer. Willard also played briefly in the 1939 World Series, which the Yankees took from the Reds in four straight wins.

Although Hershberger was batting over .300 through July of 1940, it was reported that he was "given to moods of depression ... and was said to be worried over his failure to hit consistently." On August 2, after Hershberger failed to hit in the Reds' double loss to Boston, Manager Bill McKechnie had a long talk with the catcher in his hotel suite. It was understood they discussed his current performance.

Gabe Paul, Cincinnati's travelling secretary, said that after McKechnie talked with Hershberger, the young bachelor "was in much better spirits ... and sat around the lobby with some of the players." The following morning, when Hershberger was asked by his roommate, Bill Baker, if he was going over to the park, he replied that he would show up a little late. When Hershberger failed to make it, he was telephoned and told the caller, "I'm sick and can't play, but I'll come out right away anyway.''

Later, a man by the name of Sam Cohen, a Cincinnati businessman and a close friend of Willard, went to the hotel to get him, but found the door locked. A maid finally opened the door and they found Hershberger's body in the bathroom; he had cut his jugular vein with a razor blade — a victim of suicide at the age of 29.

In Newark's second game against Toronto, Walter Brown, who had recovered from his knee injury, pitched a three-hitter and shutout the Leafs, 7-0. His performance prompted Vitt to predict 15 victories for the fat right-hander, despite his late start in the season. Although the Bears scored a total of seven runs, Bob Seeds gave Brown the third inning insurance, tripling with the bases loaded for an early 3-0 lead.

On Thursday, it took some tough pitching by reliever Joe Beggs and a two-run homer by McQuinn in the thirteenth inning to beat Toronto, 7-5. In the eighth, with the score tied, 5-5, Beggs came into the game to relieve Yocke with the bases full and two men out. He managed to squeeze his way out of the inning without letting a run score, but in the eleventh, he found himself in an even more serious jam. The bases were loaded again with two men out, but the count on Frank Madura had moved up to 3 and 0. Beggs, working ever so carefully, induced Madura to hit a ground ball to Gordon for the third and last out. Then McQuinn put it away in the thirteenth by blasting his second home run of the game. That ended the Bears' first road trip of the season. They won 9 of 12 and increased their first place lead to 3½ games.

Back in Newark, Secretary Kennedy enthusiastically talked to a group of local reporters about the Bears' performance on the road. "Gordon looks great," Kennedy said. "He had a tough time getting started in Newark, but on the road, he looked like a different player. He looked as good as he did in Florida.''

A second reporter interrupted and asked him about Nolen Richardson. "Rich has a cold in his throwing arm that gave him trouble and affected his confidence. I look for him to be O.K. as soon as the weather is warmer. I expect he'll wind up with his usual batting average. He never was a big percentage hitter, as you know, but he's dependable.''

Kennedy then switched the conversation to his outfielders. "Seeds isn't hitting as much as we expected. He probably needs warm weather, too. But that Gleeson is all anybody could ask for. And you know how Keller is going. There's a boy who gives every indication of being a great ballplayer."

"What about Dahlgren at third?" asked one of the reporters. "Time will tell," replied Kennedy. It will take him a while to adjust himself to playing in unfamiliar territory. Balls come at you at third at different angles, both on throws and off the bat, than in positions Dahlgren has been used to playing, and the hot corner calls for him making throws from positions and angles that are strange to him now. We'll have to suspend judgment on the Babe until he has had a fair trial."

"How about those pitchers on the payroll?" another reporter asked. "Say, those young pitchers look better than our veterans. That's because the veterans haven't been able to work often enough. Men like Brown, Sundra, Piechota, and Tamulis have to work about every fourth day to be at their best; otherwise, they don't have the control which is so necessary to experienced pitchers. And all those young hurlers look great. Beggs is another Makosky, the way he goes in as relief pitcher. Donald won his first five games. Yocke and Russo, two left-handers, also are delivering. An X-ray of Fallon's shoulder showed he is O.K. Spittler says he is ready. He has been pitching in batting practice without his old arm trouble returning. Everybody else on the ball club — McQuinn and Hershberger and Rosar and the others — including old Os Vitt, all look...."

"Great?" interjected a reporter.

"That's the word I've been trying to think of," Kennedy answered, tongue-in-cheek.

10.

Out In Front By Eight

ON MAY 20, THE NEWARK BEARS ENJOYED A SLIM 3½ game lead over the second place Montreal Royals. On June 9, three weeks and 21 games later, the Bears' margin had bulged to 8 and the juggernaut couldn't be stopped. They had won 17 of their last 21 games! It started with the hapless Baltimore Orioles and a brief two-game series that the Bears took by scores of 7-0 and 8-4. Atley Donald pitched a brilliant game, posting his first shutout of the year. The temperamental right-hander scattered just three hits and only allowed two Orioles to get as far as second base. It was Donald's sixth consecutive victory. As they would continue to do all year long, the Bears struck early. They scored six times in the first inning off Gordon Dusty Rhodes, capped by Buddy Rosar's three-run homer, his fifth of the season.

Marius Russo picked up the victory the next day, with relief help from Al Piechota, as the Bears won, 8-4. Russo, struggling most of the game, was whacked for twelve hits in only seven innings. Piechota retired six Orioles in a row over the last two innings to preserve the victory. And as if they needed additional help, the Yankees announced they were sending Kemp Wicker to the Bears, subject to 24-hour recall. Wicker would stay for two months and make a significant contribution to the incredible season. During this time, the lanky left-hander would win seven games before Joe McCarthy pulled the string and brought him back to New York. All totalled, Wicker pitched in 88 innings for the Yankees, winning seven and losing three with a 4.40 ERA as the "Bronx Bombers" won another pennant. Kemp also pitched one inning in the fifth game of the World Series against the New York Giants. He finished his short four-year major league career with the Brooklyn Dodgers in 1941.

On Sunday, May 23, the Bears opened a four-game series with the Jersey City Giants at the brand-new Roosevelt Stadium. Since the bitter exchange between Oscar Vitt and Travis Jackson was still fresh in the minds of the fans, many expected this first meeting to be explosive. As a matter of fact, it appeared Vitt wanted to keep the pot boiling when he commented the previous Friday, "I'm sure of only one thing, those Jersey City all-thumbers will finish in the second division, even if we have to attend to it alone." It marked the first meeting between the two rivals since 1933. Most of the 4,000 reserved seats were sold, as well as 1,200 box seats. Standing room only was expected.

A steady rain dampened the attendance that day, but not the enthusiasm. Over 20,000 wet, bedraggled but orderly fans, displaying huge "Beat the Bears" placards, cheered the Little Giants to a surprising 6-5 victory. The game started in typical Newark fashion. Joe Gordon led off with a 330-foot blast over the left field fence. In the fourth, Babe Dahlgren led off with a tremendous 410-foot homer over the center field fence. By the end of the fifth inning, the Bears were leading, 4-1, when rain halted the game for forty-five minutes.

When play resumed, Jersey City managed to pick up two runs and going into the bottom of the ninth, the Bears led, 5-3. But the scrappy Little Giants wouldn't give up, scoring three runs with two out. The game ended when Al Piechota hit Jack Redwood with the bases loaded, sending Hal Lee across the plate with the winning run. The home town fans were delighted.

After the game, Vitt was asked about some of the comments that were directed at him from the stands. Ol' Os explained he was accustomed to these epithets since it was essentially the same old stuff he had heard for ten years in Los Angeles. However, he was quick to add he did hear a few more "dems" and "deses."

Commenting on the loss, Vitt bluntly stated, "We'll beat 'em 15

Kemp Wicker joined the Bears in late May and won seven games before returning to the Yankees in July.

games out of 22. They said it was impossible to hit balls out of that park. Gordon and Dahlgren did it with plenty to spare and those outfielders caught a couple hit almost as hard. That Jersey City team is one team we can beat. We beat ourselves today.''

The joy in Jersey City was short lived. The Bears won the next three — 10-4, 9-8, and 1-0. In the 10-4 shellacking, Jimmy Gleeson, Willard Hershberger, and Bob Seeds accounted for eight of the sixteen hits, helping Vito Tamulis pick up another win. Hershberger extended his hitting streak to 11 consecutive games.

The 9-8 victory was a baffling game as the Little Giants scored seven runs off Atley Donald in the first inning, but couldn't hold the lead! The Bears slowly pecked away at the seven-run deficit, scoring in every inning except the third and sixth. Joe Beggs pitched brilliantly in relief, allowing only four hits in eight and two-thirds innings, gaining the victory and protecting Donald's six-game winning streak.

Off the field, George Weiss was as active as the Bears were on the field. The Vice President sent veteran third baseman Merrill May and the inconsistent Al Piechota to Oakland for right-hander Marvin Breuer and infielder Lewis Blair. Hy Goldberg, writing in the *Newark Evening News*, summed up the trade in these words: ''To the naked eye, it's an even swap that serves no purpose except to enrich the railroads, but the deal was made on the theory that a change of clubs frequently brings out the best in a performer who hasn't been doing as well as the cards and the stars and the numerologists say he should.''

The final game of the series saw left-hander Kemp Wicker and right-hander Glen Gabler hook up in an old-fashioned pitchers' duel. In the top of the eighth, with two out and a scoreless tie, George McQuinn and Babe Dahlgren slashed back-to-back doubles for the only run of the ball game. Wicker pitched magnificently, allowing only five hits, two of them coming in the exciting ninth. Hal Lee was on third, representing the tying run, when Elmer Klumpp hit a short fly to Bob Seeds in center field. Seeds fired a perfect strike to the plate to cut down Lee and end the game. Later it was announced that Jack Fallon, who had injured his arm in

Rochester, would be returning to the active list on Sunday. He would further strengthen an already overpowering pitching staff. Some baseball executives were claiming the Bears were as strong as a major league second division club. Would you believe first division?

The next series was played against the Syracuse Chiefs, and Newark took 3 of 5 games. Once again, Lady Luck planted a big kiss on Atley Donald and preserved his six-game winning streak. In the third game, the Bears were trailing, 6-4, with one on and two out. Francis Kelleher batted for Donald and belted a clutch home run to tie the game at 6-6. The Bears won it in the tenth when they scored two more runs. Joe Beggs received credit for the victory, his fifth of the season.

Although Beggs joined the Yankees in 1938, his nine-year major league career would fall short of the potential he exhibited in the minor leagues. In 1936, pitching for Norfolk in the Piedmont League, the sinker ball specialist turned in a great year, winning 22 and losing 9. He completed 21 games, struckout 125 batters, and registered a 3.70 ERA. In 1937, he would finish the season with a mark of 21-4. With two outstanding twenty game seasons under his belt, Joe Beggs was now pounding on the door of the major leagues.

In 1938, at the Yankees' spring training camp in St. Petersburg, Lou Gehrig tagged Beggs' sinker pitch as the "iron ball." In an attempt to hit the ball out of the park during practice, Gehrig remarked, "It feels like one of those old-time cannon balls of iron when your bat hits it."

Dahlgren agreed, recalling his earlier days with Newark. "The first day I joined the Bears, the game was called off and Beggs pitched to us in practice. That's just how the sinker ball felt — like it was made of iron. It was hard to see and seemed to plop dead when you did get a piece of it."

Beggs finished the 1938 season with the Yankees and compiled an unimpressive 3-2 mark with a weak 5.40 ERA. He started in 9 of 14 games, but managed to complete only 4. This disappointing performance assured Beggs of another year with the Bears. In 1939, he

Right-hander Joe Beggs was the ace of the staff with a 21-4 record. He played nine years in the major leagues.

turned in a mediocre season, posting a 12-10 record in 33 games and 200 innings.

But in spite of this performance, Beggs was traded to the Cincinnati Reds in January, 1940 for the fastballing left-hander, Lee Grissom. It was hinted that Grissom was coming to the Yankees in partial payment of the deal which sent Joe DiMaggio's brother, Vince, from the Yankee-owned Kansas City team to the Reds. It was also reported that Ed Barrow was quite impressed with Grissom's fastball during his short World Series performance against the Yankees in 1939.

With Cincinnati in 1940, Beggs enjoyed his greatest major league season. Used almost exclusively in relief, the right-hander posted a magnificient 12-3 record along with seven saves and a 2.00 ERA. His victory margin and seven saves were both tops in the league for relief pitchers. Beggs also helped the Reds breeze to a 100-53 record and an easy pennant. But in the World Series against Detroit, he saw very little action. He pitched one inning of the third game. The Reds went on to win the series in seven games, their first World Championship in twenty-one years.

During the next three seasons, 1941-43, Beggs was the mainstay of the Cincinnati bullpen. He pitched in a total of 261 innings, won 14 and lost 13, and recorded 19 saves. His ERA over the three-year period remained consistently low, 3.79, 2.13, and 2.34, respectively.

Shortly after the 1944 season started, the big right-hander was commissioned a lieutenant in the Navy and served through the 1945 season. When Joe returned to Cincinnati in 1946, he was taken out of the bullpen and made a starter. Apparently the new role agreed with him. He led the Reds' highly-touted pitching staff (Johnny VanderMeer, Ewell Blackwell, Bucky Walters, et al.) with 12 victories and also posted the lowest ERA at 2.32, completing 14 of 22 starts. However, as is so often the case, the fortunes of baseball change quickly. In early June, 1947, after 11 games and an 0-3 record, Beggs was traded to the New York Giants for first baseman Norman "Babe" Young.

It was the first step in bolstering Mel Ott's relief pitching staff, the key to keeping the Giants contenders in the sizzling National League pennant race. Ott felt that with Beggs' uncanny control and low sinker ball, it would be hard to loft a home run over the short fence at the Polo Grounds, particularly in the late innings. Beggs would also provide aid to overworked reliefer Ken Trinkle, who had already been in 20 games.

Beggs appeared in 32 games with the Giants that year, posting a 3-3 record in more than 65 innings. But over the winter, the 37-year-old right-hander underwent surgery on his arm and was ineffective the following spring. During the early part of the 1948 season, Beggs pitched only one-third of an inning before he called it quits. On May 10, he ended his major league baseball career, receiving his unconditional release from the New York Giants.

As quick as you could say stumblebums and smudgepots, the Bears and the Little Giants hooked up again in a three-game series. This time, Newark won all three by scores of 6-0, 2-1, and 6-5, making it six straight over Jersey City.

Joe Gordon and Babe Dahlgren teamed up to form a devastating one-two punch that gave the Little Giants fits and helped sweep the series. The first two games were a morning and afternoon Memorial Day double-header. In the morning, at Roosevelt Stadium, Kemp Wicker pitched another shutout, extending his consecutive scoreless inning skein to eighteen. Wicker scattered seven hits and allowed only one runner to reach third. Dahlgren homered and singled twice, knocking in three runs, while Gordon also homered and singled, driving in another run. In the afternoon, across the meadows at Ruppert Stadium, behind the outstanding pitching of Joe Beggs, McQuinn homered and Dahlgren tripled to drive in the winning run.

No game was scheduled for the next day and Weiss took the opportunity, as he would all season, to maneuver more players. Lewis Blair, who only a few days earlier was part of the May-Piechota-Breuer trade, was sent to Binghamton. Blair arrived Monday night from Oakland and on Tuesday, Ray Kennedy told him, "Don't bother to unpack pal, you're on your way to Binghamton." Bill

Yocke was also sent to Binghamton, where he would see much more action. The 25-year-old lefty pitched sparingly in eight games and found the Bears' solid pitching staff too tough to crack.

In the final game with Jersey City, it was the dynamic duo again — Gordon and Dahlgren. Each homered and singled, driving in three of the six runs, while scoring four between themselves. Staked to a 6-0 lead, Tamulis pitched well for seven innings, giving up only three hits. But the roof caved through in the eighth. Jersey City scored five runs on four hits, a walk, and a Nolen Richardson error. Fallon relieved Tamulis, but after Elmer Klumpp singled to start the ninth, Oscar Vitt made a quick change and brought in Walter Brown. The huge right-hander made Vitt look like a genius by retiring the next three batters.

On June 4, Newark opened a four-game set with the Syracuse Chiefs, beginning with their first night game of the season at Ruppert Stadium. Newark took the first three, but lost the fourth, 2-1, when the game was called after five innings because of rain.

Almost 14,000 fans came out to cheer the Bears under the lights and they were given a lot to cheer about. With the score tied 4-4 in the bottom of the ninth, Buddy Rosar opened with a double. Mike Kelly, the Chiefs' Manager, removed right-hander Frank Pearce and brought in 43-year-old Ray Kolp. Nolen Richardson sacrificed Rosar to third. Vitt then sent Frank Kelleher, the league's leading hitter, to bat for Joe Beggs. Now it was Kelly's turn. He yanked Kolp in favor of his ace, Jake Mooty, who proceeded to walk Kelleher. The next batter, Joe Gordon, ran the count to 2-1. Now it was Vitt's turn. The Newark Manager shocked all 14,000 fans by sending up Willard Hershberger to bat for Gordon. Hershberger hung around long enough to draw a walk, loading the bases. Mooty continued to have trouble locating the strike zone and walked his third man of the inning, Jimmy Gleeson, forcing home Rosar with the winning run. After the game, Vitt was asked how he happened to remove Gordon at such a crucial moment. "Oh, I just had a hunch," he said.

Atley Donald won the second game of the series, 7-3, for his seventh consecutive win. Chiefs pitcher Leo Mangum, a former

Newark pitcher, enviously discussed the Bears with a local reporter. "What a ball club. Power from one end of the batting order to the other, power on the bench and power on the way." The bench power Mangum was referring to was Francis Kelleher, the leading hitter in the league who couldn't crack the Newark lineup. The power on the way was Fern Bell, an outfielder from Oakland who played part of the 1935 season with the Bears and who Vitt was planning to use in a utility role. Bell, however, would only pinch hit twice for Newark before he was shipped to Kansas City.

In the four years following Newark's incredible 1937 season, utility infielder-outfielder Francis Kelleher wouldn't have time to hang his hat in one place, being shuttled back and forth between Newark, Kansas City, and Oakland. During one season, he played in all three towns, which prompted Kelleher to remark, "Why, I still have some tomato juice that I bought in Florida. It has made two trips across the country and it's none the worse for wear."

Finally, in 1941, Newark Manager Johnny Neun told Kelleher he would be the club's regular left fielder and that he could count on the job all year long. That single statement worked like magic on the 25-year-old. Playing regularly, he began to bang out home runs by the bushel. He finished the year with 37 homers (setting what was then a new record for Newark) and drove in 125 runs, four short of Charlie Keller's mark.

In spite of this outstanding display of power, Kelleher couldn't crack the Yankee outfield of DiMaggio, Henrich, and Keller. And it took until July, 1942 before he was given his big break and was sold to the Cincinnati Reds for cash, pitcher Jim Turner, and infielder Joe Abreu. Unfortunately, it would turn out to be an abbreviated major league career. Playing in only 38 games in 1942 with the Reds, Kelleher posted a pathetic .182 hitting average. Only three of his twenty hits were home runs.

On June 16 of the following year, Kelleher was optioned to Syracuse, but was recalled two months later on August 20. In nine games in 1943, the big outfielder went hitless. In 1944, Kelleher was optioned to Hollywood in the Pacific Coast League, ending a very brief two-year major league career. However, Francis Kelleher would always be remembered as a key member of the greatest minor league team in the history of baseball.

In game number three against Syracuse, Kemp Wicker ended his streak of scoreless innings at twenty-four! He allowed only five hits and one run as he chalked up his third straight win, 3-1, and his third complete game. In twenty-seven innings, the southpaw gave up seventeen hits and one run for an unbelievable .006 ERA! Oscar Vitt had mixed emotions over this performance. Of course he loved the job Wicker was doing, but he was also worried that McCarthy would take one look at the statistics sheet and Wicker would be gone. In addition, the Yankees were having pitching problems during their Western swing. They lost four of six, while the Chicago White Sox were on a nine-game winning streak, cutting the Yankee lead to one full game. It was clear the Yankees needed pitching help and Wicker was available for the asking.

Before 13,532 wet fans, the Bears lost the final game of the series, 2-1, with the game being called after five innings. Weiss continued his maneuvering as he sold right-hander Cecil Spittler, the Cranford, New Jersey native, to Baltimore. Spittler saw little action through most of spring training due to a sore arm — the same problem that forced him to sit at home most of the 1936 season.

Newark next took on the last place Baltimore Orioles for a scheduled four-game series and the rain managed to save the cellar dwellers from dropping all four. Joe Beggs won the opener, 8-6, in Baltimore's little band box by keeping the ball low and "forcing the batters to hit the ball on the ground." It was his eighth victory. Babe Dahlgren and Bob Seeds each hit three-run homers.

Steve Sundra turned in a superb pitching performance the next day by striking out ten and blanking the hapless Orioles, 6-0. Although Newark won easily, it was a costly game. In the second inning, Buddy Rosar, who was batting a gaudy .378, took the full brunt of a foul tip, badly splitting his right hand between the forefinger and thumb. It would keep him out of the lineup for ten days. With two out in the ninth, Willard Hershberger nearly repeated

Rosar's second inning performance when he took a foul tip on his throwing hand. Fortunately, the split was only under the nail and would not impair his throwing. Off the field, the hustling Weiss was operating again as a shocker of a deal was announced — the sale of Walter Brown to Cincinnati.

After the 6-0 embarrassment, the Baltimore fans were enraged. Their reactions ranged from pent-up hostility to bitter sarcasm. "Why, it's the worst ball club I have ever seen," remarked one. "I know what the trouble is," said another. "They stay out too late at night and don't keep in condition." A third put it, "They're just a lotta old men. Why don't they go out and get some young fellows." And a fourth threw out, "Aw, they oughta put 'em all against a brick wall and shoot 'em."

The next day, Atley Donald won his eighth straight game by a score of 10-5, heaping even more humiliation on the lowly Orioles. Their record now stood at 11-31 with a .260 percentage and they were buried in the cellar. Conversely, the Bears' record stood at 35-11 with a .761 percentage and they were solidly entrenched in first place. After the Baltimore series, the Bears headed north for a twelve-day homestand at Ruppert Stadium. Even with their eight-game lead, the fun was just beginning.

11.

Twelve Days At Home

THE NEWARK BEARS OPENED THEIR TWELVE-DAY homestand on a Friday evening against the Buffalo Bisons before 16,705 fans — the largest night crowd since the lights had been installed in 1930. It was also "Ladies Night" and the gals came by the thousands to watch their local heroes. They weren't disappointed, either, as the Bears walloped Buffalo, 11-3, for Kemp Wicker's fourth straight win. As usual, Newark scored early. In the first inning, Joe Gordon and Jimmy Gleeson doubled, Babe Dahlgren walked, and Charlie Keller drove the ball against the base of the brick wall in center field for a 410-foot double — probably the longest double in history. Bob Seeds singled, scoring Keller, and the Bears had a 4-0 lead. In the third, they put the game away, scoring five more times on five consecutive singles and Gordon's ninth home run, which bounced on top of the left field wall and then over.

Throughout his baseball career, Joe "Flash" Gordon was blessed with the most essential quality an athlete could possess — selfconfidence. And Gordon displayed this important trait early in his life. At Jefferson High School in Portland, Oregon, for example, when the team's regular catcher was injured early in the season, Joe volunteered for the job, got it, and then went ahead and proved he could catch. It was sheer confidence. In another situation, when Joe was looking to play a faster brand of baseball, he talked himself into the shortstop job with the East Side Commercial American Legion team. In the summer of 1931, East Side won the

State championship with the help of shortstop Gordon.

In the fall of 1932, Gordon entered the University of Oregon on an athletic scholarship, and it took only his freshman season to attract Yankee scout Bill Essick. Essick immediately liked what he saw and invited Gordon to Los Angeles to work out with the winter club. Essick was anxious to sign the classy infielder. Joe refused; he wanted to finish college. In his sophomore year at Oregon, Gordon batted a cool .418, leading his team in all offensive departments, and was one of the outstanding players in the Pacific Coast League. Still hounded by Essick and now with a bonus dangling in front of his eyes, Gordon finally relented and signed his first professional contract. Essick dashed off a wire to Ed Barrow summing up his evaluation of Gordon, "...at his best when it meant the most and the going was toughest."

Along with about sixty other hopefuls and enthusiastic youngsters, Gordon reported to Bill Meyer, manager of the Yankee's Oakland Class AA team. This didn't mean very much, since most of the young kids, including Joe, were slated for lower class ball. When Joe was told to report to the Yankee's Binghamton Class A club, the cocky and confident Gordon replied, "I can't make money that way. I want to stay with Oakland."

Meyer patiently explained to Gordon that he lacked the experience to make the grade at Oakland and that if he stayed, the best he could hope for would be to sit on the bench. Gordon insisted. Meyer obtained approval from George Weiss and for the first few weeks, as Meyer predicted, Gordon didn't play. But an injury to shortstop Bernie Devivieros forced Gordon into the lineup and 143 games later, with Devivieros still on the bench, Gordon finished the season with an even .300 batting average. The youngster's confidence once again paid off.

With young Frankie Crosetti solidly entrenched at shortstop for the Yankees and the aging Tony Lazzeri nearing the end of his career, Weiss and Barrow decided to make Gordon a second baseman, grooming the kid to eventually take over for Lazzeri. Gordon proved he could handle the job, performing magnificently for the Bears in 1937. The Yankees wasted no time and called Gordon up. When asked by a reporter whether he wasn't frightened when he heard Lazzeri was out and he was in, the confident Gordon answered, "No, I was rather pleased." The reporter continued pressing about his .280 batting average in Newark, and Gordon remarked, "I hit in a lot of hard luck, and with a little better fortune, I might even improve on those figures in the American League."

Gordon started the 1938 season with the Yankees and word quickly spread among the pitchers that he was a sucker for a high inside pitch. Naturally, that was all the kid saw. After a slow start, he was finally benched by Joe McCarthy. But a pinch-hit home run helped the rookie regain his weakened confidence and by the end of June, he was the new Yankee sensation and the talk of the town.

When reporters asked Gordon to explain the sudden turn of events, the newly-married Joe replied, "I guess it's the home cooking. Regular hours and good food are most important to a ballplayer. And you know, I'm hitting for two now instead of one!"

Although Gordon batted only .255 his rookie season with the Yankees, the slick-fielding second baseman belted 25 homers and drove in 97 runs in 127 games. Needless to say, the Yankee management was pleased.

During the next three years, 1939-41, Gordon was a solid, steady, offensive performer. He averaged 27 home runs a year, along with 100 RBI's and a respectable .280 batting average. McCarthy summed up his performance by saying, "Gordon is as great a ballplayer as he wants to be. I've never seen a better defensive second baseman. But he is a natural .330 hitter, or better, who seems to be content with a .280 mark as long as we keep winning. Most ballplayers like their hits. Gordon pays no attention to any batting average. Some day maybe he will, then watch him."

The immortal Grantland Rice described Gordon's defensive skill in these words: "Gordon has shut off more base hits than any infielder I ever saw. He is not only lightning fast with hands and feet, but an acrobat who began practicing that profession years ago. When you can make catcher Bill Dickey's eyes pop from their sockets day after day, you must be turning out a pretty fair brand of second-basing.''

In 1942, Joe Gordon turned in the greatest season of his eleven-year major league career. He batted .322 (a career high), while hitting 18 homers with 103 RBI's and 88 runs scored. This display of offensive fireworks, along with his continued defensive acrobatics in the field, led the Yankees to their second straight pennant. The baseball writers voted Joe Gordon the Most Valuable Player in the American League. Commenting on the coveted award, Gordon said, ''It's an honor I've always had ambitions to win, like any other ballplayer, but I never thought it would come this season.''

Although Gordon established three fielding records in the 1942 World Series against the St. Louis Cardinals, his batting average suffered tremendously. In five games, the MVP only managed to hit an emaciated .095. Another ballplayer would have drowned in self-pity over this embarrassing performance, but not the even-tempered Gordon. McCarthy explained it best. ''Whether he's good or bad, he never bothers about the importance of the game. Sometimes I wish he'd bother just a little more and get worried like I do. But he never does. He was the star of the World Series in 1941 and maybe the goat of the World Series the next year. But he was the same Gordon. He just figured that was the best he could do at that particular time. Things happen that way. You are not always on top when you want to be.''

If 1942 was considered an outstanding season for Gordon, then 1943 would have to be labeled disappointing and 1946 (1944 and 1945 were spent in service) a disaster! In 1943, Joe batted .249 with 17 homers and only 69 RBI's — all three records were major league lows for the star second baseman. The experts advanced more theories than Gordon collected hits. ''His eyes have gone bad. He is hitting at too many outside curve balls. The opposing pitchers finally have located his weakness. The bat he swings is to heavy. He hasn't been able to hit since he began taking flying lessons last summer.'' Whatever the reason, it still remained a puzzle and Gordon carried the slump into the 1946 campaign. In fairness to Gordon, much of his difficulties that year could be attributed to injuries — a spike wound to his left hand during spring training and a torn leg muscle later in the season. Maybe this explained it, but the fact remained that Gordon's offensive statistics dropped to even lower marks. He played in 112 games, batted .210, hit only 11 homers, and drove in a meagre 47 runs.

On top of all these difficulties, Gordon also had problems in the front office. In June, Larry MacPhail, the Yankee President, called Joe into his office and reprimanded him for his indifferent play. MacPhail remarked in particular about a ground ball which Gordon failed to field. Gordon, always an outspoken young man, in turn made a few disparaging comments about MacPhail's eyesight.

It came as no surprise, then, that in October, 1946, the Yankees sent Gordon to Cleveland in an even swap for right-hander Allie Reynolds. The trade brought together one of the prettiest double play combinations in baseball — Gordon and future Hall of Fame shortstop Lou Boudreau. Apparently the new location rejuvenated Gordon. In 1947, he played in 155 games for Cleveland, batted his customary .272, hit 29 home runs, and drove in 93 runs. Joe Gordon was back.

But the trade really paid off in 1948 when Gordon helped lead the Indians to the American League pennant and a World Series triumph over the Boston Braves. During the regular season, he batted a respectable .280, but hit 32 homers and drove in 124 runs, both career highs. It was to be Gordon's last great season. By 1950, a young 26-year-old second baseman from Mexico named Bobby Avila would help send Gordon back to the Pacific Coast League as a player-manager for the Sacramento Solons.

Eight years later in June, 1958, Joe Gordon returned to Cleveland to replace Bobby Bragan as their field leader and the Indians finished the year in fourth place. He resigned in September, 1959 over an argument with General Manager Frank Lane. But he was reinstated and then sent to Detroit in August, 1960 in exchange for Jimmy Dykes. It was a unique trade in baseball history — one manager for another.

Gordon finished the 1960 season with the Tigers and managed the Kansas City A's in 1961. In 1969, he became the first manager of the expansion Kansas City Royals, a job he held for one season, and the Royals finished fourth.

In total, Gordon managed four different teams for five years. His best showing came in 1959, the year the Indians finished second, five games behind Al Lopez's Chicago White Sox. Gordon ended his managerial career in 1969, leading Kansas City to a fourth place finish. As Grantland Rice once said of Joe Gordon, "He takes life as it comes, the good and the bad, with a grin, letting fate and nature take their devious courses."

In another key front office move, the Bears signed the 41-year-old veteran catcher Pinky Hargrave. It was the classic story of a dedicated ballplayer who possessed an undying love for the game.

Born in 1896, Pinky played ten years in the major leagues for four different teams — Washington Senators, St. Louis Browns, Detroit Tigers, and Boston Braves. He ended his major league career with the Braves in 1933, having posted a .278 lifetime batting average.

Weiss and Hargrave had known each other since the days when Weiss was owner of the New Haven Club and Pinky was their catcher in 1920-21. The following year, Weiss sold him to the Washington Senators. He remained with the Senators for three full seasons and in June, 1925, was traded to the St. Louis Browns.

Hargrave was shipped from St. Louis to Toronto in 1927, but bounced back to Detroit in the fall. The Tigers kept him until 1931, when he was traded back to Washington. The following year, he landed with Baltimore, where Weiss was then in charge of the business office. On this occasion, Weiss sold Pinky to the Boston Braves.

In 1934, the Braves sent him down to Minneapolis, where he stayed until they gave him his outright release early in 1937. By this time, Weiss was a familiar face in the Yankee organization and realized the Bears were in quite a predicament with Rosar injured and Hershberger playing hurt. To solve the catching problem, Weiss managed to coax Pinky out of retirement.

During the next few weeks, Pinky Hargrave, like Tommy

Henrich, Walter Brown, and Kemp Wicker before him, would play a vital role in the success of the Newark Bears.

Back on the field, the Bears won their next three games from Buffalo, 10-5, 7-1, and 4-3. By sweeping the series, they had won 14 of their last 15 games and had extended their winning streak to seven in a row.

The 10-5 victory was another laughter. As usual, the Bears struck early, scoring three runs in the second inning and three more in the third. In the second, Babe Dahlgren singled and Bob Seeds followed with a double. Then Willard Hershberger singled, stole second base, and scored on Joe Gordon's single. In the third inning, George McQuinn singled, Dahlgren doubled, and Charlie Keller tripled, scoring later on a fielder's choice. Jimmy Gleeson's double in the seventh gave the team 100 two-base hits in just 48 games!

On Sunday, Newark easily won the first game of the doubleheader, 7-1, behind the fine pitching of Steve Sundra, who chalked up his fifth victory. Sundra blanked the Bisons for eight innings, but lost his shutout in the ninth when he allowed a run to score on three scratch hits.

The Bears won the nightcap, 4-3, but put a scare into Oscar Vitt and the 13,443 Newark fans when George McQuinn dislocated his ankle in the second inning. Mike McCormick, the first batter for the Bisons, poked a hit over second and McQuinn, believing there might be a play at first, turned toward the bag. His spikes slid in the soft turf and his ankle snapped. Fortunately for Vitt, the ankle was not broken and McQuinn would return to the lineup a week later. At the time of his injury, McQuinn was leading the Bears in almost every offensive category. He had the most hits with 69 (34 of them for extra bases), the most doubles with 17, the most triples with 9, and the most RBI's with 39. He was also tied with Gordon in the home run department with 9. In addition, McQuinn boasted a .329 batting average and was riding the crest of a fifteen-game hitting streak. Most managers, at the loss of such a star, would have gulped down two aspirin and rested for the afternoon. But Vitt wasn't just any manager. With a talent loaded roster, he simply moved Dahlgren to first base and sent Kelleher, who was batting well over .400, to third. These were the natural positions for both players.

During the next 11 games, with Kelleher at third, the Bears would win eight and lose only three, widening their lead to 13½ games. And Kelleher would make a major contribution both in the field and at bat. Even injuries to key players couldn't slow the torrid pace set by the Bears.

The Toronto Leafs were the next team to visit Ruppert Stadium for a three-game series and surprised everyone by beating Newark in the first and third games. It was only the second series the Bears lost and the first since May 1, when Buffalo took 3 of 4 games at Newark.

One of the problems in connection with the Bears' overabundance of pitching talent (although it was a nice problem) was that there was only one mound on a field. With guys like Atley Donald, Joe Beggs, Steve Sundra, Vito Tamulis, and Kemp Wicker, it was nearly impossible for an untried rookie to break into the rotation, let alone pitch with any semblance of regularity. This was the fate that faced Marius Russo in the first game against the Leafs. The young lefty hadn't pitched since May 27 and here it was June 14. He lasted only four innings, giving up ten hits and six runs. Jack Fallon relieved in the fifth and gave up only two hits the rest of the way, but it was too late as the Bears lost, 7-4. Shag Shaughnessy, President of the International League, was on hand and commented after the game, "I came over to put the whammy on these Bears. They're ruining my league."

The next day, the Bears avenged the loss by burying Toronto, 13-7, in lightening fashion. In the first inning, they scored eight times on four walks and five hits, capped by Joe Gordon's tenth home run with two men on. Three Leaf pitchers were used in the first inning and five in the rest of the game as the Bears collected a total of fifteen hits. Willard Hershberger chipped in with three RBI's and Beggs waltzed to his ninth victory.

Toronto bounced back on Wednesday, defeating the Bears, 6-2, behind the superb pitching of Woodrow Wilson Davis. The strapping right-hander checked the Bears with six hits and two runs. Wicker took the loss, his first of the season. Once again, Shaughnessy was on hand and when asked if the success of the Bears had an injurious effect on the interest in other cities around the league, he replied in true executive fashion, "Absolutely not. We're drawing better than ever all over the circuit. The league's attendance already is past the 600,000 mark. Of course, the play-offs help.

"Anyway," concluded Shaughnessy, "the Newark club can't possibly continue at its present pace, so we don't have too much to worry about." Shag was correct. At the time, the Bears were playing .755 ball. They couldn't maintain that pace. They clinched the pennant on August 24 with a .740 percentage!

During the next three days, Newark played five games against the Rochester Red Wings — a single game sandwiched between two double-headers. In the first double-header, the veteran shortstop Nolen Richardson, not known for his hitting, caught the spirit of the Bears by winning the first game and tying the second with — of all things — his bat! Richardson, a pesky hitter, finally busted loose. In the first game, the Bears led, 4-1, on the strength of Gleeson's two-run blast in the seventh. The Red Wings bounced right back, however, with a run in the eighth and two in the ninth, sending the game into extra innings and providing an opportunity for some Richardson heroics. The Newark fans didn't have to wait long, either. In the bottom of the tenth, with the bases loaded, Nolen singled up the middle, driving in the winning run.

In the second game, with the Bears trailing, 3-2, in the bottom of the sixth with two out, the little shortstop tripled home Hershberger with the tying run. While Richardson was still trying to catch his breath on third, the heavens opened up, drenching the field and halting the game at 3-3. If the rain had arrived a minute earlier, preventing Richardson from batting, the game would have reverted to the fifth inning and a Rochester victory. It was just one of those days.

It was also interesting to note that two of the Rochester runs were due to a tall, angular 20-year-old shortstop and a 26-year-old perennial minor league first baseman. Their names were Marty Marion and Walter Alston. (Future major league stars Al Cuccinello and Johnny Hopp were also members of the '37 Red Wing team.)

The next day, Atley Donald blanked Rochester, 2-0, on a nifty three-hitter. Over the nine innings, he faced only twenty-eight Red Wings (two of the three hits were eventually turned into double plays). It was Donald's tenth straight win and talk quickly turned to pitching records. But he was a long way from the International League record of twenty in a row, set by Baltimore's Rube Parnham in 1923. Nonetheless, Atley had an excellent shot at the Newark record of twelve, set by Don Brennan in 1932.

On Saturday, June 19, the Bears ended the five-game series with Rochester by splitting the double-header. Despite home runs by Keller and Dahlgren in the first game, Russo suffered the loss as Rochester edged the Bears, 5-4. In the nightcap, Jack Fallon went the distance and the Bears came back to whip the Red Wings, 11-2. Kelleher drove in three runs for the day, two of which came in the first inning on a long homer with Gleeson on base.

The Bears ended their current homestand with a three-game set against the second place Montreal Royals. A few baseball experts tried to bill the series as "crucial," but with a 10½ game lead and the Bears picking up momentum with each succeeding day, the effort was largely in vain. If there were any skeptics still hanging around, they were all but erased as the Bears swept the Montreal series, extending their lead to 13½ games!

In the first half of the double-header, Charlie Keller thrilled the more than 10,000 fans with a perfect five-for-five game, plus three RBI's and two runs scored. In the bottom of the ninth, with the score tied, 6-6, Keller led off with his fifth hit, but was forced at second by Bob Seeds. Pinky Hargrave then singled Seeds to third, where he scored on George McQuinn's pinch-hit fly to left field. Although McQuinn won the game for Newark, it marked the end of his fifteen-game hitting streak.

In the nightcap, Seeds, Keller, and Hargrave worked their magic once again as Newark nipped the Royals, 3-2, giving Beggs his tenth win. In the sixth, Keller tied the game at 2-2 on a tremendous home run. As one reporter wrote, it was "one of the longest drives of the year at Ruppert Stadium. The ball landed in the top row of the center field bleachers, several feet to the right of the 'alley'." Keller's blast hadn't stopped bouncing when Seeds tripled and scored moments later on Hargrave's fly. Montreal's frustrated Manager, Rabbit Maranville, voiced his opinion after the double loss. "How can you beat 'em? Everything breaks in their favor. We hold the first four men in their batting order to a total of three hits in two games, but the supposedly weak end get sixteen hits."

No doubt Montreal's prayers were answered when it rained in Newark on Monday, cancelling the game. It was re-scheduled for Tuesday night, but Montreal might have played better in the rain, since the Bears crushed the Royals, 15-1. Francis Kelleher went four-for-five, including a grand slam home run, a double, and two singles. After replacing George McQuinn on June 13, the big Californian had hit at a .369 clip. The Bears broke the game wide open in the wild seventh inning, scoring eight times. In addition to Kelleher's grand slam, Dahlgren hit two homers, one before Kelleher and one after. Joe Gordon also homered, his eleventh of the season. With the score so lopsided, Steve Sundra's four-hitter was completely overlooked; it was his sixth victory.

In the summer of 1931, Cleveland scouts had been watching a tall 21-year-old right-hander named Steve "Smokey" Sundra. Sundra was in the process of compiling a phenomenal 17-1 record while pitching for the Quaker Sugars and Fisher Foods, two famed sandlot clubs. The scouts quickly passed the word on to Billy Evans, then General Manager of the Indians, who signed the kid to his first professional contract late in 1931. Steve started in 1932 in the Three-I League, leading the circuit in strikeouts, when the league was suddenly disbanded — not an uncommon occurrence in the minor leagues during the 1930's. Sundra moved next to the Mississippi Valley League, splitting his duties between Quincy and Burlington. He finished the season with an encouraging 9-3 record.

The next year, he helped lead Zanesville to the Mid-Atlantic

League pennant with a 15-12 record. In 1934, with the tail end Toledo club, Sundra posted a mediocre 7-7 record, but struck out 100 batters in 154 innings. The following year, he was optioned to the Minneapolis Millers (still part of the Cleveland chain), where he was used mainly in relief, finishing with a 5-4 record and continuing his strikeout performance, fanning 72 in 90 innings. In early August of the same year, the Indians optioned him to Newark because he wasn't getting enough work with the Millers.

Then over the winter, in an historic trade, the Yankees acquired Sundra, along with Monte Pearson, for the famed Johnny Allen. Ruppert confided later that Sundra was the man the Yankees were really after. "We told Cleveland 'Allen for Pearson' wasn't an even exchange," said Ruppert, "and we mentioned a few players we knew the Indians wouldn't give up. Then we mentioned Sundra, the man we wanted all the time." With Newark in 1936, Sundra won 12 and lost 9. He also made a token appearance with the Yankees, pitching in two innings.

After his outstanding 1937 season with the Bears, the big affable fastballer, who had an appetite to match, finally joined teammates Gordon, Beggs, Chandler, and Dahlgren at Yankee Stadium, their new home. Sundra, in his first full season with the Yankees, won six and lost four with a 4.80 ERA. It wasn't an overly impressive record, but it was enough to earn him a Yankee contract for the following campaign.

In 1939, Sundra turned in what proved to be his most outstanding season as a major league pitcher. The Luxor, Pennsylvania native led the Yankees to their fourth straight pennant by winning 11 games and losing only one for a brilliant .917 percentage (best in the league) and a 2.76 ERA. The only game Steve lost came on September 30, the day before the end of the season. Sundra also pitched in the fourth game of the World Series, relieving for two and two-thirds innings. Along with Oral Hildebrand and Johnny Murphy, he combined to shut out Cincinnati and the Yankees swept the series in four games.

After a disappointing season in 1940, the Yankees sold Sundra to the Washington Senators for a reported $20,000. "They told me they weren't dissatisfied with my work, but that I was let go to make room for some of the young pitchers coming up," said Sundra, pointing to himself and adding, "And me, considering myself a young fellow just finding myself." Ironically, the first time Steve faced the Yankees, he held them to five hits and won, 6-3. In spite of this revenge, Sundra continued his downward slide, posting a 9-13 record in 1941. By June of the following season, his record stood at 1-3 and Washington decided that was enough. The Senators traded him along with Mike Chartak to the St. Louis Browns for outfielder Roy Cullenbine and pitcher Bill Trotter.

With the lowly Browns, Sundra was given new life. He finished the 1942 season with a respectable 8-3 mark and the Browns finished in third place. The next season, he led the St. Louis pitching staff with 15 wins along with a neat 3.25 ERA. In 1944, the pitiful Browns, the laughingstock of baseball, put together a fine wartime team and managed to nose out the Detroit Tigers by one game for the pennant. Unfortunately for Sundra, after he won his first two starts in 1944, he was drafted into the Army, losing the opportunity to play in another World Series. When his Army tour ended in 1946, the big right-hander returned to the Browns. But after a month's trial, Sundra couldn't regain his pre-war form and was released by St. Louis.

Six years later, in 1952, he would die of cancer in Cleveland, Ohio at the young age of forty-two. Steve Sundra's baseball philosophy was a credit to his character. He had been traded from one level of the game to another, from a championship team to a second-division club to even a tail-ender. But what did he think of it? "It's all in a player's work," said Steve. "I mean it is all the same business whether you are on a seventh place club or a pennant winner. We can't all play for champions. There are as many second-division clubs as there are first-division clubs, and somebody must pitch and bat for them. And, if you hustle enough on a sixth-place club, perhaps you can change it into a contender."

It was a most gratifying homestand for Oscar Vitt. The Bears had won 11 games, lost three, and tied one. They now boasted a

.767 winning percentage and their record stood at 46-14, putting them 13½ games in front of the badly beaten Royals. In the meantime, armchair analysts tried to prove with fancy statistics what was known already to every Newark fan — the Bears were a great team. At the time, however, few people felt this Newark club would someday be considered the greatest of all minor league teams.

In trying to assure Vitt that the pennant was locked up, the analysts pointed to facts such as winning 13 games by one run and winning 4 out of 5 extra-inning contests. Vitt's retort was typical of the man in the dugout. "The only times I feel safe is when my club is leading the league by 22 games and winning the ball game of the moment by 23-1."

12.

Atley Donald Sets Record

AFTER THEIR SUCCESSFUL HOMESTAND, THE NEWARK Bears headed north on a short road trip to play four games in Syracuse's Municipal Stadium. The Bears won the first three, but lost the get-away game as they headed back home to Ruppert Stadium for a four-game series against the Baltimore Orioles.

Newark won the opener against Syracuse by a score of 6-5 behind the outstanding pitching of Atley Donald. The young right-hander posted his eleventh consecutive victory, one away from Don Brennan's record of twelve. It was apparent the pressure was starting to affect the youngster. The strain, as he approached the record, was taking its toll. His face was drawn. The tension was clearly visible. Couple this with an already hot temper and you could easily understand why the young man looked totally spent. Given a 6-2 lead, Donald made the mistake of inexperience and let up, allowing the Chiefs to make it a close game. But in the ninth, sensing victory, he bore down and finished strong, fanning two of three Chiefs and rapping up the victory. George McQuinn returned to first base for the first time since he dislocated his ankle. He had been out of the lineup for nine days and 11 games. McQuinn picked up where he left off with a double, two singles, and two RBI's. With the return of McQuinn, Vitt was forced to make some infield adjustments. He moved Babe Dahlgren back to third base and sent Francis Kelleher (hitting a cool .405) to the bench. But it didn't last for long. In the second inning, Jimmy Gleeson couldn't get out of the way of a pitch and was struck on the kneecap and had to be removed from the game. Kelleher immediately went to left field. In the meantime, the Bears began making arrangements to get a spare outfielder from Oakland, but the deal never materialized. And would you believe Pinky Hargrave went three-for-four, raising his average to a blistering .385.

The next day, June 25, Vito Tamulis pitched his first complete game since May 4, beating the Chiefs, 6-2. Tamulis scattered eight hits and walked five, but was particularly tough in the clutch. Over the last five innings, only one Chief reached as far as second base. Charlie Keller extended his latest hitting streak to twelve. It would end four games later at fifteen.

The third game, of what was shaping up to be a dull series, proved to be the most exciting for the fans. The fireworks started the previous afternoon when Lloyd "Whitey" Moore, a 23-year-old right-hander with a cocky attitude and a blazing fastball, predicted to the press he would strike out at least twenty-one Newark players and establish a new record for night games. The record under the lights, at the time, was twenty by Buffalo's Dave Danforth against Rochester in 1930 and Cy Blanton of Albany against Syracuse in 1934. The daylight strikeout record was set by the great Lefty Grove, who struck out seventeen Syracuse Chiefs while playing with Baltimore on April 19, 1923.

Moore first attracted attention as a strikeout artist in 1936. After a brief start with Macon, he moved to Eldorado, Arkansas in the Cotton States League, where he won 20 games and lost 5, fanning 244. He started the 1937 season with Cincinnati, but was sent down to Syracuse a week before the Bears came to town.

The young 180-pound right-hander gave the crowd of 7,500 their money's worth as they "oohed and aahed" every time he threw a strike. And he threw plenty, as sixteen Bears whiffed, leaving Whitey only four short of tying the record. If nothing else, it put some excitement back into a game and a pennant race that most baseball experts agreed was already over.

In spite of the valiant effort by Moore, Newark still beat Syracuse, this time by the score of 5-2. Kemp Wicker pitched a strong, steady game. The victory extended the Bears' winning streak to seven in a row and increased their first place lead to 15 games over Buffalo, now the second place team.

The Chiefs managed to salvage the final match of the series, 5-4, snapping the Bears' winning streak at seven games. Jack Fallon, Marius Russo, and Joe Beggs combined to give up eight hits and eleven irritating walks. Buddy Rosar, returning for the first time after missing almost three weeks, drove in two of the four runs.

Newark returned to Ruppert Stadium for a Sunday double-header against the last place Baltimore Orioles. The Bears and Jack Fallon won both games in extra innings — 8-7 in twelve and 5-4 in nine.

The first game was a nip-and-tuck thriller for twelve innings. The Bears led, 5-2, but Baltimore bounced back with four runs to take the lead, 6-5. Bob Seeds tied the score in the eighth with his second home run of the game. Les Powers put Baltimore back in front, 7-6, with another home run in the top of the ninth. But with two out in the bottom of the ninth, Jimmy Gleeson rocketed a tremendous home run over the right field fence to tie the game as the Newark fans went wild with joy. Fallon clamped the lid on Baltimore over the next three innings, getting credit for the victory, as the Bears scored the winning run in the bottom of the twelfth on a Pete Sivess balk with the bases loaded.

In game number three, Atley Donald tried for his twelfth consecutive win, equalling the established Newark record, but a streak of wildness and timely Oriole hitting put the Bears at the short end of a 4-0 score after only two and a half innings. But a 4-0 deficit to this powerful Newark team was hardly disturbing. In the bottom of the third, as quick as a wink, Gordon and Gleeson singled and Mc-Quinn hit his tenth home run, making the score 4-3. In the seventh, Gordon tied the game at 4-4 with another round tripper. Marvin Breuer relieved Donald in the fifth so the kid was off the hook again and his streak was still intact. After two perfect innings, Breuer was removed for a pinch hitter and Fallon, who won the first game, made his third appearance in two days. Gordon singled in the winning run in the bottom of the ninth, giving Fallon his second victory on this lovely Sunday afternoon in Newark.

It rained the next day, cancelling the third game of the series and setting up a twi-night double-header on Tuesday. Once again, the Bears won both ends, 5-0 in the seven inning first game and 6-2 in the nightcap, which extended their league lead to a solid 16½ games. Vito Tamulis blanked the Orioles on six hits after he escaped a bases-loaded, one out jam in the shaky first inning. Only one Oriole reached second base over the next six.

The Bears struck early, their trademark all season, by scoring four runs on five hits, including Jimmy Gleeson's two-run homer in the first inning. In the fourth, Gleeson paid for his home run when he was beaned by Bill Lohrman. Fortunately, it was only a glancing blow, but Vitt, taking no chances, removed Gleeson from the game. After an examination by the doctor, it was reported as a slight concussion and the left fielder was ordered to take a few days rest. Again, Kelleher replaced Gleeson in left field.

In the second game, Joe Beggs won his seventh straight, bringing his record to 11-1, second best on the staff behind Atley Donald at 11-0. In the second inning, Keller walked, Seeds singled, and Rosar singled Keller home. Gordon followed with a walk, loading the bases. Then Francis Kelleher, the utility man with the .400 batting average, doubled to clear the bases, giving Newark a 4-0 lead and more than enough for the victory.

The Syracuse Chiefs arrived next for a five-game series. Along with Toronto, they had provided the Bears with their toughest competition (if there was any), winning 4 of 13 games in the three previous series. This scanty success filled the Syracuse Manager, Mike Kelly, with a flourish of pride. "We have outplayed them in half the games they beat us. But we haven't outlucked them. One of these days, the breaks should start coming our way, and we are going to show some folks that we have a good ball club, too." The time was still not right for Kelly. Newark took 4 of 5, winning the first three and splitting the July 4 double-header.

Atley Donald won the second game of the series, 5-3, as 10,654 watched him register his twelfth consecutive victory, tying Don Brennan for the Newark record. Under great pressure, the young right-hander from Louisiana was magnificent. He gave up only four hits, possessed excellent control, and set the Chiefs down in order in the ninth, striking out Walter Cazen for the final out.

However, there were some anxious moments for the faithful Newark fans. The Bears were trailing, 3-2, in the bottom of the sixth when McQuinn led off with a walk and advanced to second on Babe Dahlgren's single. With Keller hitting next, Manager Mike Kelly played the percentages and took out right-hander John Pomorski and brought in lefty Fred Fussell to face the left-handed hitting Keller. Oscar Vitt, with a little strategy of his own, had Keller sacrificing, but he fouled the ball back on his first attempt. On the next pitch, Vitt switched strategy and had Keller swinging away. The muscular youth made Ol' Os look brilliant as he parked the ball far over the right field wall for a 5-3 lead and ultimately the ball game. The bewildered 42-year-old Fussell stood on the mound and shouted, "How in blazes do they play ball in this league." The Bears' lead now reached 17½ games and Vitt was heard to comment, "If they catch us now, they're entitled to win."

The next day, the Chiefs were the victims of a 10-0 drubbing. After the game, all Manager Mike Kelly could do was growl, "There ought to be a law against such a team." Steve Sundra picked up the easy win as Seeds, Hershberger, Dahlgren, and Gordon all homered.

After splitting the July 4 double-header and salvaging one game in the series, the Chiefs limped back home, thoroughly dejected. Newark moved into the new Roosevelt Stadium for the second holiday double-header on Monday, July 5 and a single game the day after. The Bears took both ends of the twin bill by identical 3-2 scores, extending the Little Giants' losing streak to eight in a row at the hands of Newark.

In the first game, with the score tied, 2-2, in the bottom of the tenth, George McQuinn led off with a double. He moved to third on Kelleher's sacrifice and then romped home on Charlie Keller's game-winning single. Kemp Wicker picked up his seventh win against only one loss. The nightcap, which began in a heavy downpour, was another squeaker, with the Bears trailing in the sixth, 2-1, due to some unusually sloppy play by Kelleher and Gordon. With the bases loaded and two out in the sixth, Buddy Rosar, batting for Marius Russo, worked the count to 3-1. The next pitch was called a strike by Umpire White. Rosar objected so strenuously that he was thrown out of the game. As he reluctantly left, a pop bottle whizzed by, narrowly "missing his head." Hargrave batted for Rosar and took the fourth ball, forcing in the tying run. The next batter was Gordon, who grounded to deep short, but the throw to third base was late and high as Seeds scored to give the Bears the lead. Russo received credit for the win, but needed help from Fallon, who pitched hitless ball over the last two innings.

Vincent Rosar, better known to the baseball world as "Buddy," was discovered by none other than Mrs. Joseph McCarthy, wife of the Manager of the New York Yankees. It was the year 1934 and Rosar was chosen to play on an All-Star team of Buffalo amateurs. It was a charity game played in the Buffalo Bisons' stadium for the benefit of the Shriners and Knights of St. John. Mrs. McCarthy attended the game and while there, did a bit of scouting on her own. She caught an eyeful of Rosar in a catching role, was impressed, and immediately passed the information to her husband. At the time, Marse Joe had his hands full in New York and couldn't bother about a kid catcher in Buffalo. But he did assign scout Gene McCann to look him over. At the same time, Ray Schalk, Manager of the Buffalo Bisons, was interested in Rosar, too. However, McCann talked bigger figures and the young catcher eagerly signed with the Yankee chain. And it all happened because of the sharp eye of Mrs. McCarthy.

Before arriving at Newark in 1937, Rosar served his apprenticeship in the low minors with Wheeling, Norfolk, and Binghamton. In 1936 at Binghamton, he batted well over .300 and left quite an impression on Manager Bill Skiff. Years later, when Rosar was in the majors, Skiff would comment, "Buddy is the best receiver in baseball. Rosar has no equal at handling wild pitches into the dirt, the difficult ones that break after passing the plate. He is the same on hard bounding throws from the outfield."

After a great season in 1937, the stocky catcher would return to

Newark in 1938, batting a sensational .387 with 15 home runs and 76 RBI's. It was good enough for the Yankees to bring him up to the majors. Rosar was used mainly to give future Hall of Famer Bill Dickey a rest during the late innings and also during the second games of double-headers. In his first year with the big club, Rosar played in 43 games and batted .276 — not a bad performance for a part-time catcher. Although Buddy would log more playing time during the next three seasons with the Yankees, he still played in the shadow of the great Dickey. On top of this, through some hard-to-explain shenanigans, he sealed his fate with Barrow and McCarthy in 1942. In one of the Yankee games, Dickey was injured and the catching duties naturally went to Rosar as his replacement. Normally, this would be welcome and exciting news to a back-up receiver. But in a shocking and unexplained move, Rosar, without permission, left the team on July 18 to travel to Buffalo to take, of all things, a police candidate's exam! After the exam, the unpredictable catcher rejoined the Yankees in Cleveland on July 21. Of course, Barrow and McCarthy were enraged, felt he ran out on them, and slapped a $250 fine on him. Rosar's explanation for his strange absence was that he felt there wouldn't be any baseball shortly, due to the war, and he wanted to make sure he could provide for his wife and family. Ironically enough, Rosar wound up failing the police exam.

It didn't take the Yankees long after the 1942 season and this silly episode to get rid of Rosar. On December 17, 1942, along with Roy Cullenbine, he was traded to the Cleveland Indians for Oscar Grimes and Roy Weatherly. No cash was involved. Observers labeled it "the perfect trade" since it filled weak spots on both teams. Grimes appeared to be the key man in the deal for the Yankees, who needed infield insurance with Phil Rizzuto in the Navy, Red Rolfe at Yale as a coach, Buddy Hassett headed for the armed forces, and Frankie Crosetti due to face a suspension for the first thirty days of the 1943 season. Rosar expressed surprise over the trade and hinted he might quit baseball. The stubborn catcher declined to say whether he would report to Cleveland or continue his present off-season job as a car inspector for the New York Central Railroad. Rosar finally reported to the team and he and Cleveland were the better for it.

With the Indians in 1943, Rosar played in 115 games, batted .283, and led the league in catching assists with 91. The following year, as the Indians dropped to fifth place, Rosar batted .263 and led all catchers in double plays with 13 and in fielding with a .989 average. There was little doubt Buddy Rosar could handle a catcher's mitt.

In early 1945, after the Indians had failed for four years to be a pennant contender, there was a widely-held opinion circulating that the Cleveland management didn't think it altogether patriotic, due to heavy losses in the armed services, to make a serious try for a pennant in a war year. The club's dealings with the players through General Manager Roger Peckinpaugh seemed to reflect this attitude. Veterans Jeff Heath, Mel Harder, and Buddy Rosar were a few of the key players who failed to report to the team's spring training camp at Lafayette, Indiana. And the Cleveland management was content to simply let them sit at home.

At the time, Rosar had a job in a defense factory in Buffalo, but was willing to report to camp on the condition his salary would start as soon as he arrived. Peckinpaugh, on the other hand, held that Rosar, who had skipped training, should first put in a probationary period to demonstrate his condition before receiving pay checks. The impasse was overcome on May 29 when Buddy was traded to the Philadelphia Athletics for another catcher, Frank Hayes.

During the next five years, playing for Connie Mack, Rosar's hitting performance was less than sensational. But during this same period, his skill behind the plate was without equal. Overall, Buddy's best year in the major leagues came in 1946. He caught in 121 games, batted a solid .283, drove in 47 runs, and led all catchers with 73 assists and a perfect 1.000 fielding average — an incredible defensive performance!

The following year, he also led the backstops with 70 assists and a .996 fielding average, and again in 1948 with a .997 mark. Catching in 313 games over a span of three years, 1946-48, this defensive genius committed only three errors!

In October, 1949, Connie Mack found himself faced with a serious problem. The A's attendance was off dramatically while the rival Phillies in the National League topped the one million mark. Mack had to rebuild the team and Rosar was one of the first to be traded. This time, he was sent to the Boston Red Sox for utility infielder Billy Hitchcock. With the Red Sox in 1950, Buddy Rosar unfortunately found himself reunited with his former Yankee manager, Joe McCarthy. He quickly became the third string catcher behind Birdie Tebbetts and Matt Batts. He caught in 27 games, but still managed to bat .298.

The following year, with both Tebbetts and Batts wearing rival uniforms, Rosar split the catching duties with Les Moss. He caught in only 58 games and batted a weak .229. It appeared that time was running out for the aging, 37-year-old catcher. It came as no surprise, then, that the Red Sox announced in October, 1951 that Warren "Buddy" Rosar had been given his unconditional release.

On July 6, Atley Donald won his thirteenth consecutive game, passing Brennan's twelve and establishing a new pitching record for the Newark Bears. But the 5-2 romp over Jersey City was gratifying for another reason, too. It afforded Donald a sweet revenge for the embarrassment he suffered earlier in the season when the Little Giants knocked him out of the box with seven runs in the first inning. Although Donald experienced a shaky start, allowing two runs in the second inning on three hits, he was not to be denied the victory. Over the last seven innings, the right-hander gave up only five hits. And during the game, he struck out five and demonstrated excellent control by walking just one batter. It was the ninth consecutive win for Newark over their Jersey City cousins.

The Bears next moved into Baltimore for a four-game series with the last place Orioles. Surprisingly enough, Newark could manage only two victories as the Orioles battled to establish a modicum of dignity to what was already a disastrous season.

Despite the near 100 degree temperature and intense humidity, over 9,000 fans turned out for the opener, which was billed as Tall Cedar Night, featuring a monstrous fireworks display and two marvelous bands. After the last Roman candle had been extinguished, the announcer at the park shouted, "And now, in a few minutes, you will see the greatest minor league club in fifteen years." The part about the "fifteen years" clearly indicated Baltimore was holding to a local tradition that the Orioles of 1921-1922 were the greatest minor league aggregation of all times. Regardless of the hoopla, however, the outcome of the game did little to support this tradition. The Bears destroyed the Orioles, 17-3, prompting Hy Goldberg, the *Newark Evening News* sportswriter who had covered the Bears all season, to claim, "There is no longer much question about the ultimate pennant winner in the International League." Although Goldberg's comment came about a month late, it aptly expressed the sentiments of the Newark fans and most of the other fans in the league. Newark had it wrapped up. The pennant race was over. Newark fans could now focus their attention on the outstanding individual performances of their beloved Bears. Interest would later shift to the play-offs and the Little World Series.

No other game during the season did more to focus attention on individual achievement than this 17-3 drubbing as the Bears hammered three Oriole pitchers for twenty-one hits and a total of forty-three bases. First, Sundra won his eighth straight ball game, which almost went unnoticed among the offensive display of fireworks. Second, Gordon belted three home runs, raising his team-leading total to sixteen. Third, McQuinn homered twice for a total of fourteen, second to Gordon. Fourth, Gordon and McQuinn each drove in five runs. Fifth, McQuinn raised his total RBI mark to fifty-six, tying him for the team leadership with Bob Seeds. Finally, Gordon led the game off with a home run, the sixth time he accomplished this feat. It wasn't a bad performance.

On the following day, the International League released team and individual averages for the first 77 games of the season. To no one's surprise, the Bears were tops in almost all key categories. They led in team hitting with an outstanding .296 average and in team fielding with a solid .971 percentage. Among the players batting over .300, there were Rosar with .398, Hershberger with .361, Keller with .355, Kelleher with .336, Dahlgren with .329, McQuinn with .326, and Gleeson with .314. In addition to this devastating hitting and flawless defense, the top four pitchers for the Bears — Donald with a 12-0 record, Beggs with 11-1, Sundra with 7-1, and Wicker with 7-1 — compiled a phenomonal 39-3 record! Is it any wonder the Bears totally dominated the International League in 1937?

While the Bears were splitting their next two games with the Orioles, the Binghamton club found themselves faced with a critical shortage of catchers. It seemed both their backstops were injured at the same time and the club was in immediate need of an experienced receiver. With both Rosar and Hershberger healthy again, Pinky Hargrave became expendable and was sent on the next train to Binghamton. The veteran catcher, during his relatively short stay with the Bears, made a major contribution to the team's success — handling the young pitching staff with finesse, hitting over .400, and in the clutch to boot. As a matter of fact, the undaunted Pinky blasted a pinch-hit three-run homer in his last official time at bat for the Bears. One could ask no more of Pinky Hargrave.

The Bears lost the final game at Baltimore, 4-3, in a wild pop bottle throwing contest. The fracas began in the second inning. With the score tied, 1-1, the Orioles had runners on first and second with two out. Bill Cissell lined a single to right, sending Hy Vandenberg lazily jogging toward the plate, while Wimpy Wilburn attempted to go from first to third. Charlie Keller in right field uncorked a throw to Babe Dahlgren at third, nailing Wilburn. The Bears immediately claimed Wilburn was tagged out before Vandenberg crossed the plate. If the call was upheld, it meant the run didn't count. Umpire Bill Kelly at third couldn't rule since he had been occupied calling Wilburn out. The Bears next appealed to the home plate umpire, Chuck Solodare, who ruled in favor of the Bears. The run didn't count! The 10,000 Oriole fans, frustrated all year as their team wallowed in the cellar, turned loose a barrage of pop bottles at the players on the field. While the bottles were flying every which way, the Orioles surrounded Solodare and continued to argue violently. At any rate and for whatever reason, Solodare changed his decision. The run did count. Out jumped Oscar Vitt from the dugout with a few choice words of his own for Solodare. In particular, he accused the umpire of being intimidated by the fans and the flying pop bottles. Apparently Solodare heard enough and gave the loquacious Vitt the old heave ho.

The ejection, however, was not the end to Vitt's trouble. He wasn't in the clubhouse five minutes when the door opened and a husky, wild-eyed man peered in, took aim, and fired a beer bottle at him. It buzzed past Vitt's ear and shattered against the opposite wall. Later, the fan was identified as a gambler and the same individual who went down to the Newark bench the previous Saturday to berate Vitt for leaving Tamulis on the mound too long. No doubt the Bears were happy to return to the friendly confines of Ruppert Stadium to face their rival patsies — Jersey City.

Newark won the first two of the five-game series, making it 11 consecutive victories over struggling Jersey City. On Monday, the Bears won, 4-3, as Joe Beggs recorded his twelfth victory, this time in relief of Atley Donald. It was his ninth in a row. Once more, Donald had his winning streak preserved when the Bears scored three runs in the ninth on three Jersey City errors.

The next day, Newark won again, 9-1, before a fair crowd of 6,319 spectators. Sundra posted his ninth straight win, giving up six hits and fanning eleven, eight over the last three innings. At this point, the big three — Donald, Beggs, and Sundra — had chalked up 35 straight victories without a loss, a truely incredible achievement. Joe Gordon and McQuinn continued their home run derby as Joe hit number seventeen and George followed right behind him with number sixteen. The slick-fielding first baseman also added three RBI's, bringing his total to sixty.

The following day, the Bears moved across the meadows to play Jersey City in a double-header at Roosevelt Stadium and were stunned out of their spikes as the Little Giants took both games, 7-0 and 2-1. It was the first shutout pitched against Newark in 83 games. It was also Newark's first double loss all season. But for the loyal Jersey City fans, it was a spectacular double victory.

It took Ben Cantwell, the Jersey City right-hander, one hour and forty-seven minutes to shutout the Bears. He allowed only six scattered hits (Keller getting two of them) as he out-pitched Vito Tamulis, who lost number five. In the second game, another right-hander, Glen Gabler, took only one hour and thirty-five minutes to edge the Bears, 2-1, in eight innings. Gabler, who even drove in the winning run in the eighth, was stingy with hits, allowing only four singles. Marius Russo took the loss, his fifth, too.

The final game of the series was rained out, giving the Little Giants a welcome split and a bit of revenge for the drubbings they had been taking at the hands of the mighty Bears. With a 17½ game lead, Newark readied for its second northern road trip, with the first stop in Buffalo, followed by Toronto, then Montreal, and finishing up with the Rochester Red Wings. It would turn out to be a most unusual road trip.

13.

The Big Road Slump

T HE BEARS PLAYED 17 GAMES DURING THEIR SECOND northern road trip of the year. And the first three games against the Buffalo Bisons went according to the script — they won them all as Joe Beggs, Atley Donald, and Steve Sundra chalked up respective victories. Oddly enough, after the three-game sweep, it was all downhill. Newark lost 9 of 14 and closed out the road trip under .500 with 8 wins and 9 losses. If nothing else, it proved the Bears were fallible. In spite of this poor showing, Newark lost only one game off their first place lead. They began the road trip 17½ games in front of Montreal, and 17 games later, they slipped to 16½. It was simply a season in which Newark could do nothing wrong and the few times they did, it made little difference to their record.

In the first game against Buffalo, Joe Beggs, the strong right-hander from Rankin, Pennsylvania, won his tenth game in a row and his thirteenth of the season against one lone defeat. Beggs relieved Wicker in the ninth and unfortunately (or fortunately, depending on whether you were Beggs or Wicker) allowed the tying runs to score, spoiling Wickers's victory and sending the game into extra innings. But it didn't last for long. Gordon, Dahlgren, Keller, and Seeds all doubled in the tenth, pushing across four runs for an exciting 10-6 victory. Earlier in the game, the 7,300 spectators watched Joe Gordon whack number eighteen over the left field fence.

In the second game, Atley Donald extended his winning streak to fourteen as he shut out the Bisons, 8-0, in their tiny park that was tailor-made for sluggers. Donald was magnificent, allowing four skimpy singles, walking four, and fanning an equal number. No Bison reached further than second base. The Bears, on the other hand, walloped three more home runs. Keller hit number seven, Gleeson hit number ten, and Dahlgren followed with number thirteen.

The next day, Newark pounded Buffalo, 12-4, making it 11 in a row over the Bisons as the Bears continued to hit and pitch their way to a run-away championship. Sundra won his tenth in a row as the big three — Beggs, Donald, and Sundra — made it 38 straight! It was a magnificent accomplishment. Again the Bears struck early, scoring eight runs in the first two innings. Hershberger belted a three-run homer and a triple, driving in four runs and raising his batting average to a team-leading .366. Gordon hit number nineteen. Of course, Oscar Vitt was delighted with the Bears' performance, but was given a momentary scare in the second inning when Dahlgren was spiked by Jack Ducker during a run-down. At first, it was expected he would be out for about a week, but the Babe healed quickly and only missed two games.

Newark finally lost the last game of the series, 6-5, with Jack Fallon, in relief of Beggs, taking the defeat. Bob Seeds belted a three-run homer in the fourth, driving in runs number sixty, sixty-one, and sixty-two, and tying George McQuinn for the team lead. McQuinn was also deadlocked with Keller for the most hits on the team with 109.

From an early age, George Hartley McQuinn demonstrated he possessed the determination and unswerving confidence it took to become a major league ballplayer. Fresh out of Washington and Lee High School in Ballston, Virginia, McQuinn was offered a scholarship to play baseball for William and Mary College. He refused, explaining that he didn't want to "waste" four years when he could be playing professional ball. That kind of statement showed the self-confidence the young player had in himself.

McQuinn's professional career began somewhat inauspiciously. Lem Owens, a native of McQuinn's hometown and a pitcher for the New Haven club in the Eastern League, recommended him to George Weiss, who was operating New Haven at the time. On Owen's advice, Weiss signed McQuinn in April, but after a miserable showing by the first baseman, released him a month later in May! Although this situation might have been disheartening to McQuinn, it certainly didn't discourage Owens. He knew McQuinn had the potential to be a major league ballplayer. So the persistant Owens tried a new approach. This time he was successful. He convinced Yankee scout Gene McCann to give the young first baseman another opportunity. It worked! Back to Virginia went McQuinn to begin his minor league career.

In his early years in the minors, McQuinn played for teams such as Wheeling, Scranton, Albany, and Binghamton, where he boasted batting averages of .280, .315, .345, and .320, respectively. Then in 1933, George McQuinn was invited to spring training with the Bears, but failed to make the club because of a first baseman named Johnny Neun, who had a tight hold on the position. McQuinn was shipped back to Binghamton, where he turned in an outstanding season, winning the batting title with a lofty .357 average and earning the Most Valuable Player award in the New York-Pennsylvania League.

In spite of McQuinn's great year at Binghamton, when 1934 rolled around, the Bears once again found themselves set at first base. This time it was the tall Dale Alexander, who boasted five years of major league experience with Detroit and Boston in the American League. Since there was no room for George, he was optioned to the rival Toronto team, where he batted a solid .331 for the Leafs, giving the Bears fits when he played against them during the regular season and again in the play-offs. Ironically, McQuinn helped Toronto edge Newark four games to three in the semifinal play-offs and also in the five-game romp over Rochester to win the International League pennant.

It didn't take George Weiss very long to know he'd made a mistake in letting McQuinn go. So back McQuinn came to the Bears, where in 1935, due to a sore shoulder, he batted below .290. It was only the second time in his minor league career that he had hit under .300.

For whatever reason, the Yankee organization let McQuinn get away once more. In November, 1935, the Cincinnati Reds purchased McQuinn on a trial basis along with Bill Raimondi. The Reds' Manager, Charlie Dressen, wanted McQuinn badly and with Lou Gehrig apparently destined to go on forever, the Yankees let George go. Dressen regarded him as the best first base prospect in the minors. "McQuinn is a finished fielder and a good hitter," remarked Dressen.

Surprisingly, McQuinn failed miserably with Cincinnati and after 38 games and a sad .201 batting average, the Reds returned him to the Bears. George explained it this way: "In the Reds' camp that spring, everyone from Larry MacPahil to the bat boy had a suggestion to make to me about my hitting. I changed bats, changed grips, changed stance, but I was so tangled up, I grew worse day by day, and Newark finally had to take me back." But George's problem didn't end at Newark. For the third time, the Bears were set at first base so McQuinn returned to Toronto. He finished the season there with a .328 average.

Apparently it was not in the cards for George McQuinn to become a Yankee, for after his fine performance in 1937 with the Bears, he was drafted by the perennial cellar dwellers, the St. Louis Browns. There were general regrets over his departure from the Yankee organization. "It would be unfair to the player to keep him out of the major leagues any longer," Yankee officials explained. "Lou Gehrig goes right along and there's simply no place for McQuinn, except on the Yankee bench."

In 1938, his first year with the Browns, McQuinn batted .324, driving in 82 runs and scoring an even 100. He also popped 42 doubles, second best in the league behind Joe Cronin's 51. In one stretch during July and August, he even hit in 34 consecutive games.

The following year, McQuinn turned in another fine performance. He batted .316, drove in 101 runs, scored 94, and belted 20 round trippers. Ironically, this would be the last time McQuinn would bat over .300 for the Browns or drive in 100 or more runs.

During the next six years, however, he was a model of consistency, hitting between .260 and .270, driving in an average of 73 runs a year, and scoring another 77.

In 1944, the Browns, the laughingstock of baseball for years, came up with a wartime team of overage and underage ballplayers and, to everyone's surprise, won the pennant, nipping the Tigers on the last day of the season. During the World Series against the Cardinals, the pennant winning team for the third straight year, McQuinn proved what a great money player he was by leading both teams in hitting and RBI's. His average for the series was .438 and he drove in five runs.

While the Browns took only two games in the series, McQuinn was instrumental in both of those wins. Despite a two-hit performance by the Cardinal's Mort Cooper, the Browns won the opener, 2-1, scoring the two runs on a fourth inning homer by George McQuinn. In the 6-2 third game victory, McQuinn again came through with three hits in three official times at bat.

The Browns finished third in 1945 and after the season, the 36-year-old McQuinn was traded to the Philadelphia Athletics for Dick Siebert. However, a back injury plagued him most of the year and in the gloom of the American League cellar, he had his worst year. He batted .225 and drove in only 35 runs. After the A's obtained Ferris Fain, the highly touted first sacker from San Francisco, Connie Mack gave McQuinn his outright release. It looked like McQuinn's career was over. There was little demand for a 36-year-old first baseman with a bad back, at least that's what a lot of people thought. But McQuinn felt differently.

In the spring of 1947, after years of slumming with the Browns and Athletics, he happily found himself hob-nobbing with the World Champion New York Yankees. Invited to St. Petersburg on a trial basis, McQuinn found out he was competing for the first base job with Nick Etten, Tommy Henrich, Jack Phillips, and Steve Souchock. Although the Yankee management was skeptical of McQuinn's physical condition, by the time the season opened, Etten had been traded, Souchock and Phillips had been shipped to Kansas City and Newark, respectively, Henrich had returned to the outfield, and McQuinn was the first baseman.

Even after he won the job, there was serious doubt whether the aging and ailing McQuinn could play through a gruelling 154-game schedule. As it turned out, however, he rarely missed a game during the early part of the campaign and didn't remain out of the lineup until the Yankees clinched the pennant in September. McQuinn turned in his best performance since 1939. He played in 144 games, batted .304 (second only to DiMaggio's team-leading .315), drove in 80 runs, scored another 84, and belted 13 homers.

Although the Yankees took the World Series from the Dodgers in seven games, McQuinn played miserably. As one sportswriter observed, ". . .there was more than a faint suspicion that he simply was weary." McQuinn collected only three hits in twenty-three times at bat for an anemic .130 average. He denied being tired. "I guess I was pressing," he declared. However, few believed the eleven-year veteran was pressing and chalked it up to a long, hard summer.

In 1948, McQuinn was no longer on trial with the Yankees, but the competition was just as keen. Souchock, a holdover from the previous year, along with two newcomers, Joe Collins, up from the Bears, and 24-year-old infielder Bobby Brown, were all taking a shot at first base. During spring training, McQuinn was asked if he was concerned about the youthful Brown.[6]

He chuckled when the question was put to him. "I'll let him have the job after one more year," McQuinn answered.

George McQuinn was true to his word. In 1948, he put in his last year in the major leagues. The 39-year-old first baseman played in only 94 games (his lowest since 1936) as age and an ailing back finally caught up with him. But he managed to finish a twelve-year career with a solid .276 batting average. In October, 1948, the New York Yankees said goodby to a great competitor and gave George Hartley McQuinn his outright release.

---

6. Brown would eventually star for the Yankees at third base, later become a renowned physician, and is currently on the Board of Directors for the Texas Rangers.

After the Buffalo series, Newark moved on to Toronto and had just about arrived when the exchange of two key pitchers was announced. Joe McCarthy, in dire need of hurlers, recalled Kemp Wicker, the North Carolina southpaw, and sent Spurgeon "Spud" Chandler to the Bears. At the time, it appeared to be an unfair exchange. Wicker had posted a 7-2 record for his two months with the Bears and was part of the starting rotation of Donald, Sundra, and Beggs. Chandler, although 5-3 with the league-leading Yankees, was troubled by a sore shoulder most of the year. However, McCarthy needed pitching and the experienced Wicker appeared to be a good choice, since he had been with the Yankees at the end of the 1936 season — long enough to pick up a World Series check for $3,500.

Actually, Chandler never reported to the Bears. He went directly to John Hopkins in Baltimore to have his arm examined. Since the doctor's report was favorable, McCarthy decided that if he could pitch for the Bears, he could pitch for the Yankees. Back went Chandler to New York before he had a chance to put on a Newark uniform. (Wicker, of course, stayed with the Yankees.)

Toronto whipped the Bears in the opening game, 6-3, as Vito Tamulis lost his sixth game against eight victories. It was only the fourth time all season that the Bears lost as many as two in a row! In defeat, however, Charlie Keller went three-for-five, raising his average to .353 and his total hits to a team-leading 112.

The two-game losing streak ended the next day as the Bears knocked off Toronto, 10-4. Russo picked up the victory as Dahlgren, returning to the lineup after missing a few games from the spike wound, tripled and singled, driving in three runs. Seeds, a steady performer all season, extended his team-leading RBI total to 65 on the strength of a home run, a double, and a single.

The final two games with Toronto were played as a twi-night double-header. The Bears lost both ends in close games, 3-2 and 2-1. In the first game, Atley Donald, trying for his fifteenth in a row, found himself hooked up with Babe Davis, the Leafs' sensational young right-hander. Going into the seventh, Donald and the Bears were trailing, 2-0. Keller opened with a single, followed by

Seeds, who walked. Hershberger then flied out and Vitt went to his bench to send Rosar in to bat for Richardson. On the first pitch, Keller stole third, but Seeds missed the double-steal signal and, in his confusion, was caught in a run-down and tagged out. Moments later, Rosar singled, scoring Keller. Now the Bears were trailing, 2-1, with a runner on first and one man out. Vitt again went to his bench. This time, he called on Kelleher to bat for Donald. Kelleher sliced one off the end of his bat into the right field corner for a triple, scoring Rosar and tying the game. Donald was off the hook for the fifth time. Beggs worked the bottom of the seventh and gave up the winning run, ironically ending his winning streak at ten, his first loss since May 23.

The night game was another squeaker. In the bottom of the eighth, Jack Fallon was guarding a slim 1-0 lead with two out when the game suddenly turned around. A walk and a double should have put runners on second and third, but Keller's throw went through Gordon and the tying run scored. The Leafs went on to win in the ninth on a double and single. It was only the third series Newark had lost all season, two of which were at the hands of Toronto.

The Bears next moved on to meet second place Montreal for a five-game series, which would have been billed as crucial, except for the fact the Bears sported a hefty 17½ game lead. On Thursday, they nudged Montreal, 2-1, and on Friday, they clobbered them, 10-0. The lead now climbed to 19½ games. In the 2-1 victory, Steve Sundra won his eleventh in a row. For almost a month, the strapping right-hander pitched extraordinary baseball. He required no relief, had a season total of ten complete games, and during the last five games, allowed a mere ten runs. In the 10-0 slaughter, Tamulis scattered six hits for his ninth victory. The Bears demolished the Royals' pitching with fifteen hits, four of which were homers. In the first inning, Dahlgren and Keller hit successive home runs over the twenty-foot-high left field wall. (Keller's shot was the first time in Montreal history that a left-handed batter cleared the wall, which was 340 feet from home plate.) In the third, McQuinn hit number seventeen and in the sixth, Gleeson ended his batting slump with a blast over the right field wall. As Bob Seeds came to bat, a French-Canadian, displaying either enthusiasm for Seeds or sarcasm for the 10-0 score, shouted, "Come on, Bob, over zee fence. One more doesn't matter."

When the Yankees sent the much traveled Bob Seeds to the Bears in 1937, a curious reporter asked the obvious question, "How do you like hooking up with this Newark outfit?"

"Oh, I like it," replied Bob, "like being bitten by a rattlesnake." It was the natural response for a ballplayer who began his professional career way back in 1926 with Enid in the Southwestern League and who bounced up and down in the majors for eleven years. Seeds' demotion was particularly disappointing since the previous October, he had picked up a quick $3,500 World Series check from the Yankees for doing nothing but sitting on the bench for six days.

The road from Enid to Ruppert Stadium was long and arduous. And in the early years, it involved familiar names like Amarillo, Kansas City, Cleveland, Chicago, Boston, Montreal, New York, and finally, Newark. Was it any wonder that Seeds was tagged with the nickname, "Suitcase Bob?" Surprisingly, his disappointment at being back in the minors after eleven years of professional baseball didn't affect his contribution to the Bears. Nor was Seeds discouraged or discontent when he found himself still in Newark on Opening Day, 1938. On the contrary, one could argue, based on his statistics after only 59 games into the new season, that it strengthened his resolve to return to the big leagues. Seeds was tearing up the International League, batting a solid .335 with 28 home runs and an amazing 95 RBI's. Actually, the home run and RBI totals were respectable figures for a full season's play and the 31-year-old outfielder had accumulated these statistics in little more than one-third of the campaign.

But it was on May 6 and 7 that Bob Seeds, as Robert Obojski recalls in his book, *Bush League*, "put on perhaps the greatest two-day batting exhibition in the history of professional baseball." The *Newark Sunday Call* echoed Obojski's comments: "Mr. Seeds closed one of the greatest, if not the greatest, individual two-day

In 1938, Bob Seeds was sold to the New York Giants for a reported $40,000.

performances in baseball history this afternoon..."

It all began on May 6. The Bears were playing the Buffalo Bisons up in Buffalo. Ironically, Bob's offensive display began quite innocently. In his first at-bat, in the second inning, he singled sharply past third base. So far it was nothing to get excited about. But what followed was history. In the fourth inning, Seeds came to the plate with none out and Charlie Keller on first base. He ran the count to 2-0 and then on the next pitch, belted a long high fly ball that just about cleared the left field fence. In the fifth, with none out and Jimmy Gleeson on second, Keller was given an intentional pass, setting up the double play. Seeds, the next batter, worked the count to 3-2 and then lined a bullet over the same left field fence, just inside the foul line. It was home run number two. In the sixth inning, with two out and runners on second and third, Keller was given his second intentional pass, loading the bases, this time setting up a force at any base. Seeds once again ambled to the plate and once again ran the count to 3-2. On the pay-off pitch, he hit a towering drive that carried far over the fence in left center. It was home run number three.

An inning later, Bob Seeds hit his fourth consecutive home run, a "looping liner" over the now familiar left field fence with Keller on first base. But the day was far from over. There existed the possibility that Seeds could get one more turn at bat if only his teammates could hit around in the next two innings. But who needed two innings? In the eighth, Newark loaded the bases again, bringing the mighty Seeds to the plate for his sixth appearance of the game. By this time, everyone in the park was rooting for still another homer, including Steve O'Neill, the Buffalo Manager. Since the Bears were leading by fifteen runs at the time, the outcome of the game was already determined. With a wild, free-throwing youngster on the mound, Seeds ran the count to 3-2 and then dramatically fouled off several blazing fastballs. On the next pitch, the kid fooled Seeds slightly, just enough to get him off balance. Bob poked a single over second base, driving in two more runs, but disappointing the thousands of screaming spectators. It was an incredible day's work, six-for-six, including four consecutive home runs and twelve RBI's.

Prior to the game, when O'Neill was going down the Newark lineup, he was overheard to comment about the outfielder, "Seeds is one batter we don't have to worry about." After the game, O'Neill was whistling a different tune as he was quick to congratulate the home run hero. "I was rooting for you to get the fifth one," said O'Neill.

"Then why didn't you leave that Kowalik in there instead of bringing in a fresh pitcher when I came up in the eighth?" asked Seeds.

Talking with the press, Bob summed up the event as "the happiest and best day of my life. I once got seven straight hits including about three homers in Newark when I was with Montreal, but never before did I get more than four hits in one game."

The next day, May 7, with memories still fresh from the previous game, Bob Seeds homered in his very first time at bat. Two innings later in the third, he astonished the thousands of spectators by hitting his sixth home run in his last seven times at the plate. Coming up in the fifth, a local photographer brazenly interrupted play to take a picture of the home run hero. Apparently this intrusion upset Bob's concentration, for all the slugger could manage was a mere base-on-balls.

Prior to the walk, Benny Bengough, the great Yankee catcher and member of the famous 1927 "Murderer's Row" team, was kept busy coaching first base. Every time Seeds hit one and started to race toward first base, Bennie would carefully follow the flight of the ball and then signal with his raised arm for Seeds to slow down, shouting, "Take it easy, its over again." In the sixth inning, Bengough was waving and shouting once more as Seeds parked still another homer over the now intimate left field fence. It was his third for the day.

In the ninth inning, Bob Seeds came to bat for the last time in the game. Don Ferris, the third Buffalo pitcher of the afternoon, was on the mound and Seeds had reached a full count. On the next pitch, he drove the ball deep into the left field stands, but it curved foul at the last minute. The crowd breathed a collective sigh of relief. Then Seeds took the last pitch, "which looked slightly inside," and Umpire Borski raised his right arm, indicating the third strike. Seeds protested bitterly, but to no avail. It was the first time Buffalo had managed to retire Seeds during the two-day massacre and it was on a questionable call at that.

In those two incredible games, Bob Seeds had gone nine-for-ten; he had driven in seventeen runs; and he had blasted seven homers. It was truly a magnificent performance! Telegrams poured in from well wishers all over New Jersey, including one from South Orange that read: "You have planted seven seeds in baseball's immortal garden."

Days later, Seeds described his unforgettable experience. "I found it a little tough in that first game in Buffalo. The bats just didn't feel right and I wasn't comfortable at the plate. So the next day I decided to try a new bat. I didn't want to break the bats of any of the fellows who were playing regularly. So I went trying and feeling the pitchers bats. I picked up a bat that felt pretty good. I asked whom it belonged to and found out it was Mickey Witek's, so I said such a little guy has no right with such a big bat. It was a Pepper Martin model, 36 inches long, or two inches longer than my own bat and several ounces heavier. I used it in practice and it felt great.

"It was even better during the game. I simply got to feeling I could put that ball over the fence any time I picked out the right pitch. I hit five of those homers on three-and-two pitches. I just got that feeling that if they put the ball where I like it, I could hit it out of the lot. It is a grand and glorious feeling, too, and the first time I ever got it in thirteen years of baseball.

"The last time up Saturday, I realized that Ferris wasn't going to give me a ball I could hit over the fence. So I decided to swing for a single and keep up that streak of nine straight hits. But the three-and-two pitch was way inside. I decided to take a walk. But that Borski called me out. I hold no grievance against him. He probably was bearing down with all, he had to be honest, for the spotlight was on us up there at the plate, but in his anxiety to make the right decision, he simply missed one."

On June 24, Seeds returned once more to the major leagues. He was sold to the New York Giants for a reported $40,000. At his hotel room prior to his departure for the Giants, the Newark players gathered around the popular outfielder, wishing him well in his new venture. Seeds, aglow with anticipation of joining his new club, proudly predicted a pennant for the national leaguers. His prediction proved overly optimistic, however, as the Giants finished third, five games in back of the pennant winning Chicago Cubs.

Commenting on his sale to the Giants, Seeds remarked, "I'm sure happy I hit that homer into the center field bleachers Tuesday night in Newark. When Bill Terry saw that one, I guess the sale was just about completed." Bob continued in his jovial mood, adding facetiously, "Since these 28 homers I hit this spring aren't going to do me any more good, I'm going to bequeath them to Atley Donald. Atley hasn't hit a homer in his life, so he can have these by proxy."

Three days after the sale, Seeds electrified almost 16,000 fans at the Polo Grounds when he propelled a 460-foot homer that landed at the steps of the Giant clubhouse in dead center field. Had he aimed a few more feet to the right, it would have made the bleachers where, according to folklore, only Babe Ruth had ever poled one up to that time. The Giants beat the Cubs that day, 5-1, for Carl Hubbell's two-hundredth victory.

Giant Manager Bill Terry, overjoyed with the win and his team's new addition, sent off a telegram to George Weiss: "Package of Seeds arrived O.K. Much better than anything Congress sends. Please send new catalogue of farm bargains."

Seeds played in 81 games for the Giants in 1938, batting .291 with 9 homers and 52 RBI's. Surprisingly enough, it proved to be the most productive season of his three with the Giants and, for that matter, his nine-year major league career. He stayed with the Giants two more years as a mediocre, part-time performer and was finally sold to the Baltimore Orioles. "Suitcase Bob" was once again back in the International League at the age of 34. A year later, in May, 1942, Seeds was released outright by the Orioles.

In the third game of the Bears' series with Montreal, the Leafs finally managed to squeeze out a 6-4 victory. Marius Russo allowed twelve hits for his sixth loss against five wins.

The following game of the series was a sad one for the Newark fans, as Atley Donald lost the first half of the Sunday double-header, 9-3, ending his consecutive winning streak at fourteen. During his streak, Donald had beaten every club at least once. He had taken four games from Buffalo, three games from Syracuse, two each from Rochester and Baltimore, and one game from Montreal, Toronto, and Jersey City. Prior to the loss, Donald had won 31 of 33 games, including the last 17 of 19 at Binghamton in 1936. It was a sensational record for any pitcher to achieve. No doubt Donald felt relieved as the tremendous pressure that had been building since April 23 finally burst like a pricked balloon. During the streak, in which he started 20 games (finishing 11), Donald lost thirty pounds. The mental strain was also evident. After a good performance in the first three innings against Montreal, he finally cracked wide open. His fast ball was gone. He couldn't find the plate with his curve. And his change of pace was nothing. Donald was simply mentally and physically exhausted. The end came in the seventh when Vitt reluctantly removed him for a pinch hitter. As reported by the *Newark Evening News*, Donald's departure was greeted by the fans in a very unsportsmanlike manner: "As he trudged sadly across the field toward the showers, there were a few stray hoots from the unfriendly and highly partisan French-Canadian gathering of 9,000. Not a hand was raised to applaud the International League's longest winning streak since Rube Parnham won 20 in a row in Baltimore back in 1923."

The Bears won the second game of the double-header, 11-3, with Joe Beggs posting his fourteenth win. The right-hander gave up seven hits and two of the three runs in the last inning. Seeds led the hitting attack with a three-run homer, bringing his RBI total to 68, one behind McQuinn. It also raised the team's home-run total to 101, just 32 short of setting a new Newark record. Dahlgren went three-for-five, raising his average to a team-leading .359. Hershberger, Rosar, and Keller followed with averages of .357, .355, and .351, respectively.

In spite of a cold, chilly evening in Rochester, more than 7,200 fans came out to watch the mighty Bears, attesting to their tremendous drawing power throughout the league. Steve Sundra lost the opener of the four-game series, 8-4. The defeat ended Sundra's eleven-game streak and marked the first time since May that a Newark player didn't have some type of hitting or pitching streak in progress. Babe Dahlgren continued his hot hitting. The third baseman went three-for-five with two 400-foot triples and a single, giving him thirteen hits over his last twenty-five at-bats and raising his average to a sizzling .363.

In a front office move, it was announced that Phil Page, a veteran left-hander from the Kansas City Blues, would be joining the Bears in exchange for Marvin Breuer. In the months ahead, Page would be used mainly in relief, providing Newark with additional left-handed pitching and mound experience that would later prove valuable in the play-offs. Page, who had kicked around the league for a number of years, had previously pitched for Montreal and Toronto. In 1936, with Kansas City, he posted a record of 15-12 with a 3.50 ERA, fifth best in the league. But he came to the Bears after 18 games with an unimpressive 3-5 mark.

Phil Page came out of Penn. State in 1927 at the age of 22 and by 1937, it was estimated that he had travelled through forty-seven of the then forty-eight states of the Union. Somehow, the lefty had missed South Dakota. During his early years in professional baseball, Page became familiar with just about every bullpen in the Eastern and Pacific Coast Leagues. He later pitched in both the International League and the American Association, and had brief appearances in both major leagues.

In his three years with the Detroit Tigers, 1928-30, Page appeared in only 25 games, mainly in relief. After a return to the minor leagues, 1931-33, the determined left-hander surfaced again in 1934, this time in the National League with the Brooklyn Dodgers. But with Brooklyn, he only pitched a measly ten innings, posting a 1-0 record. It turned out to be his last hurrah in the major leagues. Phil Page was the only member of the 1937 "wonder team" that had his major league career behind him.

The next day, the temperature in Rochester dropped below 60 degrees as the cold wave continued. But the Bears still won the game, 10-5. Vito Tamulis picked up his tenth win against six loses, striking out eight Red Wings as he went the full distance. Bob Seeds went three-for-five, driving in four more runs and bringing his team-leading RBI total to 73.

Newark ended its four-game set with Rochester before a twinight crowd of 10,481 and took it on the chin in both ends, 5-3 and 3-1. Beggs lost the seven-inning first game by allowing three runs in the fifth, bringing his record to 14-3. Gleeson and McQuinn accounted for all three Newark runs, the former with a two-run blast and the latter with a solo shot. Fallon took the loss in the night game, but it wasn't entirely his fault. The usual sure-fielding Richardson and McQuinn helped the Red Wings with key errors, giving Rochester three unearned runs. In addition, the mighty Newark bats, in one of their rare moments, fell asleep. It was only the second time in 102 games that the Bears failed to get an extra-base hit.

Even the between-game festivities turned out poorly for Newark. The highlight of the evening was the 75-yard dash, featuring Keller and Gordon for the Bears against Johnny Hopp and Red Juelich for the Red Wings. The Rochester fans were delighted by the outcome as Hopp nosed out Keller in a "photo finish." Juelich finished third and Gordon wound up fourth. Hopp, the outstanding Rochester rookie who would later enjoy a fourteen-year major league career (including five World Series and a lifetime batting average of .296), took some good natured kidding from the Newark players. They claimed he was "hopped up" as they called for a saliva test.

On the way home, the Bears stopped off to play Binghamton, their sister club, and showed no mercy, promptly trouncing them, 12-8. To baseball buffs and trivia addicts, there were two noteworthy points to the game. The first was the man behind the plate calling the balls and strikes. He was the perky John "Jocko" Conlan, the future Hall of Fame American League Umpire. The second note of interest was the 21-year-old kid in right field named John Harlan Lindell, who stood 6'-4'' and carried 200 pounds of raw-boned muscle. Big John, of course, would later star with the Yankees and enjoy twelve years in the majors as an outfielder, pitcher, and, occassionally, a first baseman.

With the double defeat, the Bears ended a very disappointing road trip and looked forward to returning to Ruppert Stadium. In the next two weeks, they would play the same four northern teams in a total of 17 games. It would turn out to be a homestand to end all homestands.

14.

Home Sweet Home

THE NEWARK BEARS OPENED THEIR SEVENTEEN-GAME homestand by sweeping the Toronto Leafs four straight, extending their first place lead to 19 games. Over 9,500 enthusiastic fans greeted the mighty Bears in the opener as Steve Sundra posted his twelfth win, scattering eight hits, including three over the last seven innings. After Charlie Keller doubled in the third, Bob Seeds hit his fourteenth home run over the left field fence. Jimmy Gleeson also homered in the eighth, far up into the right field stands. The final score went to the Bears, 6-4.

On Saturday, Vito Tamulis pitched a brilliant game, skipping by Toronto, 2-1. He gave up only five hits and one walk while fanning seven. The hard luck Toronto pitcher was Jack Berly, who allowed only seven hits, but wound up throwing one bad pitch. It came in the bottom of the eighth inning. With George McQuinn on second with a double, Babe Dahlgren whacked home run number sixteen far over the left field fence, and the ball narrowly stayed fair. Toronto Manager Dan Howley charged out of the dugout screaming foul ball, while a voice from the visitor's bench yelled to the umpire, "You must have bet on the game." Ed Rommel, the homeplate Umpire, spotted the player, Earl Caldwell, and quickly ejected him from the game. Howley continued to argue, but to no avail. The upshot of it all was that one player was banished, Howley was muzzled, and, most importantly, the home run was allowed to stand.

On Sunday, the Bears took both ends of the double-header and sent Toronto away with their tail between their legs. In the first game, Atley Donald won his fifteenth, edging Toronto, 6-5, in twelve innings. He had one bad frame, the sixth, in which Toronto scored four runs on five hits, but down the stretch, Atley was extremely tough. Seeds won the game in the twelfth with a bases-loaded single. Jack Fallon won the second game, 10-2, but needed help from Joe Beggs as he hit a streak of wildness in the fifth. And Seeds picked up three more RBI's with a bases-loaded double, bringing his total to 81.

After a well-deserved day off, the Bears resumed play against Buffalo. Guess what? They swept the Bisons in three straight. The opening game on August 3 was billed as "Radio Appreciation Night" and attracted 17,816 fans, setting a new attendance record for a Newark night game. The old record of 16,705 was set earlier in the year on June 11. Prior to the game, several WNEW radio artists entertained the spectators and a committee of fans presented Bears' announcer Earl Harper with a chest full of silver. The popular Harper was the voice of the Bears, presenting dramatic play-by-play reporting of both home and away games. As Joe Beggs recalled, "He was loved by all the players and did a great job as an announcer."

However, the feature act was the quartet of Gordon, Richardson, Tamulis, and Dahlgren — three on harmonicas and the Babe playing something described as "a whistle with a trombone slide fixture." Steve Sundra won his thirteenth and Dahlgren hit a homer in the third. On a more painful note, George McQuinn aggravated an old thumb injury. Later, X-rays revealed a chipped bone. He would be out of the lineup for at least a few weeks. The next day, Vito Tamulis, of harmonica playing fame, beat the Bisons, 6-4, for his fourth consecutive victory and twelfth of the season. It also cemented his position as the fourth member of a pitching rotation consisting of Donald, Beggs, and Sundra.

Tamulis began his professional baseball career, like so many other ballplayers, through an odd set of circumstances. The year was 1930 and Tamulis was pitching for Boston English High

School. The young lefty was having a fabulous season. He hadn't lost a game and was attracting scouts from all over. But in spite of his great pitching, the competition was so tough that the league championship would have to be decided in the final game of the season. And the hopes of a championship for Boston English rested on the shoulders of their teenage star.

On the day of the crucial game, while Tamulis was warming up on the sidelines, a gentleman approached him and inquired about his future. Did he want to continue his education or go directly into professional baseball? Tamulis described the man as a "tricky looking guy I sized up for a school principal."

Vito, who had been turning down college baseball scholarships right and left, figured this was another offer and told the man he wanted to go directly into professional baseball. The stranger said he would like to talk to him and they agreed to meet after the game.

Tamulis went out that day and beat another left-hander named Justin McLaughlin, who eventually pitched three years for the Boston Red Sox. Vito gave up five hits and fanned eleven in the 10-0 whitewash. After the game, flushed with victory, Tamulis deliberately avoided his meeting with the "school principal" because he simply wasn't interested in scholarships. On the way home, however, he accidently ran into his baseball coach, who asked, "What did McCann have to say?"

"McCann?" Who is McCann?," Tamulis asked with a puzzled expression.

The coach then proceeded to tell Tamulis he had been talking to Gene McCann, one of the top Yankee scouts. Young Vito almost collapsed! All afternoon he had been avoiding the man he would give his right arm to meet.

Fearing he had thrown away his one and only opportunity, young Vito raced back to the clubhouse. Luckily, McCann was waiting and the eager Tamulis signed on the spot.

During the next five years, Tamulis played for Chambersburg, Cumberland, Albany, Binghamton, Springfield, and Newark, always turning in outstanding records. With the Bears in 1934, he won 13 and lost 7 with a 2.74 ERA, good enough for the Yankees to call up the diminutive lefty at the end of the season. And Tamulis made the most of what remained of the season, starting, completing, and winning the only ball game he appeared in. In 1935, however, Tamulis saw a great deal more action with the Yankees, starting 19 games, completing 9, and posting an admirable 10-5 record. But in the winter of 1935, Vito Tamulis nearly saw his career come to a surprising end. He was hospitalized with a serious case of pleurisy and the illness left the chunky southpaw in a highly-weakened condition.

During spring training in 1936, Yankee Manager Joe McCarthy had this to say about Tamulis. "What I like about Vito is his coolness born of absolute confidence in his control. He has been under fire a half dozen times and always has been as cool as any big league veteran I ever saw. He has fine stuff on the ball. The only thing that worries me is his build. He is apt to become very heavy all at once and find difficulty in getting into condition. Why, nothing fazes this boy. He doesn't care whether the batter is Jimmy Foxx or Al Simmons. Some pitchers take years to acquire that poise."

Those complimentary words, however, didn't stop McCarthy from sending Tamulis back to the Bears to regain his strength from the bout with pleurisy. Since Tamulis was somewhat dejected, Manager Vitt tried to console the youth. "The only thing to do," Oscar told him, "is to get in there and show Joe McCarthy you're ready to go back."

But a slow recovery forced Tamulis to sit out most of the 1936 season. By the end of the summer, though, it looked like he had gained all his strength back and was fully recovered. Vito finished the season with Newark, posting three consecutive shutouts.

In spite of his complete recovery and a great year in 1937, Tamulis was sold by the Bears to the St. Louis Browns for cash and first baseman Harry Davis. But Tamulis didn't stay with the Browns very long. After three games and an 0-3 record, he was shipped off to the Brooklyn Dodgers for the $7,500 waiver price. With Brooklyn, Vito's luck began to change. For one, he stayed put. For another, he turned in a fine season, pitching in 38 games, winning 12, and losing only 6. During the next two seasons with Brooklyn, the little lefty won 17 and lost 13, pitching in over 150 innings each year and recording ERA's of 4.37 and 3.09, respectively.

Then in a strange turn of events, the Dodgers traded Tamulis over the winter to the Philadelphia Phillies for right-hander Kirby Higbe. The trade turned out to be a stroke of genius for Brooklyn, as Higbe led the Dodgers to a pennant, posting a splendid 22-9 record. And to make the trade even more ludicrous, during the season, the Phillies traded Tamulis back to Brooklyn for 34-year-old left-hander Lee Grissom. (Grissom went on to win 2 and lose 13 for the last place Phillies.)

Tamulis was sent down to Nashville, where he finished the 1941 season. He also played for Nashville in 1942 and then went into the service. Once again, the war effort prematurely ended a baseball career. It was the last season that the 32-year-old Tamulis played in.

The following day, it took the fast-working Joe Beggs only one hour and twenty minutes to polish off Buffalo, 4-2, for his fifteenth victory and the Bears' seventh win in a row (the fifth time they ran off seven straight). There is an old cliche that goes something like a great team will take advantage of a mistake. The Bears were a great team. In the bottom of the fifth, with Kelleher on first and Newark trailing, 2-0, Dahlgren popped up to first baseman Mike McCormick, who unexplainably dropped the ball! You guessed it. On the next pitch, Dahlgren hit number seventeen far into the right center field bleachers to tie the score. The Bears picked up two more in the sixth and won the game.

With the injury to McQuinn, Weiss decided to send the Bears a young Binghamton catcher by the name of Clyde McCullough. This move permitted Manager Vitt to use Rosar or Hershberger in the infield or outfield, positions both were capable of playing. Mc-Cullough would later star in the major leagues for fifteen years with the Chicago Cubs and the Pittsburgh Pirates.

The Bears next hosted the Rochester Red Wings in a twi-night double-header before 14,250 fans. One of the dignitaries on hand was the immortal Connie Mack, who had come over from Philadelphia to get a look at the "wonder team." Newark won the first game, 9-6, as Atley Donald posted his sixteenth victory against only one loss. It also marked the Bears' longest winning streak of the season at eight games. It didn't last, however, as Rochester won the nightcap, 4-3. Russo took the loss, his seventh against five wins, and needed help from Phil Page, who made his debut by pitching two and a half innings. Connie Mack, after watching Joe Gordon leap high and snare a line drive in the second and Charlie Keller race to the fence to make a one-handed catch in the third, paid the Bears the ultimate tribute: "Newark has a great team. I know Philadelphia fans would like to see them come to Shibe Park intact and do their playing in the American League."

During the between-game 75-yard dash rematch, Keller beat Hopp for the $25 prize, with Juelich and Hershberger finishing as also-rans. Hershberger substituted for Gordon when the young second baseman refused to race, claiming he was nearly injured during the previous one. The split of the double-header now brought the Bears' home record to 47-10 for an .824 percentage, while their first place lead bulged to an unprecedented 22½ games!

On Saturday, Jack Fallon won the three-hour, thirteen-inning, rain swept marathon. The right-hander had to work hard for the victory, particularly in the top of the thirteenth when, with the bases loaded, he struck out George Blackerby. Then in the bottom half of the same inning, Charlie Keller blasted a clutch home run into the left field bleachers to end the game.

Charles Ernest Keller, better known to baseball fans as "King Kong," would return to Newark in 1938 to lead the Bears to yet another league championship. In the process, Keller would win the batting title for the second consecutive year with a sensational .365 average, while collecting 211 hits, driving in 129 runs, and scoring another 149 — quite a performance for a kid in his second year of professional ball. The following year, the muscular Maryland farm boy would join the New York Yankees and teammates Joe DiMaggio and Tommy Henrich to form one of the greatest outfields in baseball. Oddly, Keller's first year with the Yankees was his best. In helping New York win the pennant in 1939, Keller played in 111 games and hit .334 (second best for the Yankees behind DiMaggio's league-leading .381). He collected 21 doubles, 6 triples, 11 homers, and 83 RBI's. Operating brilliantly in the outfield, he posted a .969 fielding percentage. In the World Series, Keller helped to crush the Cincinnati Reds in four games. His .438 mark led all the regulars, along with home runs, RBI's, and total bases. It wasn't bad for a kid seeing his first World Series.

Charlie was born on a 140-acre dairy farm near Middletown, Maryland on September 12, 1916. From a very early age, young Keller worked at the daily farm chores, milking cows, chopping wood, and plowing fields. This kind of activity ultimately helped develop his powerful shoulders and steel-like wrists. Years later at Newark, a reporter once asked Keller why his strong arms resembled oak tree trunks. "How'd I get 'em?" asked Keller, "Why, milkin' cows when I was a kid I guess. From the time I was seven, my father used to have me milk cows down on the farm..."

It was in the North Carolina hills that the Yankees "trapped" Keller, as Lefty Gomez once put it. Two of the Yankees' top scouts, Paul Krichell and Gene McCann, rooted him out of bed at daybreak in their haste to get the jump on a half-dozen rivals. The contract was signed while the two leaned happily against the side of a house.

There were no fabulous bonuses or salaries in those days and Keller ruefully remarked at a baseball writers dinner in his honor; "Those stories about paying off the mortgage on my father's farm were untrue. In fact, he eventually lost the property." A bystander mentioned $3,200. "The bonus was less than that," Charlie added.

At the dinner, a whistler provided the entertainment and when the microphone-shy George Weiss rose to talk, he began by saying, "I wish I could whistle."

Later, when it was teammate Tommy Henrich's turn to speak, he said, "Mr. Weiss was sorry he couldn't whistle. Well, he'll whistle a long time before he finds another ballplayer like Charlie Keller."

Scout McCann also recalled the time young Keller reported to

Sebring for spring training with Newark in 1937. The Bears had only been in Florida for about two weeks and were carrying five experienced outfielders, all capable of making the grade in the International League. Then one day a 20-year-old kid blew into the Bear's camp — not even on the club's roster. Bashfully, he registered at the Sebring Hotel. He had never been away from home before except at college, which was nearby. It was his first venture into professional ball.

"Who's the newcomer?" a reporter asked.

Vitt didn't know. Neither did the other Bears in the lobby. Up spoke McCann. "His name is Keller," said the scout, "Charlie Keller. I picked him up in the University of Maryland. And get this. He'll be the best ballplayer on the Newark team."

In spite of Keller's outstanding rookie year with the Yankees in 1939, he reached the charmed .300 circle only twice more, in 1944 and 1950, and both were abbreviated seasons. Many of the experts who saw Keller play were of the opinion the youth never fully lived up to the potential he showed in the minor leagues. Keller himself agreed when he once remarked, "I never became the ballplayer I thought I would be."

However, his failure to hit for high averages could possibly be traced to the attempts by the Yankees to change Keller's batting style. Keller, a left-handed swinger, was a tremendous left field hitter when he arrived at Yankee Stadium. Herb Pennock, Yankee ace chucker and Hall of Famer, once said that of all the southpaw swingers he had seen, only Babe Ruth could hit a ball as hard to left field as Keller. Years after Keller left the Bears, Montreal fans still recalled the home run he walloped over the left field barrier 340 feet from home plate and approximately 50 feet high. (Earlier newspaper accounts claimed the wall to be 20 feet high, but like the proverbial fish story, the wall grows with the passage of time). Montreal historians claim Keller was the only left-handed hitter who ever cleared that wall.

Another interesting story was just how young Keller developed his ability to hit to left field. It started the summer before Charlie signed a professional contract, when he was playing in the Coastal

Plain League, an independent circuit which attracted many collegians during school vacation. Keller's home team was in tobacco country, Kinston, North Carolina, and the ball park was definitely patterned against left-handed hitters. The distance to the right field fence was an out-of-sight 500 feet and the left field fence, in comparison, only a scant 300.

"I would hit long drives to right field," recalled King Kong, "and they'd always catch them. So I fell into the habit of poking the ball toward left field where it was more apt to hit the fence. I guess I never quite broke myself of the habit."

The Yankees, however, were not interested in left-handed hitters who could hit the ball to left field. The short right field wall in the stadium was too tempting to Yankee management. So they tried to make a "pull" hitter out of Keller. They succeeded to the extent that Keller collected as many as 33 homers in 1941, but his average suffered. It was interesting to note that in his first year, when he hit .334, Keller whacked only 11 home runs.

Charlie Keller was an intent ballplayer who never let up and if not a perfectionist, the closest thing to it. He batted .500 in college and couldn't understand why he was only hitting .350 in the International League. At Newark, he led the league in batting two years in a row, but still wandered around with a puzzled frown on his face. He carried this frustration into the majors, too. Keller and Joe Gordon occupied adjourning lockers in the Yankee dressing room. After a typical Yankee victory, Charlie was sitting on a bench in front of his cubicle, wearing his customary frown while Gordon was smiling and chatting with reporters referred to Keller. "If this guy doesn't get three-for-four in every game, he comes in here looking as if the building fell on him."

"Well, I should be doing better than I am," growled Keller.

Years later, Jack Fallon recalled "Keller getting three hits, then smashing a bat because he didn't get one the fourth time up."

The stories are endless. In the first World Series game, Keller tripled to win the ball game. In the clubhouse, reporters were hovering around and congratulating him on his three-base hit. "Aw, I didn't get the wood on it," deprecated Charlie. "It should have been over the fence." Always the perfectionist, he once remarked, "If you do anything well, there's a reason for it."

In spite of Keller's fame with the Yankees, he would always remain a farm boy. He found it easy to forsake the broadway lights for the peace and quiet of his home. "I couldn't wait to get home when the season ended," he recalled. "It was like getting out of the Army every year."

However, the incident which provided the best insight into the character of Charlie Keller occured after the incredible 1937 season. The Bears were returning from Columbus, after winning the Little World Series, when Colonel Jacob Ruppert sent word to Secretary Ray Kennedy, aboard the Eastbound train, that he was giving a party in New York to celebrate the Newark triumph. As the players, reporters, and photographers strolled out of the Pennsylvania Station, Charlie quietly commented, "You know, this is the first time I've ever been in New York." It was a remarkable and candid admission. Charlie had played in Newark for about six months and hadn't troubled himself to take a twenty-minute train ride for a look at the greatest city in the world.

"I'm a farm boy," he went on to explain, "and I'm really not interested in cities. I can't wait to get back home."

Although Keller remained a farm boy, he was not without a touch of class. In 1950, Keller, after turning down a job offer by the Yankees to manage in the minor leagues, signed with the Detroit Tigers. Manager Red Rolfe, recognizing that Keller, hobbled for years by a back injury, would not contribute heavily to the Detroit cause, remarked, "I don't know whether or not he can play ball. But I got him because he'll lend a touch of class to my team." Keller batted .314 in 50 games, pinch hitting for the most part, as the Tigers battled the Yankees for the pennant, but lost.

The most revealing incident which best exemplified the class character of the Maryland farm boy took place in Yankee Stadium. It was Charlie Keller Day, arranged by the loyal Maryland alumni. On such occasions, it was customary to shower the honored player with elaborate gifts, usually topped by a brand-new expensive automobile. But Keller insisted that, except for a plaque he could hang in his trophy room, all contributions be turned into a fund that would educate as many boys as possible at the University of Maryland.

Although Keller officially retired in 1952, the muscular, long ball hitting outfielder was only a shadow of himself until then. In June of 1947, while with the Yankees, Keller was leading the league in home runs and RBI's and appeared on his way to another outstanding season. But that was before his fateful game in Detroit. Keller explained it this way: "I was caught in a rundown at Detroit and something snapped. After that, I just couldn't run." The problem was diagnosed as a ruptured disc in the spine. It was a tough break that forced Keller to undergo surgery in July, putting him out of action for the rest of the season. Although the surgery was a "success," Keller's mobility was significantly reduced. No longer could he swing with the kind of authority that demanded respect, if not actual fear, from opposing pitchers. Taking the extra base was now a bad memory, while the amount of ground he could cover in the outfield was quickly shrinking.

Used mainly in pinch-hitting roles in 1950 and 1951 with Detroit, Keller finally returned to the Yankees in 1952, but only played in two games before he hung up his spikes at the age of thirty-five. Keller played a total of twelve years in the American League, ten with the Yankees (not counting the two games in 1952) and two years with the Tigers. He finished with a lifetime batting average of .286. But Charlie "King Kong" Keller would always be remembered by the millions of baseball fans as an important link in one of the all-time great major league outfields.

The double-header on Sunday ended the Red Wings stay and, like Buffalo and Toronto before them, they left with their tails between their legs. Rochester lost both games by scores of 8-4 and 4-1. Sundra posted his fourteenth win in the first game, while Gordon belted number twenty and Seeds number fifteen.

Tamulis won the second game, scattering five hits, only one of which did any damage — Hopp's long home run to the right field bleachers in the third inning. It was Tamulis' fifth straight victory and his thirteenth of the season. "These fellows will make fifteen runs in a double-header," said Tammy. "How can you lose with them?" Newark ended the long day with a total of 113 home runs in exactly 113 games — respectable power in any league. They also increased their first place lead to 24 games with an incredible 83-30 (.735) record.

Montreal next moved in for a long five-game series that would end the Bears current homestand. The Royals had a new manager and a different roster, but it didn't change the way they played. The Bears walloped the Royals in the first game, 11-1. Beggs picked up his sixteenth victory against only three losses and narrowly missed a shutout. For the record, the game ended in the third inning when Joe Gordon hit a vicious line drive into the left field bleachers with the bases loaded, capping an eight-run rally. It raised his RBI total to 73, second only to Bob Seeds, who led the league with 87. Out in front by 25 games, Oscar Vitt blandly announced he thought the Bears would win the pennant. "You can quote me," he said.

It rained the following day, forcing the scheduling of back-to-back double-headers. But on Wednesday, it was still raining in Newark, postponing the first double-header, which now meant two games would have to be played in Montreal since this was the last trip the Royals would make into Newark. Rabbit Maranville, the Montreal Manager, future Hall of Famer, and all-around clown, was not that unhappy with the games being scheduled for Montreal. But the way Newark was playing, it really didn't matter where the game was played. "You know," he said, "it may not rain in Montreal when the Newark club comes to town, but we still have lots of sprinkling cans in the city." Maranville's comment was a throwback to the days of John McGraw and the New York Giants. Rabbit couldn't resist telling the story about McGraw's watering system whenever the Giants found it inconvenient to play a ball game. "Boy, we'd walk along Broadway about noon in a bright sun. Not a cloud in the sky. Pretty soon, we'd have lunch, ride a subway to the Polo Grounds, and find the diamond was practically underwater. Funny how it used to rain up there when the sun was shinning everywhere else in New York, especially when the Giants had run out of well-rested pitchers.'' Rabbit smiled. ''You never know, it might rain in the Montreal Stadium next week.''

Apparently the two days of inactivity had a detrimental effect on the mighty Newark bats. When the rain finally ended and play resumed, Montreal took both ends of the double-header, 8-2 and 2-1. A pair of nifty left-handers turned the trick, allowing Newark a total of only eight hits *all day*. In the first game, Harry Smythe allowed five hits, with both runs coming in the first inning, but then blanked the Bears the rest of the way. It was Atley Donald's second loss. In the next game, ex-Newark pitcher Marvin Duke allowed only three hits, one of which was a home run by Bob Seeds. Duke retired the last nine in a row to end the game. Fallon took the loss.

Although the Bears ended their homestand on a sour note, they had still managed to post an outstanding 12-3 record. Their front-running lead slipped to 23 games, but with only 38 left to play, it appeared the Bears would clinch the pennant on the road, as they headed north for 17 games.

15.

Clinched!

ON AUGUST 13, THE NEWARK BEARS BEGAN THEIR LAST northern road trip of the season. Ten days and 15 games later, on August 23, they mathematically clinched the International League pennant, in anything but championship fashion. They backed into the pennant (if one can label a 25-game lead as "backing in") by losing to the Buffalo Bisons, 9-2, while second place Montreal was splitting a double-header with Baltimore. It was the first time in the history of the International League that a team clinched the pennant as early as August 23. The true greatness of this feat is measured by the fact that it has stood the test of time. Over forty-three years later, it is still an International League record.

Actually, the Bears' quest to clinch the pennant started on a bad note. After losing the double-header to Montreal at Ruppert Stadium, they travelled to Toronto and lost the opener, 3-2, in twelve innings. This three-game losing streak, the longest all season, prompted Vitt to jokingly say, "I knew I shouldn't have claimed the pennant when we had that 25-game lead. First thing you know, they'll cut us down to 20 games and then that league leadership will really be in danger."

Although Vitt was obviously kidding, Spud Chandler had a different opinion of his soon-to-be manager. "I remember we were leading the league by some 20 games late in the season and the opposing club scored a couple of runs and he had every available pitcher warming up. He became real excited and afraid we would lose the game. I don't believe he trusted his players as he should have, and every player had great potential.''

In the second game of the series, Toronto's Earl Caldwell handcuffed the Bears over twelve innings, allowing seven hits and two unearned runs. Sundra started for Newark, but was relieved by Russo in the ninth, with the lefty taking the loss. In spite of this rare hitting drought, Newark still boasted the top four hitters in the league — Hershberger with .359, Keller with .350, Dahlgren with .343, and Rosar with .335. In addition, Seeds was leading the league with 87 RBI's.

The next day, the Bears avenged their loss by whipping Toronto in a double-header, 6-3 and 4-2. In the first game, Tamulis got his fourteenth victory and his sixth in a row. It was not an elegant performance, however, as the namesake of a Lithuanian king was racked for ten hits while walking eight. But he was particularly effective with men on base, which helped his cause immensely as Toronto stranded fourteen. Phil Page started the second game (his first starting appearance as a Bear) and turned in an excellent job, allowing only two hits and two runs. Keller broke the 2-2 tie with a single, scoring Kelleher and Dahlgren.

Before Newark moved on to Montreal, they obtained three additional players to strengthen their club for the upcoming play-offs. Spud Chandler rejoined the team from the Yankees, John Niggeling, a right-handed knuckleballer, came from Kansas City, and an outfielder by the name of Joe Gallagher was sent up from Binghamton.

During the next three days, in an unusual scheduling quirk, the Bears played Montreal in three consecutive double-headers, winning the first and splitting the next two. Beggs won number seventeen, beating Montreal, 6-0, for his first shutout of the season. Russo won the second, 10-6, with a rare relief appearance by Atley Donald. (With six games in three days, it was surprising Vitt didn't pitch.) Rosar led the assault with a home run, a double, and a single for four RBI's, helping to extend the Bears lead to 24½ games.

The next day, Montreal won the twilight game, 3-1, as Spud Chandler, still feeling an occasional twinge of pain in his arm, took the loss. Jack Fallon, the tall right-hander from Quincy,

Massachusetts, posted his eighth victory against five defeats in the night cap. This prompted Vitt to heap some high praise on Fallon and in the process, Oscar claimed he was the second best pitcher in the league behind Whitey Moore of Syracuse. One wonders what the reaction was of Beggs, Donald, and Sundra to all this. Rosar continued his torrid hitting pace with a triple and three singles, leading the fourteen-hit attack.

The Bears won the first game of the final double-header, 10-6, as Page posted his second win in four days, relieving the veteran Niggeling who was hit hard. Gleeson belted his fourteenth home run of the season. Montreal won the second game, 7-1, as Sundra gave up twelve hits for his third loss against fourteen wins. The Bears took the seventh and last game from Montreal, 7-6, as Donald chalked up his seventeenth victory against only two losses. Their lead now swelled to 25½ games and the end was drawing near.

The Bears moved into Rochester and in rapid succession, beat the Red Wings three straight — 7-2, 5-1, and 6-5. Tamulis won his fifteenth and seventh in a row as Dahlgren hit number eighteen and Seeds drove in his ninety-first run. Next, Beggs won number eighteen, narrowly missing a shutout. And John Niggeling won the third game of the series, his first as a Bear. The big blow of the game came in the eleventh when the newly-acquired Joe Gallagher blasted one over the left center field fence to win the game. With Niggeling and Gallagher making key contributions, it was simply a case of the rich getting richer.

On Sunday, August 22, the Rochester Red Wings knocked off the Bears, 8-4, while second place Montreal took a double-header from Jersey City, 5-4 and 2-1, delaying the inevitable one more day. Jack Fallon, plagued by wildness all season, gave up four walks and was hammered for ten hits and eight runs. Although Vitt was not happy with the loss, what really upset him was the discouraging news concerning Atley Donald and George McQuinn. Donald, troubled with a sore arm, was scheduled to be examined by trainer Doc Painter in New York. As it turned out, he went to John Hopkins instead, where it was disclosed he had a sore spot under his pitching shoulder. The report on McQuinn was just as disturbing. The chipped bone in his elbow was not healing properly and there was a good chance he would have to be operated on in the fall.

But the bad news was temporarily forgotten the following evening when Newark clinched the pennant on the strength of Baltimore's defeat of Montreal in the second game of their doubleheader. It was the fourth pennant for the Bears in six years under the dynamic leadership of George Weiss. Since this was 1937 and the Newark Bears were a minor league team (in name only), the traditional champagne celebration was still in the future.

But the clubhouse was still a happy scene of raucous laughter, back slapping, and superlatives, as the mighty Bears celebrated with four cases of beer. There was an amusing story behind that beer. It so happened that a local Buffalo bowling association made arrangements to sponsor a "field meet" prior to the game between the two teams. As it turned out, the Bears copped all the events except the 100-yard dash, when Mike McCormick nosed out the sorearmed Chandler. Seeds and Keller were one and two in throwing accuracy from the outfield. Hershberger and Rosar were one and two in firing from the plate to second. Finally, the four-man Newark relay team won a walking race around the bases. The prize for winning the field meet was four cases of beer. And it couldn't have arrived at a more timely moment.

Vitt, no newcomer to the managerial ranks, commented after the game, "They're the finest bunch of fellows I ever managed." For the veteran pilot, this was no idle boast. It was his third flag in thirteen years. He had previously led Hollywood to back-to-back pennants in 1929 and 1930 in the powerful Pacific Coast League.

Oscar Vitt started his baseball career through a bizzare and unfortunate set of circumstances, namely, an earthquake and subsequent fire. It all began back in San Francisco in 1906. Vitt was a struggling architect who played semiprofessional ball on Sundays and was sought by several clubs in the tough Coast League. As was often the case in those days, however, his parents objected to his playing ball for a living. They wanted him to be a "professional man." With Oscar just about on the brink of becoming an industrious architect, the earthquake struck and put him out of work. Right then and there, his parents decided to let their little Oscar select his own vocation. Vitt naturally chose baseball.

He began his professional career in earnest when he joined the Oakland club of the California State League. Later, when that league disbanded, he latched on with the Three C League and eventually, in 1909, signed to play with the San Francisco Seals. Vitt got what he considered to be a "fat contract," calling for $125 a month. Three years later, the Detroit Tigers drafted him.

Oscar Vitt, the man with the "perpetual smile," joined the Tigers in 1912 as a 22-year-old rookie third baseman.

"I didn't think myself so lucky," commented Vitt. "Up with a team of world beaters — Cobb, Veach, Crawford — I was considered a mediocre hitter. Jennings [Detroit Manager] yelled to me the first day out, 'You're lead-off man. Don't you try to hit; take two, wait the pitcher out, get on there; Bush, Cobb, and Crawford will drive you in.' I never hit .300 in my life; as a result, pitchers had two strikes on me all the time. But I learned discipline and team play. Hughey bawled me out many a time before I learned to play third base to suit him."

Vitt played with the great Ty Cobb for seven years and amassed a number of legendary Cobb stories. There were two in particular that he enjoyed recounting the most. Both clearly revealed Cobb's blatant obsession for wanting to be number one!

Ty Cobb often took exception to the way some of his infielders put the ball on runners, particularly when it could mean an assist for him. One day, when Vitt failed to tag a man, Cobb threatened to blow the head off the little third baseman's shoulders. Vitt, fresh and cocky, came right back at the great Cobb, who bolted from the bench to belt little Oscar. But he never got started. Big Oscar Stanage, the Tiger catcher, blocked the way. "You big bully," said Stanage. "Get this right: any time you hit little Ossie, you hit me. From now on, pick on fellows your own size." Cobb wisely backed down.

The other incident occurred against the Yankees at the Polo

Grounds. Vitt was on second when Cobb drove a clean single to center. Oscar legged it all the way to the plate with plenty of time to score, but burly Les Nunamaker was blocking home and Vitt "bounced off to one side." He was tagged out before he could scramble back to the plate. Cobb stopped at third.

As Vitt shook the cobwebs from his stunned brain, Cobb yelled to him, "Watch me get the big duffer on the next play, kid. I'll even it up for you."

"A moment later," Vitt recalled, "the ball was hit to an in-fielder. Cobb, taking a desperate chance as the infield had been playing in, dashed for home. Sure enough, Nunamaker blocked the plate.

"Well, sir," said Vitt, "I have seen some mighty football backs hit a line, but never have I seen anything quite like that impact. Cobb came in high and virtually undressed Nunamaker. Ty's spikes were so high he tore the chest protector completely off the big Yankee backstop as his mask went flying in one direction and Nunamaker rolled half way to the Yankee bench.

"Of course, Cobb scored, making up for the run Nunamaker had stolen from me. Ty continued to play, never showing a sign he had been hurt. But in the clubhouse after the game, I happened to be near him when he unpealed his socks and baseball pants. His leg had been skinned the same as though you had taken a keen razor blade and removed the cuticle. He had to tear off the blood clots. Yet he never had whimpered.

"I have seen Cobb play when he was so cut and bruised from spikings, another man would have been out for weeks. The old boy could take it. There'll never be another just like the Georgia Peach."

In 1918, Oscar Vitt was traded to the Boston Red Sox for catcher Eddie Ainsmith, outfielder Chick Shorten, and pitcher Elmer "Slim" Love. He played three years for the Red Sox, never hitting above .243. And it was with Boston that Vitt first met up with Ed Barrow, who was the Field Manager of the Red Sox at the time. No doubt this association with Barrow later played a role in Vitt's selection as the Newark Manager. But Vitt's memories of the Red

Sox in 1919-21 inevitably revolved around tales of the great Babe Ruth.

Vitt loved to tell the story of how he and shortstop Everett Scott helped Ruth get his first chance as an outfielder.

"George Whiteman, an outfielder for the Sox, was ill during the spring of 1919 and we were about to play a series with the Giants. Ruth came to Scott and myself and asked us to put a plug in for him as an outfielder. We both asked Ed Barrow, then Manager, and he almost fell over."

"Do you want that guy to get killed out there and ruin a perfectly good left-handed pitcher?" Barrow asked.

"However," Vitt continued, "after a while, Barrow consented, and Ruth hit a home run at Tampa, Florida. I think it sailed almost 600 feet — clear out of the race track. Ruth never was a regular pitcher after that game. He got twenty-nine homers that year."

After the miserable 1921 season when Vitt's average scraped bottom at .190, the Red Sox waived Oscar out of the league. Since Salt Lake City of the Pacific Coast League needed a third baseman badly, the union was inevitable. Years later, Vitt, always the optimist, would recall his Salt Lake City days with fond memories.

"I should have played ball in the rarified atmosphere of Salt Lake City all my life. In the majors, I was a cheap .250 hitter (or less), but out there, my average suddenly soared to .315 and, in 1925, to .345. Why, I had to steer shy of scouts, who thought I was having a second blooming and deserved another major league trial!"

In a surprise move, Bill Lane, owner of Salt Lake City, named Vitt to manage his club. Oscar made rapid strides as a manager. While a fun-loving, practical joker off the field, he demanded a high brand of hustling from his players and was very strict once the game began. During the next eleven years, Vitt, the high spirited showman, managed Salt Lake City, Hollywood, and Oakland. He won pennants in 1929 and 1930 with Hollywood.

As a manager, Vitt's greatest discovery was a broad-shouldered youngster from the Telegraph Hill section of San Francisco named Tony Lazzeri.

"I sold Lazzeri to my friend, Ed Barrow, for $50,000. Yes, Lazzeri was my baby. He was the greatest ballplayer I ever handled and I have followed his career with deepest interest."

In 1934, after managing the Hollywood Stars for nine years, Oscar Vitt was fired. It was a shocking turn of events. One Los Angeles sportswriter summed up the fans' feelings: "I can't believe it. There must be something wrong. Maybe it is only a dream. It is unbelievable. He has had a magnificent record as a manager."

It wasn't a dream and it was believable. Vitt was fired all right, but as he later admitted, it was much of his own doing. Three times, Oscar had been in line to manage the Boston Red Sox and once, he narrowly missed a shot at the Detroit Tigers. The final straw came when Larry MacPhail, the Director of the Cincinnati Reds, chose Charlie Dressen over Vitt for the Reds' job. Vitt was so disappointed, he decided that a change in scenery would be the best thing for him. So he set the price of his 1934 contract with Hollywood so high that his old pal, Lane, had to let him go.

Oscar was not unemployed for very long when he signed with the Oakland Oaks — his first step on the road to piloting the Newark Bears and the legendary 1937 team that would eventually lead to the major league managerial job he so eagerly sought.

On October 19, 1937, shortly after Newark's incredible Little World Series victory, President Alva Bradley of the Cleveland Indians announced the appointment of Vitt as Cleveland's new manager, replacing Steve O'Neill. The appointment climaxed the ambition Vitt had cherished ever since the end of his major league playing career.

Ray Kennedy said the news of Vitt signing with the Indians was a complete surprise to the Newark club officials.

"I am sure George Weiss knew nothing about it. In fact, the first news the Bears had was when the *Newark News* called," Kennedy said. "Ossie was given permission to get a major league job when he told Colonel Ruppert he had been approached by several major league clubs. Of course, we are happy. Vitt deserved a chance in the majors. He'll make a good manager. Well certainly miss him here in Newark."

Vitt, anxious to start the season, poured on the charm to the press. "I hope to convince my new bosses and the Cleveland fans that the right man was picked. I have no recommendations as to changes at this time and will make none until I have gone over the situation closely with President Bradley." The outspoken Vitt continued, "I don't want any lazy players on my club. If the boys won't hustle, out they go."

The new manager arrived in Cleveland, bubbling over with ideas. As he did in Newark, he captured the imagination of the Cleveland sportswiters. He was always good copy. During his first two years, 1938-39, the loquacious and hard-driving Vitt led the Indians to two third place finishes. Both were respectable showings and it looked like 1940 might just be the year Cleveland would go all the way. The lineup was sprinkled with a mixture of young and old. Hal Trosky was at first, Ray Mack at second, Lou Boudreau at short, and Ken Keltner at third. In the outfield, it was Ben Chapman in left, Roy Weatherly in center, and Beau Bell in right. Behind the plate was Rollie Hemsley. The pitching staff was led by Bob Feller, Mel Harder, Al Milnar, and Al Smith. It was a good, solid team capable of winning a pennant. But suddenly an event occured that shook the city of Cleveland and the rest of the baseball world. It was an action "believed unprecedented in major league baseball."

On June 12, 1940, after Cleveland lost 8 of 13 games on a disastrous road trip East, a group of "veteran members of the Indians personally laid before President Alva Bradley a demand that Manager Oscar Vitt be fired."

The mass protest by twelve players was led by Bob Feller, Mel Harder, Al Milnar, Hal Trosky, and Rollie Hemsley. "They told Bradley they could not play the kind of baseball of which they are capable as long as Vitt remained at the helm. Their charges, according to *The Plain Dealer*, included insincerity, ridiculing of players, and caustic criticism."

"Naturally, I am going to look into the matter," said Bradley, "but until I have investigated thoroughly, I can't say what action will be taken."

The specific charges laid down by the "Cleveland Crybabies," as they were later dubbed, included the following:

That Vitt had ridiculed his players in conversation with newspaper writers, fans, and opposing players and managers;

That he had undermined the confidence and spirit of the individuals by sarcastic comments on their failures;

That he had proved himself insincere in his dealings with the players;

That he is a 'wild man' on the bench, storming up and down, voicing caustic comments on his players' actions, and communicating his 'jitters' to the players;

That his antics have made him a laughingstock among other teams and that the Indians have lost dignity and pride thereby; and

That he has persisted in comparing the Indians unfavorably with minor league teams he has managed, notably the Newark Bears of 1937, who won the International League pennant by twenty-five and one-half games.

In the days that followed, both sides of the controversy voiced specific charges and counter charges. The players cited the time Vitt stormed around the dugout and hammered the bat rack as the Red Sox were clubbing Bob Feller.

"Look at him. He's supposed to be my ace. I'm supposed to win a pennant with that kind of pitching," shouted Vitt.

Another time, after Mel Harder was knocked out of the box at Boston, he said, "It's about time you won one, the money you're getting." And still another comment made by Vitt was, "You guys aren't fit to wear Newark's sweat shirts."

In reality, Vitt's downfall began as early as June, 1939. In his book, *Strikeout Story*, Bob Feller writes: "Vitt was losing his popularity among the Indians because of his emotional reaction to defeat. He couldn't forgive the fumblers and the futility ot some of his men, even when they weren't intentional.''

In his own defense, Vitt offered the following, in part, as a rebuttal. ''And that Bob Feller! Never in my life have I thought — much less said — anything that would hurt that kid. Oh, maybe I groaned in the dugout when Bob was being beaten, but certainly it was no reflection on him.'' Vitt continued, ''Sure, I've been nervous in the dugout. What do the fellows want? A manager who doesn't care whether they win or lose?''

President Bradley, at least on the surface, put an end to the controversy when he spoke to the players in the clubhouse following a double-header. ''There can be no action now. I want you to sign a paper withdrawing charges against Vitt. This will not mean that the matter has been completely closed, but it will be the best for all concerned.''

Days later, in a statement signed by all but three players, the team called off its sensational rebellion against Vitt. The statement read:

> We, the undersigned, publicly declare to withdraw all statements referring to the resignation of Oscar Vitt. We feel this action is for the betterment of the Cleveland baseball club.

The players' agreement seemingly ended one of the strangest episodes in major league baseball. However, the die of dissension had been cast. Although Vitt finished the season, many baseball experts believed the player rebellion cost the Indians the pennant as they finished in second place only one game behind the Detroit Tigers.

Then on October 27, 1940, the Cleveland Indians closed out one of the most bizarre chapters in baseball history by firing Oscar Vitt. At his home in Oakland, Vitt commented, ''I can't exactly say that I am surprised. At no time were next year's plans discussed with me, and I knew long before the close of the season that unless drastic changes were made, it would be impossible for me to work under the present circumstances. It doesn't look as though these changes are being made, so I am just as well satisfied.

"I made plenty of money for the Indians in the last three years and I have no regrets. Unless I get a job that will pay me well, I presume Old Os will just retire. Whoever gets the job has my best wishes — also my sympathy. Just let the boys back there know I don't intend to apply for unemployment compensation." Once again, the spunky, outspoken, and often loveable Oscar Vitt had the last word.

The Bears finished the Buffalo series and their northern trip by winning the next two games, 6-2 and 5-4. In the first game, Tamulis won his sixteenth and eighth straight. Beggs, although hit hard at times, won the 5-4 game for his nineteenth of the season, inching closer to the magical twenty mark. In an unusual move, Rosar played third base in both games. It all started with the injury to Mc-Quinn's thumb, which forced Dahlgren to first and Kelleher to third. Then with the injury to Kelleher's forefinger, Rosar was summoned to the hot corner. He was not totally unfamiliar with the position, however, since he had played 30 games in the infield at Binghamton in 1936. The catcher-turned-third baseman showed a hot bat in both games. He tripled and doubled twice in the first and blasted a ninth inning, game-winning home run in the second.

The Bears headed home with only 19 games remaining in the season — 13 at home and 6 away. With the pennant tucked neatly in Vitt's back pocket, interest naturally shifted to team and individual statistics. The Bears record at Ruppert Stadium was a cool 51-12 for a phenomenal .810 percentage. The 1921 Baltimore Orioles claimed the record with 68 wins and 18 losses (.791). So the Bears had an excellent opportunity to establish a new International League record at home by winning their last 10 of 13. They were to play six games against Jersey City, five games against Baltimore, and two against Syracuse.

The batting title was another area in which fan interest was keen. Charlie Keller, the college kid in his first professional season, Babe Dahlgren, first basemen-turned-third basemen, and outfielder Lou Scoffic of Rochester were locked in an exciting race for the batting honors. Leaving Buffalo, Keller and Scoffic were tied at .344, with Dahlgren trailing at .339. In another individual battle, Bob Seeds, with 97 RBI's, was trying desperately to overtake Baltimore's Ab Wright, who led with 101.

The pitching staff was not to be denied, either. Beggs, Donald, and Tamulis all had shots at winning 20 games. Beggs, of course, had the best opportunity since he had already won 19, but Donald also had a good chance, needing only three more victories to boost his 17-2 record over the top. However, his sore arm was still giving him trouble, which added a serious element of doubt. Tamulis was the least likely to reach the magical goal, having posted only 16 wins. But with 19 games remaining, it was certainly possible and Vito would make a gallant effort.

16.

Batting Title Comes To Newark

OVER 10,000 NEWARK FANS GREETED THE RETURN OF their conquering heroes to Ruppert Stadium, and as their thank you, the Bears walloped three Jersey City pitchers for a lopsided 11-2 victory in the opening game. Steve Sundra scattered ten hits, notching his fifteenth victory. Joe Gordon belted number twenty-two and Bob Seeds number seventeen — each driving in two runs. Ray Pascall, President of the Sebring Chamber of Commerce and often referred to grandiosely as "Mr. Sebring," attended the game and appeared to enjoy every minute. He was also overheard discussing the Bears incredible season and jokingly commented, "You know where they trained."

The following day, Newark split their double-header, losing the first game, 6-3 (Pascall was nowhere to be found), and winning the second, 5-2. The 6-3 win was the first for Jersey City at Ruppert Stadium all season and even this took a monumental effort — three runs in the seventh and two in the eighth to overtake the Bears' 3-1 lead. Phil Page took the loss.

In the second game, the Bears immediately jumped all over the Little Giants. Gleeson's double and Keller's triple, along with four singles, produced four runs in the first and Newark was never headed. Spud Chandler picked up his first win as a Bear and was working on a shutout until the sixth. Bob Seeds brought his RBI total to 100, but still trailed Ab Wright, the power-hitting Baltimore outfielder.

The next day was Sunday and "Oscar Vitt Day" at Ruppert

Stadium. Newark fans came from all over to honor their colorful manager and present him with a magnificent gift of silver. The pregame festivities were an absolute delight. Al Schacht, the famous clown prince of baseball, put on a thirty minute show which had the crowd in stitches. In the competitive events, Newark did extremely well. The fleet-footed Keller won the 75-yard dash in 8.1 seconds and clocked the best time in the race around the bases, 14.1 seconds. Bob Seeds was second at 14.5 and Joe Gordon followed with 14.6. For his winning efforts, Keller was presented with a new suit and a wrist watch. Jersey City copped all three places in the outfield-to-home plate accuracy throwing contest. Lincoln Blakely, Joe Dwyer, and Hal Lee finished one, two, and three, respectively. Willard Hershberger flipped the ball into a barrel at second base to win that event, while the team of Atley Donald and Jack Fallon captured the three-legged race. Spud Chandler finished first in the 50-yard "dash" running backwards! The quartet of Nolen Richardson, Babe Dahlgren, Gordon, and Donald were too much for the Little Giants as they won something called the heal-and-toe relay race. But the event that attracted the most attention was between Vitt and Travis Jackson, the Little Giants' Manager. Ol' Os came out on top, displaying unusual skill pushing a wheelbarrow from second base to home plate — blindfolded. Vitt would also get the best of Jackson in the game, as the Bears fattened their batting averages by banging out nineteen hits, coupled with the magnificent pitching of Vito Tamulis. The young lefty blanked Jersey City, 9-0, on only five singles. It was his ninth consecutive victory and seventeenth of the season. His quest for the traditional 20 was now within sight. Gordon blasted his twenty-third and twenty-fourth home runs in the fifth and sixth innings. However, Keller hit the longest round tripper of the afternoon, a mighty blast into the bleachers in right center field, while Francis Kelleher put one into the uncovered section in left field. In addition to his home run, Keller went three-for-five, raising his league-leading average to .349. Dahlgren, not giving ground, poked out two hits in five trips to the plate for a .338 average.

The Bears sped on to Syracuse for a twi-night double-header. It was to be their final appearance of the regular season in Syracuse. The Chiefs won the first game, 9-2, as Joe Beggs missed his twentieth victory. He would have to wait for another chance. The game was lost in the seventh when Syracuse scored eight times, the most runs scored against the Bears in one inning all season. But it took four errors and six hits to do the job.

In the second game, Marius Russo, the young left-hander from Brooklyn who worked infrequently all year, pitched a brilliant three-hit, 1-0 shutout. It was the Bears' one-hundredth victory of the season! Newark scored its only run in the sixth when Dahlgren tripled and Keller singled.

Although Russo was used sparingly in 1937, the 23-year-old rookie would find a lot more work for the Bears in 1938. He would lead them to another first place finish, posting a 17-8 mark with a 3.15 ERA. In spite of this fine performance, the Brooklyn-born youth found himself still pitching for the Bears in 1939.

Perhaps the reason was simple, but not necessarily palatable to the kid. The Yankees had won three straight World Championships from 1936 to 1938. With a staff of Red Ruffing, Lefty Gomez, Monte Pearson, and Spud Chandler, there was little room for an inexperienced pitcher. But despite his inexperience and youth, there were many who felt Russo displayed the poise of a veteran. He was cool in the clutch, lacked emotion, and took everything in stride.

So Russo started the 1939 season once again with Newark. By June, he had posted what appeared to be, at least on the surface, an unimpressive 5-4 record. However, three of his defeats were by 1-0 margins. His true skill was more accurately measured by his astonishing 1.97 ERA! In the Yankee camp, what looked like a solid pitching staff three months before now showed signs of disintegrating. McCarthy quickly forgot the inexperience and called up Russo.

Marius responded brilliantly. He finished the season with an 8-3 mark, winning seven in a row as he helped the Yankees to their fourth consecutive World Championship. The youth was being hailed by baseball men as the best southpaw to come to the major

Marius Russo pitched a brilliant three-hit, 1-0 shutout over Syracuse for the Bears one-hundredth victory of the season.

leagues in 1939. He appeared in 21 games for the Yankees, 10 of them in relief. His early success prompted Yankee catcher Bill Dickey to comment, "He is a control pitcher, knows how to pace himself, and has a good change of pace delivery. Good left-handers aren't coming up fast. He's a great prospect and I haven't a doubt he could get by as a starter, after handling him twice in relief roles."

Russo did more than just "get by as a starter." He finished 9 of 11 starts and turned in a 2.41 ERA. It was a remarkable performance for a kid who only three years before was pitching for Long Island University. Russo stated it this way: "I'm only thinking what a lucky break it was for me the day I gave up trying to play first base and decided to try my hand at pitching. You know, I never pitched in high school, nor the first three years at college. I'm a pretty lucky stiff."

Russo's personal life had moved swiftly, too — he had met and married a Newark girl by the name of Stasia Syndek. Oddly enough, it was reported that the marriage came about on a dare. It was in June, 1938 that Stasia was attending the Newark-Rochester game at Ruppert Stadium with some friends. Marius, of course, was pitching that night, but after being roughed up pretty badly by Rochester, he was removed from the game. He was heading for the showers when Stasia's friends dared her to ask the local hero for his autograph. Considering the situation, it was not a very discreet thing to do.

Stasia vividly recalled what took place. "He was in bad humor and said, 'You're a brat, beat it.' I wouldn't have minded so much, but my friends got such a kick out of it I was red. An usher at the park happened to pass just then. I told him what I thought of Rus and he told him. I was surprised when Rus came up shortly afterward and apologized. He took me out for a soda and it all began."

In 1940, the Yankees finished third, one game in back of Cleveland and two games behind the pennant winning Detroit Tigers. In spite of the third place showing, Russo (along with Ruffing) led the pitching staff with a 14-8 record and a 3.28 ERA. This exceptional season inspired one of his teammates to comment to

Joe DiMaggio, "Someday that kid is going to be as important in pitching to the Yankees as your bat and fielding skill, mark my words."

"You're telling me," blurted Joe, "I am glad we don't face him during the regular season. I never did have much luck with southpaws."

The Yankees bounced back in 1941 to win the pennant by 17 games. Russo pitched in 210 innings, the most on the staff, and posted a 14-10 record and a 3.09 ERA. However, his greatest achievement came in the third game of the World Series against the Brooklyn Dodgers.

The 40-year-old Freddie Fitzsimmons hooked up with young Russo in a classic mound duel. Both pitched six impressive shutout innings. Then in the top of the seventh, with the score still deadlocked at 0-0, Russo came to bat and lined a pitch off Fitzsimmons' kneecap. Jim Ogle of the *Newark Star-Ledger* described the action: "...the courageous veteran was knocked out of the game and series when a torrid line drive from Russo's bat hit him just above the left kneecap. The ball bounded 30 feet in the air to become a pop fly out for Pee Wee Reese and end the inning. Fitz was helped from the field and was all through for the day..."

In the top of the eighth, with Fitzsimmons out of the game, the Yankees scored twice and went on to win, 2-1. Russo finished the game, allowing only four hits and one run. It was a sparkling performance by the gritty left-hander and gave the Yankees an important 2-1 edge, which some felt was the turning point in the series.

After the game, surrounded by reporters, Russo reflected on the sweet victory. "It's too bad Fitz was hurt. He pitched a great game and I'm sorry he went out that way." Concerning his own feelings later in the game, Russo said, "I was most scared in the ninth with Pete Reiser leading off. He gave me the most trouble during the afternoon. Well, I finally fanned him, but I wasn't breathing right until Joe Medwick and Cookie Lavagetto were out of the way, too. I was so tense I was afraid of grooving one through the center or making a boner. But Bill Dickey, who deserves more credit for the victory than I, kept me on the right track."

Dickey, self-effacing as usual, refused to take any credit. "Russo did the pitching, I didn't, and that's the whole story," he told newsmen. "Russo had good stuff and fine control. He mixed them up and his fast one was taking off. It was his best pitch of the game. I'm glad he took his time out there and didn't get excited in his first series competition."

Asked to compare the Dodgers with an American League team, Russo frankly stated, "They just don't fit. I would not call them a team of good hitters. They did not bother me much, and I am not bragging. In fact, they did not impress us throughout the series as a good hitting club against any of our staff.

"However, I have one grudge. Those Brooklyn fans sure took it out on me because my line drive hit Fitzsimmons on the leg and crippled him so he had to quit when we were having a red-hot pitchers' battle.

"Most of the Dodger fans are all right, but some can be mean. One lady writer was particularly hateful in a letter to me. She claimed I had deliberately aimed that line drive at Fitzsimmons. Maybe I get a hit now and then, but I'm not that good!"

The 1942 season was a disappointing one for Russo. He injured his arm in May against the White Sox and aggravated it again against the Senators in early August. That finished him for the season. Marius pitched in only 45 innings, posting a 4-1 record with a 2.78 ERA. The Yankees still managed to win another pennant, but lost the World Series to the St. Louis Cardinals, led by future Hall of Famer Stan Musial.

His arm still ailing, Russo suffered through his most disappointing season as a Yankee in 1943. He turned in a sub-par 5-10 record. With Spud Chandler, Ernie Bonham, and Johnny Murphy having good years, the Yankees won still another pennant, earning the right to face the Cardinals again in the World Series. This set the stage for the second brilliant World Series pitching performance by the cool left-hander. With the Yankees leading the Cardinals, 2-0, in the series, Russo got the nod from McCarthy to pitch the third game. Russo met the challenge, scattering seven hits and allowing one unearned run as the Yankees nipped the Cardinals,

2-1, for their third series victory. The next day, Chandler shut out the Redbirds for the Yankees' tenth World Championship.

Coming home from St. Louis after the series, McCarthy kidded a few of the sportswriters. "The big surprise of the series to me," he said, "was the way you guys figured I was taking a long shot in naming Russo to pitch the third game. It was obvious that his arm was right again — he'd proved that in recent weeks — and everybody and his brother knows what a helluva pitcher he is when he's in shape.

"Oh, I know he won only five and lost ten this year, but four of those wins were low-hit affairs in the last weeks of the season. He was just coming on as the season ended. He was ripe. I knew it and he knew it. I never lost a wink of sleep over the decision."

Russo, like so many of the ballplayers at that time, was tagged for military service in early 1944. Upon returning to civilian life approximately two years later, the still lame-armed southpaw underwent surgery for the removal of bone chips in his left elbow that he picked up in the Pacific.

The operation in January, 1946 was declared successful and full recovery was eagerly anticipated by both Russo and the Yankees. But it was not in the cards. Russo would struggle through a little more than eighteen innings, posting an 0-2 record with a 4.34 ERA. In August, the Yankees gave up on their one-time star and optioned him to Kansas City in the American Association. The move ended Russo's major league career.

After the short Syracuse series, Newark headed for Baltimore to play the Orioles — all but ace right-hander Steve Sundra. The fifteen-game winner remained in Newark and checked into the Presbyterian Hospital complaining of stomach pains, which turned out to be nothing more serious than an attack of appendicitis. At five a.m. on September 1, Sundra underwent an operation for the removal of his appendix. At the time, it was obvious he would not be ready for the play-offs. But many fans were hoping the right-hander would be available for the Little World Series. It turned out to be nothing more than hope. Sundra missed both the play-offs and the Little World Series, forcing Vitt to make adjustments in his pitching rotation.

The twi-night double-header at Baltimore attracted 14,000 fans into a park that was built to hold only 10,000. There were two reasons for this tremendous turnout. First, it was "Bucky Crouse Night" and the Oriole Manager was to be presented with a brand new automobile. The second reason was that fourth place Baltimore was guarding a slim lead over fifth place Buffalo. The Bisons were trying desperately to make the play-offs, so from that standpoint, the game was critical to Baltimore.

The fans were spread all over the playing field, resembling the game held earlier in the season at Ruppert Stadium. They were stacked along both foul lines and strung across the outfield, which forced the umpires to establish a temporary ground rule: any ball hit into the crowd was an automatic double. Although this makeshift rule didn't affect the outcome of the game, it did turn many a single into a two-base hit as the fans often ran after the ball before it reached a player.

It was another typical wild and unruly Baltimore crowd which forced the second game to be cancelled. Trouble started when the locals began heaving bottles at Jimmy Gleeson, who was trying to catch a fly ball in left field. The exciting and dramatic finish of the extra-inning game also helped to ignite the crowd. In the top of the fifteenth, Joe Gordon smacked number twenty-five over the left field fence to give the Bears a temporary 6-5 lead. But the Orioles came right back with two runs in the bottom of the inning for an exciting 7-6 victory. The action was far from over, however. For no apparent reason, a Baltimore fan hauled off and walloped Vitt with a sneak rabbit punch as the Newark Manager was stooping to enter the dugout. If that wasn't enough for one night, Crouse's new car was driven to home plate and was immediately surrounded by the unruly crowd. Only two cops were available and tried helplessly to control the wild mob. Crouse made a few attempts to reach his car for the presentation, but finally gave up in disgust. With the 11:15 curfew drawing near, the second game had to be called off.

The next night, the Bears swept both ends of the twi-night

double-header. Tamulis, determined to win 20 games, chalked up his tenth straight victory, bringing his record to an outstanding 18-6, but he needed relief help from Chandler.

This was a different Tamulis than the one McCarthy sent to spring training in Sebring. In March, Tammy was bitter, but now his attitude was more understanding. The month before, he commented, "I didn't feel right this spring, either. I didn't run enough when I was down with the Yankees. Well, to be perfectly honest, I didn't want to run much. I felt I'd rather stay in the International League another year and get completely over the effects of that pluerisy and then go up when I knew I was ready. I'm ready now."

When a reporter asked why his fastball was so effective, Tamulis shot back, "Running. Vitt has had me running my legs off and I'm in shape. I'm stronger than I was when I was up with the Yankees and I'm bigger."

Nolen Richardson was the unlikely Newark batting hero. The veteran shortstop tied the game at 3-3 with an RBI single in the fourth and again with an RBI double in the sixth. He then topped both clutch hits two innings later. In the eighth, with the Bears trailing, 7-6, he singled to right field, scoring two more runs for an 8-7 lead.

Nolen Richardson was the 34-year-old veteran of the club. Before Newark purchased him during the winter of 1934, Richardson had shuttled back and forth between Detroit and Toronto for several years. His best year with Detroit came in 1931 when the part-time player batted .270 in 38 games. The following year, however, he was still with Detroit and the tall, lanky shortstop played in 69 games with his batting average sinking to an anemic .219.

From 1935 through 1937, Richardson served three full seasons at Ruppert Stadium (in addition to 12 games for the Yankees in 1935). Despite his weak hitting, Richardson never let it affect his play in the field. He was usually the unanimous choice for the All-Star team.

At the end of the great 1937 season, Ray Kennedy, Secretary of the Bears, made a surprise announcement to the press. Richardson had been sold to the Baltimore Orioles in a straight cash deal with no other players involved. It looked like the end of the trail for the aging shortstop.

However, Nolen surfaced once again in the majors, this time with Cincinnati. He played in 35 games for the Reds, batting a surprising and respectable .290. It turned out to be Richardson's last hurrah as the Reds sold him to Indianapolis, ending his short six-year, 168-game major league career.

In spite of the Richardson heroics, the victory over Baltimore was a bittersweet one. In the fourth inning, Dahlgren sprained his ankle as he stepped on the catcher's mask crossing the plate. He would miss the next nine games and in that period, Keller would raise his average to over .350, virtually eliminating Dahlgren from the batting title. During this same period over in Rochester, Scoffic would watch his average dip below .325, blocking his chances for the title, too.

Atley Donald won the second game, 6-3, which was called after five innings — the 11:15 curfew again. It was the first time the sore-armed Donald pitched since August 18 and the right-hander was obviously rusty from inactivity. He gave up four hits and three runs, and during streaks of wildness, walked five. But he still had enough to notch his eighteenth victory against only two losses. However, it would be seven days before he started again, as Vitt began to prepare for the critical play-offs by resting his pitching staff. This rest all but ended Donald's quest for a twenty-game season.

In the final game of the series, Joe Beggs posted his twentieth win as the Bears topped Baltimore, 5-2. And to think it was only a year before that the tall Rankin right-hander was pitching in Class B in the Piedmont League. Beggs had an easy time of it as he scattered seven hits, walked three, and struck out four. He was seldom in serious trouble. Newark won the game in the first four innings, collecting six hits and four runs, including a home run by Bob Seeds. Keller picked up three more hits.

The Bears happily left Baltimore and returned to friendly Ruppert Stadium for their last nine games of the season. In a doubleheader on Monday, September 6, Newark whipped Jersey City in short order. They won the first game, 4-2, in an hour and a half, and the second game, 1-0, in sixty-five minutes. This brought the Bears' record against their last place push-overs to 16-4 and their home record to an unbelievable 56-13 (.811)! Russo won his eighth in the first game as Seeds drove in the winning runs in the home half of the eighth, bringing his RBI total to 105. Phil Page won the second game, allowing four hits and two walks, while his teammates picked up an unearned run in the fifth. As it turned out, this was the only run Page needed as the left-hander brought his record to 3-1.

Syracuse next invaded Newark for their final two games at Ruppert Stadium and surprisingly won both, dropping the Bears home record to 56-15 (.788), three percentage points below the league record .791. The Bears lost the first game on Tuesday, 7-6, as Harry Craft, in the top of the ninth with the bases loaded, smacked an outside fastball from Jack Fallon into the right field stands for a 7-6 lead and eventually the game.

In the second game, Tamulis went after number nineteen, but came up empty when he was rapped for thirteen hits and seven runs in seven and one-third innings. Niggeling relieved, but was no improvement, getting bombed for seven hits and eight runs the rest of the way. Seeds hit number twenty (bringing the team's home run total for the season to 138, tying the 1934 Newark record) and added three more RBI's to bring his total to 109.

The Baltimore Orioles then came to Newark for their final five games of the season at Ruppert Stadium. In the first of two, Atley Donald got a chance to pitch again and turned in a sterling performance. He allowed the Orioles four hits and one run — Woodley Abernathy's home run in the first inning — and won the game, 10-1, for his nineteenth victory. McQuinn slapped a home run in the first with Gleeson on board, which gave Newark a new record of 139 homers for one season.

In the seven-inning second game, Joe Beggs posted his twenty-first win, blanking the Orioles, 4-0, on five hits. Bob Seeds drove in three runs, with two-for-three, bringing his RBI total to 112. It would remain at 112 as Vitt rested Seeds over the last three games. Since Wright finished with a league-leading 122 RBI's, it would have taken a minor miracle for Seeds to overtake him.

The next day, Baltimore beat Newark, 7-1. It was the Bears' forty-third loss (only the sixteenth at home) and erased their chance to establish a new International League record. Chandler, still bothered by a sore shoulder, started the game and took the loss, lasting only five innings.

In hindsight, one wonders why Vitt didn't give the nod to a healthy Vito Tamulis, who hadn't pitched since September 3. It was reported in the press that Oscar wanted to rest his front line pitchers for the play-offs, but even so, Tamulis wasn't used in the semifinals until the third game, which was five days after the Bears' loss to Baltimore. This would have given Tamulis four days of rest. And since the Bears beat Baltimore in a double-header the following day, Vitt's pitching choice certainly raised some skeptical eyebrows. But in all fairness to Vitt, the play-offs were foremost on his mind in light of Newark's disastrous showing over the last four years. Apparently Ol' Os was taking no chances and if he could steal a few days of rest for his pitching staff, an International League record was a small price to pay.

From Baltimore's standpoint, however, it was an important victory, since it clinched a berth for the Orioles in the play-offs. Their exact place (third or fourth) would not be determined until the final day. As it turned out, Baltimore finished fourth with a 76-75 record, dropping two games to Newark on the last day as Syracuse split with Jersey City and finished third with a 78-74 record. Since the first place team played the third place team in the Shaughnessey Play-offs — namely, Newark and Syracuse — many Baltimore fans were not overly disappointed in their fourth place finish.

The Bears' loss to Baltimore did have a bright spot, however. Keller clinched the batting title with two-for-four and finished the double-header victory the next day with three-for-seven, raising his final league-leading batting average to .353. It was the first time a rookie won the batting title in the history of the International League. Dahlgren finished second with a solid .340.

The book was now closed on the Newark Bears' regular season. And what an incredible season it was. The list of team and individual achievements were a mile long.

In addition to Keller winning the batting championship and leading the league with 189 hits, the *Sporting News* presented the young rookie with the Most Valuable Player award, a plaque inscribed as follows:

Charles Ernest Keller
Outfielder of Newark International League Bears

Cited by *The Sporting News* as the leading minor league player in 1937 for the achievement of leading the International League with a batting average of .353, including 34 doubles, 14 triples, 13 home runs, 120 runs scored and 88 runs batted in, during his first year in Organized Ball.

By finishing 25½ games in front of Montreal, Newark won the pennant by the greatest margin in International League history.[7]

INTERNATIONAL LEAGUE
1937 FINAL STANDINGS

	W.	L.	PC.
Newark	109	43	.717
Montreal	82	67	.550
Syracuse	78	74	.513
Baltimore	76	75	.503
Buffalo	74	79	.484
Rochester	74	80	.481
Toronto	63	88	.417
Jersey City	50	100	.333

7. The 1920 St. Paul team in the American Association holds the all-time record of 28½ games.

Charlie Keller received the Most Valuable Player award from The Sporting News. The rookie led the league with the highest average .353, and the most hits, 189.

The Bears won 109 games and lost 43 for a percentage of .717, becoming the eighth International League club since 1888 to finish above the .700 mark. Here again, the Bears missed several marks by narrow margins. Their 109 victories left them one short of the league record for a 154-game schedule established by the 1920 Baltimore Orioles. At home, the Bears won 60 out of 76 games for a percentage of .789, a new Newark record, but again narrowly missing the all-time high of .791 set by the 1921 Orioles.

Newark had a strangle hold on top individual performances. They possessed the four best pitchers in the league with respect to wins and losses and their combined percentage was an unbelievable .820.

	W.	L.	Pct.
Atley Donald	19	2	.905
Joe Beggs	21	4	.840
Steve Sundra	15	4	.789
Vito Tamulis	18	6	.750
Combined	73	16	.820

In the offensive department, Newark dominated the league with their sensational hitting statistics.

	G.	AB.	R.	H.	HR.	RBI.	AV.
Charlie Keller	145	536	120	189	13	88	.353
Babe Dahlgren	125	482	107	164	19	86	.340
Buddy Rosar	72	232	31	77	8	39	.332
George McQuinn	114	459	95	151	21	84	.329
Willard Hershberger	96	314	53	102	5	66	.325
Francis Kelleher	93	295	47	90	11	50	.305
Bob Seeds	151	565	98	171	20	112	.303
Jimmy Gleeson	143	558	101	166	16	81	.299
Joe Gordon	151	634	111	177	26	84	.279
Nolen Richardson	153	534	54	138	—	65	.258

In addition to Keller, five other regulars and a utility man all hit over .300. In the charmed circle were Babe Dahlgren, Buddy Rosar,

George McQuinn, Willard Hershberger, Francis Kelleher, and Bob Seeds. Jimmy Gleeson missed it by a single percentage point, but he had the distinction of leading the league in doubles with 47, only 10 short of the league record. Joe Gordon and Nolen Richardson were under .300, but Gordon led his teammates in home runs with 26.

It was truly a balanced effort on the team's part. While four players scored over 100 runs and five banged out more than 15 homers, the crowning glory was in the RBI category, led by Bob Seeds, who knocked in over 100 runs (112 to be exact). However, six Bears drove in more than 80 runs — simply an incredible achievement.

Collectively, the Bears finished at the head of the league in two-base hits with 285, in triples with 81, and in double plays with 159. Their 142 home runs, while failing to lead the league, established a new record for Newark, bettering by 4 the Newark Bears of 1934.

It was a fabulous season, which few clubs had the privilege of enjoying either in the minor or major leagues. In spite of this, the real challenge — the play-offs — were yet to come. For if the Bears were to lose the play-offs, as they had since 1933, their incredible season would be immeasureably tarnished. The play-offs represented one more hurdle to greatness and in the days ahead, the Bears would face this challenge with the poise and self-confidence that was their hallmark throughout the season.

17.

Semifinal Play-Offs
Syracuse Chiefs

T HE NEWARK BEARS, WHO HAD JUST COMPLETED ONE OF the most successful baseball seasons in the history of the International League (or for that matter, any league), would enter the 1937 play-offs with mixed emotions — and for good reason. In the first four years of post-season competition, the Newark Bears had failed to survive even the first round! In 1933, the Rochester Red Wings needed only four games to whip Newark after the Bears finished tops in the league. In 1934, the Bears finished in first place again, but the third place Toronto Leafs knocked them off in a series that went the limit. Finishing fourth in 1935 didn't change matters much as Syracuse embarassed the Bears in four straight! And it was the same story in 1936: in quick fashion, the Buffalo Bisons won 4 out of 5 from the hapless Bears.

In spite of this poor showing over the last four years and the uneasiness that memories fostered, an air of optimism still prevailed. This was a different Newark team. It had power hitting, strong pitching, and above all, confidence under pressure. All season long, when the Bears were 20 and 25 games in front and a let-down would have been excused, they played with the same coolness and determination. This indeed was a different Newark team and they were ready for the play-offs.

Syracuse, with a mediocre record of 76-74, barely nosed out Baltimore for third place. The Chiefs finished fourth in team batting, third in team fielding, and 30 games behind the Bears! It was a .500 ball club that simply represented no threat to Newark.

However, the Syracuse lineup did boast of a number of future major leaguers such as Harry Craft, Eddie Joost, Al Glossop, Frank McCormick, Dee Moore, Jimmy Outlaw, and Lee Gamble. But the kid who had everyone buzzing was a 23-year-old left-hander named Johnny VanderMeer. VanderMeer had been named the outstanding rookie in the country in 1936.

Glossop, Moore, and Gamble were journeymen who played briefly in the big leagues. McCormick, Joost, Outlaw, Craft, and VanderMeer had long and distinguished careers. Craft was the one exception — a weak hitting outfielder who played for the Cincinatti Reds for only six years, but was fortunate enough to play in two World Series. The first was in 1939 when New York swept four straight games from the Reds and the cry at the time was "break up the Yankees." The second came in 1940 when the Reds edged the Detroit Tigers, 2-1, in the seventh game. Craft ended his active playing career in 1942, but returned to the major leagues in 1957 as the manager of Kansas City in the American League. He also managed Chicago and Houston in the National League, finally packing it in after seven years and finishing no higher than seventh.

"Buck" McCormick, a towering giant of a man, played first base for thirteen years in the National League, ten of them with the Reds. From 1938 to 1940, McCormick slugged National League pitching mercilessly. In 1938, he batted .327 and drove in 106 runs. The following year, he raised his average to .332 with 128 RBI's. And in 1940, he hit .309 and drove in 127 runs. He finished with a respectable lifetime batting average of .229 and played in three World Series, two with Craft in 1939-40 and again with the Boston Braves in his last year in the majors.

Outlaw played ten years in the majors, two with the Reds, one with the Boston Braves, and the last seven in the American League with the Detroit Tigers. In 1945, he played against the Chicago Cubs in a World Series characterized by wartime players and sloppy fielding, prompting one sportswriter to comment, "Neither team can win this Series." He was wrong. The Tigers won it in seven games.

Eddie Joost's major league career spanned seventeen years and four clubs. Never much with the bat, but a great infielder, Joost finished with a life-time average of .239. At shortstop, he was considered one of the best, but was ironically involved in a celebrated error with Paul "Big Poison" Waner. On June 17, 1942, the Braves were playing the Reds in Boston. Waner's hit total for his career stood at 2,999. The next hit would be the big one and move him into the charmed circle of 3,000. Arthur Daley, in his book, *Inside Baseball*, recalled the incident: "Waner slammed a sharp grounder to the left of second base. Eddie Joost, the Cincinnati shortstop, got his glove on the ball but couldn't field it cleanly. All eyes turned to the press box where the official scorer was faced with a very tough decision. It was one of those hairline things and there would have been criticism if he had scored it a hit for Waner or an error for Joost. He hesitated momentarily and jerked up his forefinger, the signal for a hit."

The umpire picked up the ball and raced to first to present it to Paul as a souvenir of the historic occasion. Waner was standing on the bag, hands cupped against his mouth, shouting toward the press box, "No, no, don't give me a hit on that. I won't take it." Obligingly, the official scorer reversed himself and gave Joost an error on the play. Smiling, Waner commented, "I want my three-thousandth hit to be a clean one." That was one error Eddie Joost didn't deserve.

The best known of the bunch was VanderMeer, who early in 1937 had pitched in 19 games for Cincinnati, compiling a 3-5 record before he was sent down to Syracuse. Less than a year later, on June 15, the 23-year-old husky left-hander from Midland Park, New Jersey rocked the baseball world by pitching his second consecutive no-hitter.

It all started on June 11, 1938 when VanderMeer shut out the Boston Braves, 3-0, without a hit. Years later, VanderMeer would recall, "...I had good stuff and my ball was tailing. I was hitting that low and outside spot consistently all day and a lot of balls were hit on the ground. Harry Craft made a nice catch in center field during the game to rob somebody of a base hit, otherwise it was pretty much a routine ball game."

The second game was entirely different. It was June 15, the first night game ever in Ebbets Field. The ball park was jammed with over 40,000 fans. The game was held up for twenty-five minutes as tickets were still being sold. People were sitting in the aisles and standing all over. They came for two reasons — to watch Johnny VanderMeer and to be part of the first night game in Ebbets Field. As Roscoe McGowan, sportswriter of the *New York Times*, wrote, "...Johnny VanderMeer, tall handsome 22-year-old (sic) Cincinnati southpaw pitcher, stole the entire show by hurling his second consecutive no-hit, no-run game, both coming within five days and making baseball history that probably never will be duplicated."

In spite of these ballplayers, if there were any doubts about the Bears' superiority, the All-Star selections announced by the *Star-Eagle* on the eve of the play-offs erased them. Nine Bears made the team by overwhelming margins and Newark players were mentioned at all thirteen positions! Only at the shortstop, left field, and pitching positions were there any doubts. Charlie Keller was a unanimous choice.

The All-Star team selected by managers' Oscar Vitt, Ray Schalk, Mike Kelly, Travis Jackson, Bucky Crouse, Rabbit Maranville, and Dan Howley shaped up as follows:

First Base	George McQuinn, Newark
Second Base	Joe Gordon, Newark
Third Base	Babe Dahlgren, Newark
Shortstop	Nolen Richardson, Newark; Greg Mulleavy, Buffalo; Chet Wilburn, Baltimore
Right field	Charley Keller, Newark
Center field	Bob Seeds, Newark
Left field	John Hopp, Rochester
Catchers	Willard Hershberger and Buddy Rosar, Newark
Pitchers	Steve Sundra and Joe Beggs, Newark; Marvin Duke, Montreal

8. Ray Blades of Rochester was the only manager who didn't participate. He was en route to his home and couldn't be reached by the Star-Eagle.

If the Bears needed additional confidence, the All-Star selections certainly didn't hurt. All that remained before the start of the play-offs was Vitt's choice of a pitcher. It was a toss-up among Beggs, Donald, and Tamulis.

"Of course, Tamulis is going to be in there," said Vitt. "I still have confidence that he will deliver when the chips are up, but after the shellackings he has taken in his last two games, I don't think it would be wise to open with him." With this thought in mind, Vitt narrowed his choice to Beggs and Donald.

"There was little to choose between the boys' pitching," said Vitt. He was referring to the last time each pitched. Beggs shut out Baltimore in seven innings and Donald allowed four hits and one run in nine innings.

Vitt continued, "But since Beggs pitched the short game, I will start him Tuesday and come back with Donald Wednesday night."

Game 1

OSCAR VITT, AS PREDICTED, SELECTED JOE BEGGS, HIS LEADING hurler and twenty-one-game winner during the regular season, to face the Syracuse Chiefs in the opener. Chiefs' Manager Mike Kelly gave the nod to right-hander Earl Cook, who had posted a 9-8 record on the year.

Through the first four innings, Beggs and Cook matched goose eggs. But in the top of the fifth, center fielder Harry Craft, who earlier in the year had a short stay with the Cincinnati Reds, belted a long home run to break the scoreless tie.

After seven and a half innings, the Chiefs and Cook held on to this slim lead. But in the bottom half of the eighth, with Cook tiring, it looked like the roof might cave in. The Bears loaded the bases on three walks with two out. Vitt sent Buddy Rosar to bat for Willard Hershberger. But Rosar ended the Bears' hopes by dribbling a grounder to Al Glosson at second.

The Chiefs went out easily in the top of the ninth. Entering the bottom half of the inning, it looked like their one run would hold up. Cook quickly retired Nolen Richardson and pinch hitter Vito Tamulis as the meager afternoon crowd of 2,500 headed for the exits. Joe Gordon next stepped up to bat, representing the Bears' fading hope. Murray Robinson, Sports Editor of the *Star-Eagle*, picked up the following action: "Up came Joe Gordon, young Newark second baseman who had rapped out singles in the third and fifth innings, but who had been called out on strikes in the seventh. The score was 1-0 against the Bears and two were down. It was now or never. Cook wound up confidently and the ball started for the plate in a lazy arc. But it never reached there. *Boom!* There was the explosion which we had been waiting to hear all afternoon

— the just, if grisly, punishment for toying with TNT. The slim crowd stiffened and, as though hypnotized, followed the flight of the ball with eyes only and in momentary silence as it sailed over the left field wall. But voices croaked and cackled hysterically as Gordon trotted around the bases with the tying run.

"Another G-Man — Jim Gleeson — awaited Gordon at the plate, shook his hand, and moved up into the batter's box. Out there on the mound, Cook was viciously punching his gloved hand with a ball — *not* the one he had thrown to Gordon. He took his wind-up and tossed a tentative sort of pitch to the Bear outfielder. Umpire VanGraflan called it a ball. He wound up again, and — *boom.* Gleeson's drive rose lazily against the slanting rays of the late afternoon sun, showed white against the blue of the sky, and then settled comfortably in the left field bleachers. He trotted around the bags with the winning run, to be met halfway between third and home by a shrieking mob of fans and fellow players."

On three pitches, the Bears had won the opener, 2-1. The Chiefs were stunned. In the clubhouse after the game, the Bears were delirious. As Hy Goldberg wrote in the *Newark Evening News*, "It's impossible to conceive a more dramatic finish to a ball game. Write it for a fiction periodical and they'd throw it into the wastebasket as too far fetched."

Game 2

GAME NUMBER TWO WAS PLAYED UNDER THE LIGHTS AT RUPPERT Stadium as Oscar Vitt sent his big, strong right-hander Atley Donald, 19-2, to the mound. Facing Donald was Jersey's own Johnny VanderMeer, the most widely heralded rookie in the country in 1936. At Durham in the Piedmont League, VanderMeer won 19 and lost only 6, at the same time striking out a phenomenal 295 batters. Over 12,000 Newark fans turned out to root for the Bears as much as their own home-grown Johnny.

Newark jumped out to an early lead off VanderMeer, picking up a run in the bottom of the second inning. Buddy Rosar doubled and scored on Nolen Richardson's single.

Syracuse came right back in the top half of the fourth with an unearned run to tie the score. Babe Dahlgren set it up with a bad throw. Going into Newark's half of the fourth, it looked like the game was shaping up to be another pitching duel and a repeat of the first game.

But it wasn't for long. The Bears exploded for four runs on five hits, a wild pitch, and an error. The wild and woolly fourth inning was capped by Joe Gordon's second home run in two days, a towering drive over the left field wall.

Newark picked up two more runs in the fifth, padding the lead and putting the game out of reach. Donald allowed the Chiefs another run in the top of the fifth, but shut the door over the last four innings. It was not one of Donald's better games. The right-hander allowed nine hits and walked four. He was constantly in trouble with men on base, but always seemed to be able to find that something extra to get out of the jam. Syracuse, frustrated all evening, stranded a total of eleven runners. The final score went to

Newark, 7-2. On the minus side, Buddy Rosar, who had wrenched his knee while sliding, left for Newark the following day for X-rays. As it turned out, Buddy wouldn't play again until the second game of the Little World Series.

VanderMeer was a big disappointment. Despite all the widespread publicity and local interest, the kid couldn't finish the game and the Bears roughed him up for eleven hits and seven runs. Every man in the Newark lineup collected at least one hit except Donald. It was rough treatment for the local boy as the Bears made it 2-0 in the play-offs. Cries of "four straight" could be heard in the Pullman as the train pulled away from the Lackawanna station and headed for Syracuse.

Game 3

THE THIRD GAME OF THE PLAY-OFFS WAS A LAUGHER! LED BY THE brilliant pitching of Vito Tamulis, 18-6 during the regular season, and the continued "money" hitting of Joe Gordon, Newark buried Syracuse, 8-0.

Apparently Tamulis' experience in the three previous play-off games came in handy. He had pitched in 27 innings, winning two games and losing one, while compiling a remarkable 0.33 ERA.

In this game, the Lithuanian left-hander allowed a single in the first inning and another in the second. After that, he retired the next seventeen men in a row! In all, Tamulis allowed three hits, one walk, and struck out seven — an outstanding clutch pitching performance.

Once again, Gordon, the Bears' solid second baseman, led the fifteen-hit attack with a triple, a double, and a single which drove the celebrated Whitey Moore to an early shower. In the first three games of the series, Gordon went eight-for-fourteen for a .571 average with two home runs and four RBI's. Ironically, Gordon finished next to last among the Newark hitters during the regular season with a .279 average.

After the third straight defeat, the chance of Syracuse winning a game, let alone the play-offs, seemed hopeless. Manager Kelly announced he would start Earl Cook the following night in hopes of extending the series to a fifth game. No doubt Kelly was looking for another brilliant performance from Cook, similar to the one he had pitched in the first game.

Manager Oscar Vitt, with a 3-0 play-off lead, could afford to gamble as he announced that Brooklyn-born Marius Russo, the rookie left-hander, would be his mound choice for the fourth game. But how much of a gamble was the shrewd Vitt really taking? Still fresh in his mind were Russo's last two victories of the season, one of them a three-hit, seven-inning shutout performance against the Syracuse Chiefs.

Pitchers John Niggeling (left) and Marius Russo. Niggeling, a right-handed knuckleballer, helped down the stretch, while the young Russo posed an 8-8 record.

Game 4

IT WAS A COLD, DAMP EVENING AS A MERE 1,500 SPECTATORS, MANY wearing overcoats, filed into Syracuse Municipal Stadium to watch their Chiefs take on the Newark Bears in game number four. True to his word, Vitt sent Marius Russo, the 23-year-old rookie southpaw, to the mound, while Mike Kelly's hopes rested with veteran Earl Cook.

In the third inning, Newark managed to pick up an unearned run. With two out, George McQuinn bounced a hit off the glove of shortstop Eddie Joost. Then Babe Dahlgren grounded to Joost and first baseman Frank McCormick muffed the throw, allowing McQuinn to reach third. When Charlie Keller hit one in the hole between first and second, Al Glossup made a fine play and threw to McCormick in time, but big Frank dropped the ball as McQuinn crossed the plate. It was a frustrating inning for the Chiefs and their giant first baseman.

The Bears added a run in the sixth when the Chiefs' nemesis, Joe Gordon, hit another home run off Cook. It was a tremendous shot to deep right center that rolled to the scoreboard, allowing Gordon to circle the bases for an inside-the-park homer. That was all that Russo needed, even though the Bears picked up an insurance run in the ninth.

Russo pitched brilliantly. The lone Syracuse run came in the seventh on a double by McCormick and two successive fly balls. It was the first run scored by the Chiefs in twenty-two innings! Young Marius allowed five hits, gave up one run, and struck out eight as his fast ball was popping all night. But the amazing statistic for this kid was that he didn't walk one batter over the full nine innings — an outstanding exhibition of control!

The Newark Bears swept the Syracuse Chiefs four straight in devastating fashion, repaying them for their sweep in 1935. Devastating is almost too mild an adjective. Newark pitching allowed only four runs in thirty-six innings, with all four starters — Joe Beggs, Atley Donald, Vito Tamulis, and Marius Russo — turning in complete games.

And the hitting was overpowering. Newark finished the series with an even .300 team average, collecting forty-five hits, twelve of which were for extra bases. Individually, the four top hitters playing in all four games were:

Joe Gordon	.474
Charley Keller	.471
Babe Dahlgren	.375
George McQuinn	.333

It was a fitting and proper ending to an incredible year. Yet there was still more to come, as the Bears moved on to the final play-offs.

18.

Final Play-Offs
Baltimore Orioles

O SCAR VITT, ALWAYS FAST WITH A QUIP AND A comment, was the center of interest after Newark's first successful play-off series in five years. At a gathering of the press in Syracuse, one enthusiastic reporter was gushing about the remarkable finish to the Bears first play-off game, the 2-1 victory on two homers in the ninth.

"That was unusual," Vitt admitted. "But once when I was managing Oakland, we were seven runs behind with two out in the ninth and nobody on base. *And we won the game.*"

Vitt also had the reporters buzzing back in Newark. It started when a long distance phone call from Cincinnati arrived after he had left Syracuse. The Reds were eagerly looking for a manager since Charlie Dressen was fired in early September by General Manager Warren Giles. The dismissal was provoked by Dressen's insistence that Giles give him a commitment for the 1938 season. The speculation was whether the manager Cincinnati was looking for was Vitt.

After arriving in Newark early in the morning, Vitt was asked if he was interested in the Cincinnati job, where losing managers didn't last long. Vitt said he was. "Naturally, I'll listen to any proposition that would advance me in my profession," he said. "But it will have to be very attractive to induce me to leave Newark and the Yankee organization, because I have been treated 100 percent by the fans here and by my bosses, George Weiss and Colonel Ruppert."

During the next week, the Bears would patiently wait for the outcome of the Montreal and Baltimore series, which the Orioles finally won. Vitt tried in vain to schedule light workouts to keep his athletes in fine tune, but rain kept spoiling his plans. The St. Louis Browns even agreed to come to Newark to play an exhibition game after their series with the Red Sox in Boston. Rain in Boston, however, forced the Browns to stay longer to finish the series. The idleness did have its bright side, though. Beggs, Donald, Tamulis, and Russo, the heart of the Bears' pitching staff, were fully rested and ready to meet the Baltimore Orioles.

As was the case with Syracuse, there seemed little point in comparing Newark and Baltimore on the basis of regular season play. Baltimore finished an outlandish 32½ games behind Newark! In the 22 games in which the teams faced each other, the Bears won 18. As one sportswriter put it, "On the strength of that, Newark should be about an eight-to-one shot."

A twenty-to-one shot seemed more realistic. Although Baltimore defeated Montreal 4 out of 5 games, the series left them with some serious scars. Baltimore's playing Manager, Bucky Crouse, was forced to use at least two pitchers in each game, leaving a badly battered staff. As a matter of fact, Crouse himself would only be available for pinch hitting duty due to a wrenched knee. Milton Gray, a .230 hitter, would take his place behind the plate.

Nonetheless, every situation has its bright side, and the case of Baltimore was no different. After losing the opener to Montreal, the Orioles won four straight and the press was touting them as the "hot" club. The other subtle plus that was bandied around was the worn-out cliche, "anything can happen in a short series." The truth of the matter was that the Orioles had one significant and potent weapon going for them — the long ball. They led the league with 159 home runs to the Bears' 142. It wasn't a tremendous advantage, but one that could pose a real problem. However, some felt the shorter distances in Baltimore naturally provided the Orioles with homers. This was partially true, but some credit had to be given to their sluggers.

Right fielder Ab Wright led the Orioles with 37 home runs and

122 RBI's; ex-Newark left fielder George Pucinelli blasted 24 (with 102 RBI's); third baseman Joe Martin belted 22 (with 72 RBI's); first baseman Les Powers had 21 (with 93 RBI's); and right fielder Woodley Abernathy chipped in with another 21 (with 71 RBI's).

Here were five dangerous batters capable of hitting the ball out of the park at any time, spelling sudden victory. The Newark pitchers would have to work carefully to these sluggers, particularly in Baltimore, or it could turn out to be a difficult series for the Bears.

Final Play-Off score card — Newark vs. Baltimore, 1937. Note the 5ᶜ Muriel cigar. They were the good old days.

Game 1

A SLIM CROWD OF 5,000 TURNED OUT AT RUPPERT STADIUM TO watch the Newark Bears take on the free and easy swinging Baltimore Orioles — the team with everything to gain and nothing to lose. In the stands were a number of baseball dignitaries — Yankee Manager Joe McCarthy, scouts Paul Krichell and Gene McCann, William DeWitt, Vice President of the St. Louis Browns, and coach Gabby Street. It was rumored DeWitt was interested in acquiring several of the Bears.

Oscar Vitt, as he did against Syracuse, opened this important series with his twenty-one-game winner, Joe Beggs. Bucky Crouse chose his tall right-hander, Hy Vandenberg, who had posted a 15-17 record over the regular season.

After three and a half innings, the score stood tied at 0-0. Both right-handers were practically matching each other pitch for pitch. Beggs had a slight edge as he retired twelve consecutive Orioles and looked unbeatable. In the bottom of the fourth, Baltimore's defense fell apart. Joe Gordon led off with a scratch hit. Jimmy Gleeson then smacked a routine double play ball to Bill Cissell at second. Cissell threw to shortstop Chet "Wimpy" Wilburn to get the force on Gordon, but Wimpy's throw to first was wild, sending Gleeson to second base. George McQuinn failed to hit for out number two. However, he was followed by Babe Dahlgren, who singled over second to put Gleeson at third. Vandenberg, not helping his own cause, uncorked a wild pitch past catcher Milton Gray. When Gleeson tried to score, Gray's throw to the plate was also wild. Gleeson scored and Dahlgren wound up on third. Charlie Keller then drove in the second and final run of the inning with a double to left field and the Bears led, 2-0. They wouldn't score again during the game.

But it really didn't matter. All eyes were fixed on Beggs. It was his night. In the fifth, the Orioles went down in order again — fifteen in a row! Beggs was invincible. In the sixth, he mowed them down again — eighteen in a row! Beggs was brilliant. The slim crowd could feel the tension mounting, they could sense history in the making.

First up in the seventh was shortstop Wimpy Wilburn, a .255 hitter. Wilburn timed a change of pace and lined it back off Beggs' shin. The ball deflected to McQuinn near first base, who fielded it a split second too late to get Wimpy, who had crossed the bag for a base hit. Ironically, Beggs would retire the next nine batters in a row without a ball leaving the infield! It was the best performance by a Newark pitcher in thirty-one years.

"It was the best game of my life," Beggs commented later, "and no one's fault but my own that I didn't get a perfect game. Wilburn hit a butterfly (a half-speed drooper), but it wasn't hit hard. The ball hit me on the shins and rolled off my wrist as I tried to get my glove on it."

The final statistics showed that Beggs had pitched to twenty-eight Baltimore batters, allowed no runs, gave up one hit, struck out eight, walked none, and allowed only one ball to reach the outfield, a high lofter easily gathered in by Bob Seeds. It was the best performance of his three-year professional career and one of the most important nights of his life.

After the game, McCarthy, who must have had pleasant thoughts all night, was asked what he thought of Beggs. "What can you think of a fellow after he pitches a one-hit game?" was Marse Joe's laconic reply. Beggs had a quip of his own. Knowing of McCarthy's presence, Beggs jokingly told the press, "I thought I better work hard."

Game 2

A MERE 3,500 FANS CAME OUT TO RUPPERT STADIUM ON THURSDAY afternoon to watch game number two against the Baltimore Orioles. Ironically, one of the 3,500 was Frank Shaughnessy, the league's President, who would later be an eyewitness to an unusual rhubarb. Oscar Vitt sent Atley Donald to the mound while Bucky Crouse selected his best pitcher, Bill Lohrman (20-11), to try and stop the Newark machine.

Through the first eight glorious innings, the taste of victory grew more delicious for Newark as the Bears showed little respect for Lohrman. The 24-year-old right-hander was battered for fourteen hits and six runs. Meanwhile, Donald was pitching a strong ball game. Except for the fourth inning, when the Orioles roughed him up for two runs on three hits, Donald had the game well under control.

The top of the ninth began quite harmlessly. Although Babe Dahlgren booted George Puccinelli's ground ball, the next two batters, Glenn Chapman and Ab Wright, failed to hit. Puccinelli eventually reached second. Donald was only one out away from victory. Bucky Crouse prolonged the outcome by singling. Puccinelli scored and the game sat at 6-3. The next batter was third baseman Joe Martin, who had hit 23 home runs during the regular season. Joe promptly picked out a pitch he liked and — *bang* — the score was 6-5. Apparently Donald was tiring. Crouse next sent up Woodley Abernathy, who had hit 21 home runs, to pinch hit for Lohrman. Vitt, fully aware that Abernathy could tie the game with one swipe of the bat, elected to stay with Donald. Abernathy singled to center. Vitt had seen enough. He signaled for Spud Chandler.

With the tying run on first, Chandler would face Wimpy

Wilburn. The little shortstop in his three previous appearances had fanned all three times. He was way overdue. Chandler worked carefully to Wilburn, ultimately setting him up for the controversial pitch, which moments later Umpire Bick Campbell called a third strike. Wilburn, frustrated all afternoon, became enraged and began pushing and swinging at Campbell. Several Orioles joined into the melee, with eventually both benches getting into an uncontrolled free-for-all. It took cooler heads and the special police to break-up the fight.

After the game, eyewitness Shaughnessy gave his complete support to Campbell and put full blame for the fist fight on Wilburn.

"The ball was right through the middle," the President said, referring to the third strike. "But for the fact that none of his swings hit the umpire and the club would suffer more than the player, I would give him a suspension that he would long remember. However, I am going to fine him after I receive an official report from the umpires, and he may remember that long enough to realize that the International League will not tolerate such conduct under any circumstances, and in this case there wasn't any excuse for even a word of protest, let alone a fight." Wilburn was fined $25.

Many thought the Wilburn-Campbell incident would make the third game scheduled for Oriole Park in Maryland an ugly affair. Baltimore possessed highly partisan fans who often threw pop bottles at visiting players and umpires with or without provocation. Twice during the regular season, the Bears found themselves in the middle of such riotous scenes. They were well prepared, at least mentally, for the fireworks when they arrived in Maryland for game number three.

Game 3

THE PITCHING ROTATION FOR THE THIRD GAME CALLED FOR VITO Tamulis to open at Oriole Park, but Manager Oscar Vitt decided to start lanky right-hander Jack Fallon instead. Tamulis had never been very successful in Oriole Park, while Fallon had beaten Baltimore four times, twice in relief during the regular season. This move also gave Vitt the flexibility of using Tamulis in an emergency situation, if necessary. Pete Sivess, the right-hander with a 15-5 record, went to the mound for the Orioles.

Baltimore nibbled away at Fallon for one run in the first and two more in the third. Two of the three runs were unearned. The Bears picked up a run in the second and another in the fourth on Charlie Keller's mammoth home run over the 387-foot center field fence. The score remained 3-2 in favor of Baltimore through the first six innings.

The seventh inning started off innocently enough — with two out and Nolen Richardson on first base, thanks to Wimpy Wilburn's error. Sivess next faced clutch hitting Joe Gordon, who promplty doubled, sending Richardson to third. With runners on second and third, Sivess still had an opportunity to get out of the inning by retiring Jimmy Gleeson. The big left fielder had other ideas, however, as he singled to center, scoring both runners and putting the Bears out in front, 4-3. As center fielder Glenn Chapman bobbled the ball, Gleeson alertly took second. George McQuinn was then given an intentional pass, setting up the force at second or third. But Sivess, pitching too carefully to .340 hitter Babe Dahlgren, walked him to load the bases. Now he had to face Keller, the league's leading hitter at .353, who had singled and homered in his two previous trips to the plate. Keller, with one swing of the bat, doubled in two more runs, giving the Bears a 6-3 lead.

But the Orioles weren't giving up easily. They came right back to score two runs in the bottom of the seventh, narrowing the Bears' lead to 6-5. John Niggeling, the 34-year-old veteran, came on in relief of Fallon. The knuckleballer turned in a brilliant clutch performance, retiring all eight men he faced. However, he did have some help from Keller in the crucial seventh inning. With two runs already home and the tying run on second, the rookie right fielder made the prize catch of the game and maybe the series, a "leaping one-handed grab" of Hy Vandenberg's liner.

The Bears added an insurance run in the eighth, with the final score ending at 7-5. Fallon gained the victory. Newark's third straight win set the stage for the dramatic fourth game under the lights. If the Bears won, it would be the first time in the five-year history of the International League play-offs that a team had made a clean sweep of both series.

Righthander Jack Fallon (left) and southpaw Phil Page. Young Fallon impressed Vitt so much during the season that he called him his "best pitcher." Veteran Page joined the Bears late in the season, but proved valuable in the play-offs.

Game 4

IN THE WILD AND WOOLLY FOURTH GAME, THE NEWARK BEARS made International League history by defeating the Baltimore Orioles, 10-7, for the second consecutive sweep in the play-offs — eight straight victories. The Bears outhit, outscored, outfielded, and even outran the Orioles, confirming their superiority all season over the entire league. As Hy Goldberg reported in the *Newark News*, "The minor leagues seldom have seen a mightier 'money' ball club."

It was an unusual game from a number of standpoints. First, Baltimore scored all their runs and collected all their hits in the sixth inning — seven of each. At the time, they were losing, 5-0. Never losing heart, this determined bunch of athletes managed to explode for seven runs off starter Marius Russo to momentarily take a 7-5 lead. Second, some daring base running by Charlie Keller and Bob Seeds resulted in two runs. In the second inning, Keller scored from second base on a routine fly to right field when Ab Wright made a careless return. Another run was set up when Seeds raced from first to third on Willard Hershberger's sacrifice bunt in the ninth. Third, knuckleball specialist John Niggeling relieved for the second consecutive night (apparently Vitt couldn't get enough of a good thing) and turned in another outstanding performance as he pitched to only nine men over the last three innings, protecting the slim lead.

If there were any individual heroes in the game, one would have to consider Seeds along with Niggeling. The center fielder accounted for six runs — scoring three and driving in three. In the seventh, his three-run homer, the first in eight play-off games, put the Bears out in front, 8-7, and all but broke the heart of the

Orioles.

After eight consecutive play-off victories, Manager Oscar Vitt, looking over the Newark statistics, was no doubt shaking his head in amazement. The Bears were red hot. Charlie Keller and Joe Gordon led the team in hitting, while Joe Beggs and Atley Donald had each posted two victories — tops on the pitching staff. As a team, the Bears batted .305 in the eight games, with the four leading hitters compiling the following records:

	G.	AB.	R.	H.	2b.	3b.	HR.	RBI.	AV.
Charlie Keller	8	33	6	15	2	1	1	7	.455
Joe Gordon	8	39	7	15	4	1	3	7	.385
Jimmy Gleeson	8	32	8	11	2	1	1	3	.344
George McQuinn	8	34	6	11	0	0	0	6	.324

In the first eight play-off games, Newark had things all their way. When they needed pitching, they got it. When they needed hitting, they got it. And when the big defensive play was called for, they got that too. With the Little World Series near at hand, the Bears were confident, poised, and at the moment, unbeatable. In addition, they were now almost at full strength. Buddy Rosar, injured with a wrenched knee since the second play-off game against Syracuse, was in uniform and said he was ready to play. But Vitt wouldn't use him until the third game. On the minus side of the ledger, there was very little. Starter Steve Sundra, out of action since the removal of his appendix late in the season, was still on the inactive list, but he was the only exception. So the Bears were entering the Little World Series at the top of their game, mentally and physically. But unlike Syracuse and Baltimore, Columbus represented a much tougher opponent. Newark was in for an early and unexpected surprise.

Back Row: Marius Russo, Steve Sundra, Phil Page, Jack Fallon, Nolen Richardson, Bob Seeds, Babe Dahlgren, Charlie Keller, Atley Donald. **Front Row:** Jimmie Mack, trainer, George McQuinn, Jimmie Gleeson, Francis Kelleher, Joe Beggs, Oscar Vitt, Manager, Willard Hershberger, Vito Tamulis, Joe Gordon, Buddy Rosar, Joe Fixter, and announcer.

19.

Little World Series At Newark

PRIOR TO THE PLAY-OFFS AND LONG BEFORE THE NEWARK Bears swept both Syracuse and Baltimore, George Weiss and Colonel Ruppert engaged in a brief, but revealing telephone conversation. "Four straight in each play-off series suit you all right, Colonel?" asked Weiss. "I always vote a 'four straight' ticket," answered the Colonel. "And see that you do the same thing in that Little World Series."

Whether Weiss and Ruppert were serious about this or just joking, one will never know. It is a fact, however, that at least half the conversation did come true and Manager Oscar Vitt and the Bears were anxious to fulfill the other half by sweeping the series against the Columbus Red Birds, the pennant winners of the American Association.

Realistically, another sweep seemed unlikely, particularly if history was any indicator. In every previous Little World Series, only one club made a clean sweep and that was Toronto's 1926 team, which took five in a row from Louisville. At that time, a nine-game series was played.

The 1937 Little World Series was more than just a classic confrontation to determine supremacy in the minor leagues. It provided, for the first time, an interesting clash between two great chain organizations — Ruppert's New York Yankees and Branch Rickey's St. Louis Cardinals. In a much larger sense, it was the Yankee empire taking on the far-flung Cardinal farm system. It was the Yankee brain trust against the Cardinal brain trust. It boiled down to Ruppert versus Rickey.

Not surprisingly, the two teams were closely matched, with the Bears holding a slim edge. One American Association expert claimed that if the Bears' outfield was better than the Red Birds', it didn't belong in the minor leagues. That expert was closer to the truth than he realized. Many baseball experts believed the entire Newark team could easily hold their own in the major leagues. The Columbus outfield consisted of Enos Slaughter in right, Johnny Rizzo in left, and Lynn King in center. Slaughter and Charlie Keller had amazingly similar records. Both were only twenty-one years of age and both were rookies in Double A ball. Each led his respective league in batting: Slaughter with a towering .382 and Keller with a handsome .353. Slaughter, like Keller, would eventually star in the major leagues.

Enos "Country" Slaughter was a Cardinal institution for thirteen exciting years between 1938 and 1953, with three years out for military service. He remained in the major leagues for nineteen years, finishing with a lifetime batting average of an even .300. He also compiled a .291 average in five World Series. He was a hard-nosed competitor, right out of the old "gas house gang." Winning was everything to him. Even during the twilight of his career with the Yankees, Kansas City, and Milwaukee, when he was often relegated to pinch hitting roles, Slaughter would beat you with the clutch hit. It's no surprise, then, that Slaughter ranks tenth among major league players with the most pinch hits — 77.

Johnny Rizzo, the Columbus left fielder, was no slouch, either. He was third among American Association hitters with a .358 average. Rizzo belted 38 doubles, 18 triples, 21 homers, and drove in 123 runs — not a bad season's work. Unlike Slaughter, Rizzo's major league career was that of a journeyman. He played for five years with four different teams — Pittsburgh, Cincinnati, Philadelphia, and Brooklyn.

Ironically, Johnny turned in his best major league performance during his rookie year in 1938. With Pittsburgh, he batted .301, smacked 23 homers, and drove in 111 runs. After that, it was all downhill. However, he did finish with a lifetime batting average of

.270.

Sandwiched between the two power hitters was center fielder and lead-off man, Lynn King, who sported a .302 batting average during the regular season. King's major league career was much shorter than Slaughter's and Rizzo's. He played for the Cardinals for only three years before hanging up his spikes in 1939.

In the infield, Newark had the edge in both batting and defense. For Columbus, Dick Siebert, a .318 hitter, was at first base, Jimmy Jordan (.285) played second, Jimmy "Skeeter" Webb (.286) played shortstop, and Justin Stein (.274) was at third. This was an outstanding infield that would eventually find its way to the major leagues. Jordan and Stein both had abbreviated careers, while Siebert and Webb played considerably longer.

Siebert was a major league first baseman for eleven years and turned in consistent seasons with the Philadelphia Athletics from 1939 to 1945, ending his career with a respectable .282 average. Webb played eleven of his twelve years in the American League with four teams — Cleveland, Chicago, Detroit, and Philadelphia. The highlight of the tiny shortstop's career came with Detroit in 1945. Skeeter played in 118 games during the regular season and in all seven World Series contests as the Tigers whipped the Cubs for the World Championship. This was the Tiger team that boasted such great names as Hank Greenberg, Rudy York, Roy Cullenbine, Hal Newhouser, Virgil Trucks, Dizzy Trout, and Stubby Overmire.

Behind the plate, the Bears seemed to have another marked advantage. They had youth while Columbus had experience. Jack Crouch, at the age of thirty-four, batted .223 in 89 games, while Frank Grube at thirty-two hit .213 in 17 games. Obviously, the careers of both catchers were behind them. Crouch had short stays in the majors dating back to 1930 and Grube went back to the 1931 Chicago White Sox.

It was in the pitching department, however, that Newark excelled. In spite of Steve Sundra's absence, it was still virtually impossible for Columbus to match the remarkable records posted by Atley Donald (19-2), Joe Beggs (21-4), and Vito Tamulis (18-6). The Red Birds did have a well balanced staff, however, with Bill

McGee (17-7), Max Lanier (10-4), Max Macon (21-12), John Chambers (12-7), Mort Cooper (13-13), and Nelson Potter (11-11).

Aside from Chambers, the rest of the Red Birds went on to enjoy major league careers beyond 1937. Mort Cooper was the most celebrated pitcher, starring for eleven years in the majors and finishing with an extraordinary record of 128-75. Cooper strung three twenty-game seasons together from 1942 to 1944, posting records of 22-7, 21-8, and 22-7, respectively. Lanier was a respectable pitcher, too. The rangy southpaw pitched twelve of his fourteen years with the Cardinals, winning 108 and dropping 82. Ironically, Max never won 20 games in a season. Potter pitched in both the American and National Leagues for twelve years, putting together three fine seasons with the St. Louis Browns during the war. From 1943 to 1945, he won 44 and lost 23 and his ERA was always under 3.00. McGee spent eight years in the National League, turning in impressive performances in both 1939 (12-5) and 1940 (16-10). Macon pitched six years with three different National League teams — St. Louis, Brooklyn, and Boston — but only managed a flimsy 17-19 lifetime record.

The manager of the Columbus Red Birds was none other than Burt Shotton, the man who eventually became the toast of Flatbush. By 1937, Shotton had already managed six full seasons (unsuccessfully) for the Philadelphia Phillies from 1928 to 1933 and one game (successfully) for the Cincinnati Reds in 1934. Shotton's fame, however, came in 1947 when he piloted the Brooklyn Dodgers to a pennant while Leo Durocher, suspended for one year by Commissioner Albert "Happy" Chandler, sat in the stands in Ebbets Field. The following year, "The Lip" was back and Shotton was out. But he wasn't gone for long. Halfway through the 1948 season, Durocher shocked the baseball world by agreeing to manage the bitter rival New York Giants and Shotton was back again. This time, the Dodgers finished third. The next year, Shotton won another pennant, but lost the World Series to the Yankees. After finishing second in 1950, Shotton retired, ending his eleven-year career as a major league manager.

So the scene was set for a classic match-up between the exciting

and spirited Columbus Red Birds and the mighty Newark Bears —
a club the Newark fans had stamped with the mark of invincibility.

Little World Series score card (outside) — Newark vs. Columbus, 1937. Back cover features the men of the media who covered the Bears all season — Hy Goldberg of the Newark Evening News, Mike Gaven, Newark Star Eagle, Gus Falzer, Sunday Call, Willie Klein, the Newark Ledger, and announcer Earl Harper.

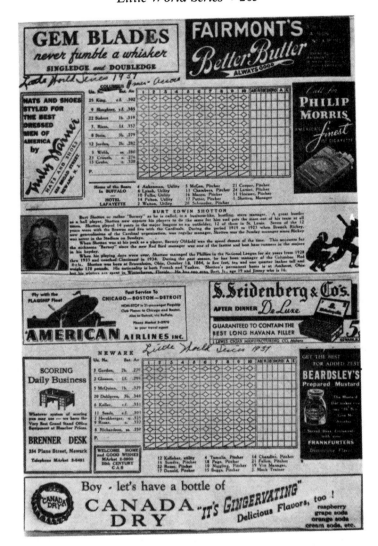

Little World Series score card (inside) — Newark vs. Columbus, 1937. The photograph at the left is of the smiling Burt Shotton, Manager of the Red Birds.

Game 1

IT WAS A WARM, BRIGHT SUNNY DAY AT RUPPERT STADIUM AS Newark Mayor Meyer C. Ellenstein tossed out the first ball to open the nineteenth Little World Series between the International League and the American Association.

A disappointing 6,370 paying customers were on hand to watch the opener, no doubt reflecting a weekday game and possibly fan overconfidence in the "unbeatable" Bears. Whatever the reason for the slim turnout, it was not lacking in dignitaries. The Yankee official family was represented by Colonel Jacob Ruppert, Ed Barrow, George Weiss, Joe McCarthy, George Perry, and scouts Paul Krichell, Gene McCann, and Bill Essick.

As expected, Manager Oscar Vitt chose his ace right-hander, Joe Beggs (21-4), while the studious-looking, bespectacled Burt Shotton pulled a fast one — switching suddenly from the left-handed fastballer Max Macon (21-12) to right-hander Jimmy Chambers (12-7), a junk pitcher with a good curve.

In the bottom of the third, the Bears picked up a quick run off Chambers. Nolen Richardson led off with a double to left center, advanced to third on Beggs' sacrifice bunt, and scored when Joe Gordon lined a bullet to Johnny Rizzo in left field.

But Columbus came right back in the top of the fifth to tie the score at 1-1. Newark bounced back in their half of the inning, scoring two more runs and gaining a temporary 3-1 lead. Gordon doubled down the left field line, Jimmy Gleeson walked, and George McQuinn dropped a perfect bunt between Chambers and Stein. All hands were safe. With the bases loaded, Burt Shotton brought in Nelson Potter, a tall right-hander. Potter quickly fanned Babe Dahlgren, but Charlie Keller flied to Enos Slaughter in right, scoring Gordon. When third baseman Justin Stein allowed Slaughter's throw to get by, Gleeson scampered home with another run.

The Red Birds were not to be denied, however. In the top half of the seventh, Jimmy Jordan doubled down the left field line and Skeeter Webb reached first on Dahlgren's boot. Jack Crouch then dumped a bunt between Dahlgren and Beggs, which neither could field, and the bases were quickly loaded. That brought Potter to the plate and forced Shotton to make a crucial decision. Shotton, realizing his powerful fastballer was in command, let him bat for himself. Potter promptly repaid Shotton for his confidence with a sharp single up the middle, scoring Jordan and Webb and tying the score at 3-3. Lynn King sacrificed and Slaughter, the American Association's leading hitter, received an intentional pass, loading the bases with only one out. Dick Siebert wasted no time, smacking a long single to center that scored two more runs, chasing Beggs and giving Columbus a 5-3 lead.

The Bears made a valiant effort in the ninth when Gordon belted a solo shot into the left field stands, making the score 5-4. But that was all Newark could get. Potter shut the door. Pitching superbly, he allowed only two hits over the last five innings. The final score went to Columbus, 5-4.

After the game, Vitt offered a frank and honest excuse. "We should have scouted them. But now that we have lost and in doing so found out what they have, we have charged that loss up to experimental work, and shall proceed to go to work on them starting tonight.

"We were given to understand that we had to worry about only two batters, Enos Slaughter and John Rizzo, and we found out all we could about what they liked and did not like to hit. As a result, we pitched to them perfectly, but the last four guys in the batting order, including a relief pitcher, got seven of their nine hits. If those fellows could hit like that every day, they would be higher in the batting order and their averages would be something more than .280. And I might add, a few of their blows were nothing to brag about.

"Beggs had terribly tough luck; they had only one clean hit off him until the seventh and I'll shoulder full responsibility for leaving him in there to lose the game after they loaded the bases with none out," continued the Newark Manager.

"I went out there with all intentions of bringing in Russo to pitch to that Potter. But Joe says, 'Os, I still have plenty.' What was I to do? The boy had pitched out of more difficult situations all season. Nine times out of ten he would have got out that big apple knocker [meaning Potter, whose single tied the score] and I believe in playing percentage. As long as he said he still had his stuff, I was willing to string along with him. Why, no one had hit a ball really hard in a month.

"Then he allows those two hits and he has to lose his ball game. When Siebert hit him square on the nose and brought in those winning runs, I knew he was through. Up until that time, he pitched as well as he had in either of those play-off games, but the boys made it too tough for him. As for our mistakes, both offensively and defensively, there's nothing much to say. We simply made 'em and I hope we won't make 'em again.

"Every Newark fan knows better than to guard third and let the winning run go to first base, and Keller could take the same chances on the bases in a dozen games and not get caught. It simply wasn't our day.

"I made a mistake myself by putting in Tamulis to bat for Niggeling instead of a right-hander hitter. Having never seen Potter before, I didn't realize his screwball was as tough as he showed up. He also made Jimmy Gleeson look bad in the ninth, but next time, a right-hander hitter, say Rosar or Kelleher, would probably murder him. Gordon really hit it, didn't he? Say, if you want to write about something, why don't you write about Gordon?"

The next day, with the defeat behind him, Vitt's comments to the press were much more optimistic. "But why all the hue and cry? Donald will get them tonight and we'll win the next three after that. Obviously both clubs were tightened up yesterday. They should be more natural this evening."

Game 2

THE NEWARK FANS CAME EARLY FOR GAME NUMBER TWO UNDER the lights. They came by the hundreds, by the thousands. They came from Newark, from Jersey City, the Oranges, West New York, Hoboken, Plainfield. They came from New York City; they came from Brooklyn. They came from Staten Island and Long Island. Over 17,000 partisan bodies jammed Ruppert Stadium, a near-capacity crowd.

As Vitt told the press earlier in the day, Atley Donald, who finished the regular season with a superb 19-2 record, would start on the mound to stop Columbus. Burt Shotton countered with his winningest pitcher, left-hander Max Macon (21-12).

By the sixth inning, the surprising Red Birds had built a 4-0 lead and one could sense the 17,000 fans were getting restless. Although Donald was far from sharp, the rookie right-hander deserved a much better fate. All four Columbus runs were unearned! It was a case of continued sloppy defense.

Inspired by the hometown crowd, the slumbering Bears came to life. They scored single runs in both the sixth and seventh innings, narrowing the lead to 4-2. But in the bottom of the eighth, Newark really gave the 17,000 something to scream about. Nelson Potter, who had stood the Bears on their ears the previous afternoon, was back on the mound in relief of Macon. George McQuinn led off the inning and was safe on an error by first baseman Dick Siebert. Babe Dahlgren followed by lashing a double to left, sending McQuinn to third. With the Newark crowd still screaming, an overenthusiastic fan jumped from the lower grandstand and raced to second base to offer Babe a drink. Time was called as the umpires led him back to the stands. When play resumed, Potter had lost his concentration, couldn't find the plate, and walked the dangerous Charlie Keller. The bases were now loaded with nobody out and the fans were going wild.

Shotton went out to the mound and sent Potter to the showers. In came right-hander Bill McGee (17-7), making his first appearance in the series. The first batter to face McGee was Bob Seeds. McGee blew a third strike by him for out number one. Buddy Rosar, in the lineup for the first time since injuring his knee in the second play-off game against Syracuse, fouled to catcher Frank Grube for the second out. The Bears hadn't scored and the faithful Newark fans let out a disappointing sigh. With the bases still loaded and two men out, it all came down to the weakest hitter on the club, shortstop Nolen Richardson. The situation looked bleak as McGee put Richardson in the hole with two quick strikes. On the next pitch, however, the .258 hitter lined a sharp single to right, scoring McQuinn and Dahlgren with the tying runs. The roar of the crowd was deafening as the inning ended with the game deadlocked, 4-4.

Spud Chandler then came on the mound to pitch for the Bears. Both teams failed to score in both the ninth and tenth innings. In the top of the eleventh, as the *Newark News* reported, "Chandler encountered misfortune similar to that which befell Donald earlier in the evening," Johnny Rizzo opened with a single to center and when Seeds bobbled the ball, he raced to second with the potential lead run. As everyone anticipated, Justin Stein sacrificed Rizzo to third. There was one out. Vitt brought his infield in for a possible play at the plate. With the infield drawn close, Jimmy Jordan lined a shot that barely got by Gordon's outstretched glove. Rizzo scored the go-ahead run.

In the bottom of the eleventh, McGee fanned the good hitting Vito Tamulis, who was batting for Chandler, and then struck out the long ball hitting Gordon. Jimmy Gleeson walked, putting the tying run on first and keeping the Bears' fading hopes alive. But Bill McGee rose to the occassion, chalking up his third strikeout of the inning by fanning the always dangerous George McQuinn. The final score again went to Columbus, 5-4.

After Newark's second straight defeat, a disheartened Oscar Vitt waxed philosophical. "Why must we suddenly encounter a slump at a time like this?

"We pounded along all through the season, winning game after game and series after series, and I'd say to myself, 'They have to crack sometime,' but they didn't let up even when we were miles in front of the rest of the league.

"And I began to think that here was a ball club that felt neither stress nor strain under any circumstances and simply couldn't slow down. But that mid-season slump finally caught up with us and at a very bad time indeed."

Branch Rickey, in victory, commented magnanimously on the Bears' early demise. "Newark has a great ball club," he said. "It's bound to come along and I don't believe this series is in the bag for us yet, although we have a two-game lead."

A local sportswriter was not quite as kind in his remarks about the Bears. "Last night, in a comedy of errors, they lost their second in a row to the American Association champions by a score of 5-4 in Ruppert Stadium, and the stay-ups blinked in amazement as Os Vitt's bright young men floundered about in confusion."

Game 3

ANOTHER BUMPER GATHERING OF OVER 17,000 PARTISAN spectators turned out to witness game number three. Regardless of the outcome of the series, it would be the last ball game to be played at Ruppert Stadium in 1937. The total three-game attendance figures reached 40,717, exhibiting solid support for the local heroes.

Oscar Vitt chose southpaw Vito Tamulis, 18-6 over the regular season, to try to stop the confident red-hot Red Birds. Tamulis was well rested; he hadn't pitched in fourteen days. His last outing had been the third game of the semifinal play-offs against Syracuse when he spun a brilliant three-hit shutout, winning the game, 8-0. Burt Shotton selected his strong, fireballing right-hander, Mort Cooper (13-13).

Columbus reached Tamulis early, scoring two runs in the first inning, much to the disgust of the Newark fans. With one out, Enos Slaughter and Johnny Rizzo rapped back-to-back singles. Dick Siebert then bounced back to the box — an easy double play ball. Tamulis wheeled and fired to second, but the usually reliable Nolen Richardson dropped the throw! The bases were now loaded. Justin Stein followed with a looping fly to short right and Charlie Keller received an error as he failed to hold it, allowing Slaughter to score the first run. Moments later, Jimmy Jordan flied to Keller and this time Charlie caught it. But it didn't stop Rizzo from tagging up and scoring run number two.

The Bears fought right back in their half of the first, however. Jimmy Gleeson doubled. George McQuinn singled. Babe Dahlgren doubled. Charlie Keller walked. Then Bob Seeds flied to right and Willard Hershberger singled to left. When the inning was finally over, three runs had crossed the plate, Cooper was taking a shower, the Bears were on top, 3-2, and the Newark fans were delighted.

Through the next five innings, it looked like that was all Tamulis would need as the chunky southpaw blanked the Red Birds. But in the top of the seventh, Vito faltered slightly and the Red Birds took advantage of the opportunity. Lynn King walked to open the inning. The next batter was Enos Slaughter, the league's leading hitter at .382. The "Country" farm boy was held hitless in two previous games and during the second game, he embarrassingly struck out four times! The dangerous Slaughter was overdue and everyone knew it. Tamulis reared back and fired a fastball. Slaughter swung and lifted a lazy fly to deep right field, which moved Keller back against the wall. As the ball descended, Keller leaped high and extended his outstretched glove as far as it would go, but the ball eluded him by "inches," dropping into the front row of the bleachers. Columbus was back on top, 4-3. The Red Birds added two more insurance runs in the eighth, giving them a more comfortable 6-3 lead.

Although no one knew it at the time, the turning point in the game came early. In the bottom of the first inning, when Cooper was blasted from the mound, Shotton once again made the perfect call to the bull pen. This time it was Max Lanier, a 21-year-old southpaw who had won 10 and lost 4 during the season. The rookie pitched brilliantly, blanking the powerful Bears for seven and one-third innings and yielding three skimpy singles. But he did need some help in the bottom of the ninth. With a 6-3 lead, Shotton was taking no chances. With two out, Justin Stein booted Babe Dahlgren's roller to third and a walk to Bob Seeds caused Shotton to replace the kid with the Red Birds' ace reliever, Nelson Potter — his third straight appearance. Potter easily induced Willard Hershberger to loft a lazy fly to center to end the game. Again the final score went to Columbus, 6-3.

20.

On To Columbus

I MMEDIATELY AFTER THEIR THIRD STRAIGHT DEFEAT IN THE series, the Newark Bears hopped on a Pullman and sped westward to Columbus, Ohio. They were a dejected lot of players. A few of the more hearty ones tried to smile and present an optimistic face. But most found it too difficult to hide their true feelings. In their hearts, they were horribly ashamed of their pitiful exhibition.

Fans and casual spectators who had seen the Bears rise to such glorious heights all season long couldn't believe what was happening. Their hitting was weak and untimely. Their pitching was only fair. Their defence was dreadful. In short, they were not the same ball club. It was hard to imagine this talented team could experience such a total collapse. No ball club in baseball history was ever built up so high for such a terrible let-down.

The Bears were on the brink of elimination. Down in the Little World Series, 3-0, the odds were heavily stacked against them. To win four straight at Columbus against the now jubilant and confident Red Birds would take a miracle.

Forty-two years later, Jack Fallon recalled the gloomy atmosphere. "After losing three straight to Columbus, I do not think anybody thought we would emerge the Little World Champions. Evidence this by the fact that we all made preparations to bring our wives to Columbus, prior to the third game in Newark. None made the trip."

In spite of the hopeless outlook, Oscar Vitt tried to maintain a spirit of courage. He selected Joe Beggs to pitch game number four in Columbus. "He was our mainstay all season and if we are going down, we are going down with our best," commented the Newark Manager.

Bob Seeds, on a more optimistic note, remarked causally in his Texas drawl, "We've won four straight ball games several times this year. Perhaps we can do it again."

Center fielder Bob Seeds (left) and shortstop Nolen Richardson. Seeds led the team in RBI's with 112 and Richardson was the glue in the infield.

Game 4

TRUE TO HIS WORD, ON THIS SATURDAY NIGHT IN COLUMBUS, Oscar Vitt sent Joe Beggs to the mound in one last valiant effort to stop the Red Birds. Burt Shotton gave the nod to Bill McGee, the right-hander who struck out the side in the ninth inning of game number two.

Through the first five innings, Beggs and McGee hooked up in a tough pitchers' duel with the Bears desperately hanging on to a slim 2-1 edge.

But in the top of the sixth, more than 10,000 partisan Columbus fans saw the roof cave in on McGee. Jimmy Gleeson opened the inning with a single to right. George McQuinn then flied out. Trying to build an insurance run, Vitt gambled and gave Gleeson the green light. The fleet-footed left fielder stole second, putting him in scoring position. This brought Frank Kelleher to the plate. Kelleher was playing third base in place of Babe Dahlgren.

In the first three games, the Babe had gone two-for-fourteen and had committed three errors. Vitt made the switch and left Kelleher in the cleanup slot. The move paid off. Kelleher bounced a single up the middle to score Gleeson from second. Charlie Keller followed with a double to right center, sending Kelleher to third. Bob Seeds then rapped a clutch single to center, driving in both Kelleher and Keller. The fourth and final run of the ining scored when Enos Slaughter dropped Willard Hershberger's long fly to right and Seeds romped home. Shotton brought in Nelson Potter for his fourth consecutive game to get the last two outs of the inning.

From that point on, the game was a breeze. Newark added single runs in the seventh and ninth innings, but they had more than enough as Beggs kept the Red Birds well under control. The Pennsylvania right-hander went the full distance, scattering eight hits, walking one, and allowing one unearned run. It was an outstanding clutch performance and the Bears picked up their first victory, avoiding a sweep of the series and excruciating embarrassment.

The 10,201 partisan spectators went home disappointed — not only by the loss of the game and a clean series sweep, but also by the loss of their peppery second baseman, Jimmy Jordan. In the fifth inning, Jordan fractured his right ankle when Hershberger spiked him on a force play at second. He was carried off the field and replaced by utility man Pat Ankenman.

It was a rough day for the high-flying Red Birds. They committed five errors, lost the game, 8-1, and watched their star second baseman suffer an unfortunate injury. However, most baseball people still thought it was simply a matter of time. Columbus needed to win only one game in their own park. They felt it was impossible for the Bears to win four straight.

It rained the following day in Columbus, which turned out to be a break for Newark since it gave Atley Donald some more time to rest. In addition, the shellacking the Bears handed out the previous evening seemed to recharge the club. Even some of the usually quiet players, who hadn't spoken two words all season, began to voice their optimism.

"We broke out of that terrible batting slump Saturday night and no Columbus pitcher is going to stop our young sluggers now," said Nolen Richardson.

"And that rain yesterday means as much to us as our errors meant to Columbus at Newark," added Bob Seeds.

"Yes, sir, Atley Donald has now had three full days of rest and the Columbus boys are surely not going to find him any easier to hit than they did in the second game. And it is almost impossible for us to hand them as many runs as we did in that game," uttered Keller.

"Nice talking," said a beaming Vitt. "More like the old spirit. If they can go out and win that one tonight, Tammy will even the series up tomorrow night and Joe Beggs will take 'em in the seventh. Great guys in the clutch, Tammy and Beggsie, and they should be a breeze with three days rest, providing, of course, our fielding is up to par."

Game 5

IN GAME NUMBER FIVE, ATLEY DONALD, THE BEARS' STRONG right-hander who won 19 and lost 2 during the regular season, hooked up with left-hander Max Macon (21-12) in a classic mound duel, described by Hy Goldberg of the *Newark News* as "... the most thrilling and best pitched contest of the series."

Surprisingly, in the very first inning, it looked like the Bears were going to send the 22-year-old Macon to an extremely early shower. Joe Gordon and Jimmy Gleeson opened the inning with back-to-back singles. Then George McQuinn dragged a bunt past the outstretched glove of Macon and the bases were loaded with nobody out. Babe Dahlgren, Charlie Keller, and Bob Seeds were the next three power hitters coming up in the inning, which had all the earmarks of something big.

Dahlgren, the next batter up, rapped a sharp grounder to Pat Ankenman at third (Stein, the regular third baseman, had moved to second, replacing the injured Jimmy Jordan). Ankenman fired home to force Gordon at the plate and the slim crowd of over 4,100 took a deep breath. Then Keller, in a rare lapse of concentration, got caught looking at a third strike for the second out. Macon, buoyed by the Keller strikeout, reached back for that something extra and induced the long ball hitting Seeds to roll a weak one out to first. With the bases loaded, none out, and a golden opportunity to bust the game wide open, the Bears had failed to score. Oscar Vitt vividly displayed his utter frustration by throwing his hands up in disgust.

Columbus failed to score in their half of the first, too, after Enos Slaughter singled with one man out. In the second inning, Willard Hershberger led off for the Bears with a single and then stole second. Nolen Richardson and Donald, however, both failed to produce and once again it looked like Macon would get himself out of another jam. But the lefty wasn't as lucky this time. Gordon, the "money" player, singled to left and scored Hershberger.

That one run was all Atley Donald needed. The International League's leading pitcher turned in a "masterpiece." He completely baffled the Red Birds through nine innings, allowing only three singles and one walk. He also struck out six, including Slaughter three times. Donald faced only thirty-one batters out of a possible twenty-seven!

Years later, Spud Chandler recalled this mound performance as the key to the series. "Atley Donald deserves much credit for us winning the series as he pitched the fifth game, beating Max Macon, 1-0."

Jack Fallon agreed. "There was a quiet determination to give it a good shot, and after the great 1-0 win by Atley Donald, we were certain we would win the whole thing."

Atley's excellent pitching performance couldn't have been more timely, either, since young Macon was almost as tough, scattering eight hits and allowing only one run (unfortunately, the losing one). Over the last seven innings, the Columbus left-hander faced only twenty-three Bears.

Thanks to Donald, Newark was still alive, but barely hanging by a thread. It still remained an uphill battle. Complicating the struggle even further was the announcement by Oscar Vitt that Vito Tamulis, the Bears' eighteen-game winner, had a sore arm. The left-hander was scheduled to pitch the sixth game. Vitt would now have to make a crucial pitching selection.

Game 6

IN SPITE OF NEWARK'S TWO CONSECUTIVE VICTORIES, IN GAME number six, Oscar Vitt was confronted with a serious problem. Vito Tamulis, his scheduled starting pitcher, turned up with a lame arm! It was certainly not the time to begin looking for a replacement. But once more, destiny tapped the Bears on the shoulder. Spud Chandler, the ex-Yankee, approached the manager and proudly announced: "You don't have to look any further. I'm ready."

Justifying the selection of Chandler (as if there were a number of options opened to him), Vitt commented, "Spud realized the importance of the game. He knows his own arm better than any one else. If he wasn't sure he could beat those Birds, he wouldn't put himself on the spot or ruin the boys' chances. If his arm doesn't bother him, he is a big league pitcher, and I feel he is going to be a big league pitcher tonight."

Chandler had started the 1937 season with the Yankees, but was troubled by a sore shoulder most of the year. In spite of this, he managed to post a 7-4 record. Then, late in the season while pitching in Cleveland, he injured his arm. The Yankees, in the midst of a pennant race, were doubtful Chandler could pitch any more during the season. To strengthen their pitching staff, they picked up Ivy Andrews from Cleveland for $7,500 and sent Chandler to Newark for the remainder of the season to work out his problem.

Chandler met the challenge head on and pitched a splendid game, scattering seven hits and allowing only one run. Years later, the modest Chandler recalled, "I never felt important to the club as they had it won when I came down from the Yankees. I contributed very little other than relieving in a few games and winning one game in the series. In a way, it was a blessing for me, as my arm responded without any after-stiffness or pain. I knew that I would be ready for the 1938 season..."

And ready he was. Chandler posted a 14-5 record to lead the Yankees to another American League pennant along with team-mates "Red" Ruffing, "Lefty" Gomez, and Monte Pearson.

Chandler's clutch performance, although appreciated, was completely overshadowed by the Bears' relentless offensive machine. The Newark bats, silent most of the series, literally exploded. In an awesome display of batting power, the Bears pounded out fourteen hits, including four doubles and two triples, and scored ten runs.

Mort Cooper started the game and was blasted from the mound before he knew what happened. Doubles by Joe Gordon and a triple by Babe Dahlgren accounted for two quick runs. Newark picked up three more in the fourth, two in the sixth, and led, 7-0, before Chandler gave up a run in the bottom of the sixth inning. The Bears showed no mercy as they added three more runs in the ninth, demolishing Columbus, 10-1, and tying the series at three games apiece. How quickly fortunes can change. Only a few days earlier, the Bears were all but counted out. But with clutch pitching and steady and relentless hitting, Newark was on the brink of achieving the impossible.

Burt Shotton, in a fruitless effort to stop the Bears' attack, followed Cooper with pitchers Max Lanier, Ed Heusser, and Ed Schroeder. By using his pitching staff sparingly, the crafty Shotton was already planning for the final and deciding seventh game. He would have most of his front line pitchers available for duty if needed.

Game 7

AFTER 152 REGULAR SEASON GAMES, EIGHT PLAY-OFF GAMES, AND six Little World Series games, the entire 1937 season for the Newark Bears rested on the seventh and deciding game of the Little World Series. This single contest would determine the champion, the best team in the minor leagues. Oscar Vitt, as he had done all season long when he needed a key victory (even in the play-offs and series), sent Joe Beggs to the mound. Burt Shotton, going with the percentages, chose Nelson Potter, who had pitched extremely well against the Bears in previous series outings. Although the crowd was slim, slightly under 4,000 (it rained hard an hour before game time), the tension throughout the park was evident. This was it. The string had run out. There would be no next game.

Newark drew first blood in the top of the second inning when Charlie Keller walked and scored on Bob Seeds' long double. Columbus failed to come back in the bottom of the inning. In the top of the third, Jimmy Gleeson blasted his first home run of the series, a towering 390-foot shot over the right field wall, for a 2-0 lead. Moments later, the Bears scored another run when George McQuinn walked and Babe Dahlgren and Keller drove him in with singles. Shotton quickly yanked Potter and replaced him with Bill McGee. With Newark leading, 3-0, it looked like another rout as Beggs set the Red Birds down without a run in the third inning. But in the fourth, Columbus finally scored two runs and managed to load the bases with only one out.

That was all for Beggs. In a surprising but shrewd move, Vitt called for the veteran southpaw, Phil Page. In a crucial situation like this, Vitt wanted experience more than anything else. He was playing the percentages all the way. Enos Slaughter and Dick

Siebert, two left-handed batters, were coming to the plate for Columbus. With the left-handed Page, Vitt had the odds stacked in his favor. It appeared to work, too, as Page fanned Slaughter for the second out. The next batter was Siebert, who topped one of Page's deliveries and sent a slow grounder towards second base. Joe Gordon charged, scooped, and flipped the ball all in one motion to nip Siebert for the third out. It was the fielding gem of the game.

In the fifth, Dahlgren singled and Keller doubled him over to third. McGee was now in trouble. Bob Seeds flied to Johnny Rizzo, but when the left fielder dropped it for an error, Dahlgren scored from third. Willard Hershberger then laid down a neat sacrifice bunt that put both Keller and Seeds in scoring position. Nolen Richardson grounded out, but Keller managed to score on the play. Page, adding to his pitching heroics, singled to score Seeds for the third and final run of the inning. The Bears had padded their slim lead to 6-2 and Page proceeded to put the Red Birds down in the bottom of the inning.

In the top of the sixth, the Bears scored three more runs in lightening-like fashion! McQuinn and Dahlgren walked and Keller and Seeds smashed doubles in rapid succession. McGee was through. Columbus was finished. The Newark Bears had achieved the impossible. The final score easily went to Newark, 10-4.

The 32-year-old Page had pitched a whale of a game. He gave up a total of three hits in five and two-thirds innings — the first one coming in the eighth — and allowed single runs in the eighth and ninth. By that time, the game was virtually over.

In the final analysis, the Newark Bears won the Little World Series the same way they had won games throughout the regular season and into the play-offs. It was a combination of brilliant pitching, solid hitting, and tight defense. The Bears won the last four games by scores of 8-1, 1-0, 10-1, and 10-4. They scored 29 runs and collected 46 hits, while Newark's pitching finally showed its class by limiting Columbus to six runs and 27 hits! It was a fitting climax to a miraculous season.

Newark sportswriters summed up the series and the season in these magnanimous words: "It was, in our opinion, the most dramatic triumph in the recent history of baseball — or any sport.''

Another writer simply put it: "Newark baseball club has reclaimed its title — Wonder Team of the minor leagues.''

And finally, there was this flamboyent accolade: "Hail the wonder team! Hail Newark's greatest team! Hail the greatest minor league club ever!''

As a footnote to the baseball era, each of the Newark players received a little more than $600 from the proceeds of the Little World Series, while the losing Red Birds received slightly over $400 apiece. How times have changed!

21.

The Parade

ON OCTOBER 7 AT 4:30 P.M., IT WAS ESTIMATED THAT 3,000 to 5,000 delirious fans awaited the arrival of their beloved Champion Newark Bears at Pennsylvania Station. Over fifty special policemen were assigned duty on the upper platform. Another fifty were needed. Spud Chandler was the first to leave the ballplayers' special Pullman car. Pandemonium broke loose. At the same time, a brass band started in with *Happy Days Are Here Again.*

The railroad police were having a difficult time trying to keep the crowds from being swept off the platform and onto the tracks. The city police had "their hands full keeping the wild-eyed fans, many of them children ranging from 10 to 16, from tearing the clothes from the backs of the Bears."

Through all this bedlam, the players somehow managed to push their way from the depot to the automobiles waiting at the street. There they joined Deputy Mayor William L. Fox on a parade through downtown Newark. With the band still playing *Happy Days Are Here Again,* the cars packed with ballplayers slowly pulled away, maintaining a five-mile-an-hour pace. Every few minutes, mounted police would have to chase away eager youngsters seeking autographs. Some fans even made it as far as the running boards of the cars.

When the parade reached Raymond Boulevard, employees in the Raymond Commerce and Federal Trust Building emptied wastebaskets out of the windows. Others showered ticker tape and bits of paper on their local heroes. The motor parade continued along

Broad Street, past City Hall, and finally wound up at the Parkhurst Hotel.

Later that evening, at the Hotel Commodore in New York City, the players were the guests of honor at a banquet tossed by Jacob Ruppert. They were toasted with the best champagne the Colonel could buy and it was observed that the celebration "compared favorably with the Yankees' World Series victory dinners..." Babe Dahlgren probably best summed up the feelings of everyone in a short but sentimental statement.

"It is a shame that a ball club such as ours can't go on together. Give us another season together and we will win the World Series. But it just can't happen. Never in my seven years was I so sorry to see the season end. Sorry to have to say good-bye to a great bunch of fellows and the best young ballplayers ever assembled."

It was a day and a night that would long be remembered. It was a year never to be forgotten.

L. Bamberger & Co. had the entire 1937 Pennant winning Bears as luncheon guests. Seated at the head table are (l. to r.): Nolen Richardson, Captain; William J. Wells, President of Bambergers; Oscar Vitt, Manager, and Leo Cluesmann, Secretary to Commissioner Michael B. Duffy.

Postscript

THE 1937 NEWARK BEARS DREW THE LAST OF THE GREAT BASEBALL crowds to Ruppert Stadium. In the seasons that followed, even though the Bears produced some exceptional teams and outstanding players, attendance began to drop. Various reasons were cited — increased interest in radio, improved transportation to New York ball parks, and the ultimate crusher, television.

The slide in attendance continued steadily. The 1948 team, which battled for the pennant all season long, drew a total of only 170,560 spectators — less than all but two Double A clubs. At the end of the season, the Yankees placed the franchise on the market. But there were no takers and the Yankees continued to run the club through 1949. Despite a vigorous promotional effort by Parke Carroll, the Bears' General Manager, attendance tumbled to a new low of 88,170 as the Bears finished in the cellar. At the end of the 1949 season, the Yankees again announced the club was for sale.

This time they were successful. On January 12, 1950, the Chicago Cubs purchased the Newark Bears from the New York Yankees. The price for the franchise and players was "variously reported between $450,000 and $500,000." The Cubs planned to move the franchise to Springfield, Massachusetts.

In a terse statement to the press, George Weiss, General Manager of the Yankees, commented, "Attendance did not warrant our continuance of a Newark club in the International League. There could be no doubt about the brand of baseball produced under Yankee ownership, for we had seven league champions."

Mayor Villani of Newark expressed regret that the Bears decided to leave the city. "I'm very sorry to see them go," Villani said. "The City Commission and I did all within our power to induce the

Yankees to keep them here. We hope some day they'll be back in Newark.''

Ruppert Stadium, the scene of so many thrilling baseball games, was now officially empty. Approximately two years later, on December 31, 1952, the Newark Board of Education purchased the stadium from the New York Yankees for a reported $275,000. Six months later, Ruppert Stadium was renamed Newark Memorial Stadium in honor of the Newark citizens "who lost their lives in the defense of freedom.''

Although the City of Newark had honorable intentions and elaborate plans for the stadium, by 1967, the former home of the Newark Bears had sadly deteriorated to a resting place for pigeons. Broken glass, rusted cans, and pieces of brick and wood were strewn about the stands and concrete ramps. The nine tall poles, which once held hundreds of lights, now held nothing. They stood like sentinels guarding memories of the past. Paint was peeling everywhere and splinters protruded from almost every seat.

The final step came in the fall of 1967 when the heavy steel ball of the demolition crew toppled the stadium walls. For some, it marked the beginning of industrial redevelopment in Newark and a new sign of economic growth. For others, the razing of Ruppert Stadium represented the final passing of the Newark Bears and in a much larger sense, a baseball era.

On the evening of June 20, 1979, the Meadowlands Sports Complex in Rutherford, New Jersey was the setting for an event that honored the Newark Bears' organization. Although the ceremony was planned to commemorate a great baseball club, most of the attention centered on the glory team of 1937.

Brendan Byrne, the Governor of New Jersey, and Monte Irvin, who represented Baseball Commissioner Bowie Kuhn's office, payed fitting tribute to the Bears. In attendance were some of the 1937 players who helped write the greatest chapter in the history of minor league baseball — Charlie Keller, Joe Beggs, Jack Fallon, Spud Chandler, Atley Donald, Jimmy Gleeson, Babe Dahlgren, and Marius Russo.

It was a glorious reunion. Wonderful memories were shared and countless baseball stories were swapped. As the players reminisced about their incredible season, they even shed a few tears. It was a legend revisited.

The evening and the team were best summed up by Beggs and Donald. "There's no doubt in my mind that this was the best team in minor league history," remarked Beggs. "It was an incredible team," added Donald.

...and the legend lives on.

Left to right: Joe Gordon, Jack Fallon, and Buddy Rosar. A visit to a St. Petersburg pier after a Yankee spring training workout.

Bibliography

Books

Allen, Lee. *The Cincinnati Reds.* New York: G.P. Putnam's Sons, 1948.

Allen, Lee and Meany, Tom. *Kings of the Diamond.* New York: G.P. Putnam's Sons, 1965.

Barrow, Edward Grant and Kahn, James M. *My Fifty Years in Baseball.* New York: Coward-McCann, 1951.

Baseball Encyclopedia, The. New York: Macmillan, 1976.

Clements, John. *Chronology of the United States.* New York: McGraw-Hill, 1975.

Creamer, Robert W. *Babe.* New York: Simon and Schuster, 1974.

Daley, Arthur. *Inside Baseball.* New York: Grosset & Dunlap, 1950.

Durant, John. *The Yankees: A Pictorial History of Baseball's Greatest Club.* New York: Hastings House, 1949.

Editors of American Heritage. *The American Heritage History of the 20's and 30's.* New York: American Heritage, 1970.

Editors of Time-Life Books. *The Fabulous Century 1930-1940.* New York: Time-Life, 1969.

Feller, Bob. *Strikeout Story.* New York: Grosset & Dunlap, 1947.

Golenbock, Peter. *Dynasty.* Englewood Cliffs, New Jersey: Prentice-Hall, 1975.

Graham, Frank. *The New York Yankees: An Informal History.* New York: G.P. Putnam's Sons, 1943.

Green, Stanley. *Ring Bells! Sing Songs! Broadway Musicals of the 1930's.* New York: Arlington House, 1971.

Honig, Donald. *Baseball Between the Lines.* New York: Coward, McCann and Geoghegan, 1976.

Honig, Donald. *Baseball When the Grass Was Real.* New York: Berkley Publishing, 1976.

Leichtenburg, William E. and Editors of Life. *New Deal and Global War*. New York: New York Times, 1964.

Linton, Calvin D. *The Bicentennial Almanac*. New York: Thomas Nelson, 1975.

Miers, Earl Schenck. *Baseball*. New York: Grosset & Dunlap, 1973.

Mooney, Michael M. *The Hindenburg*. New York: Dodd, Mead and Company, 1972.

Morris, Richard B., Ed. *Encyclopedia of American History*. New York: Harper and Brothers, 1953.

Obojski, Robert. *Bush League*. New York: Macmillan, 1975.

Smith, Robert. *Baseball*. New York: Simon and Schuster, 1970.

Sobol, Ken. *Babe Ruth and the American Dream*. New York: Random House, 1974.

Newspapers

The Newark Evening News. (Newark, New Jersey, 1931-38.)
The Newark Star-Eagle. (Newark, New Jersey, 1931-37.)
The Newark Star-Ledger. (Newark, New Jersey, 1941, 1953.)
The Newark Sunday Call. (Newark, New Jersey, 1931-37.)
The New York Times. (New York, 1937, 1940.)

Articles and Periodicals

"Baseball and Beer: Two of Ruppert's Ventures." *Newsweek*, Vol. 13 (January 23, 1939), 30.

Gross, Milton, "Money Player: Joe Gordon." *Collier's*, Vol. 110 (July 18, 1942), 18.

Other Sources

Mayer, Ronald A. Correspondence with John F. Redding, Librarian, National Baseball Library, Cooperstown, N.Y.

Mayer, Ronald A. Correspondence with Jack Fallon, Quincy, Massachusetts.

Mayer, Ronald A. Correspondence with Spud Chandler, St. Petersburg, Florida.

Index

Abernathy, Woodley, p. 52, 226, 249, 252.

Abreu, Joe, p. 138.

Ainsmith, Eddie, p. 206.

Alexander, Dale, p. 49-51, 53, 54, 58, 171.

Allen, Johnny, p. 152.

Allen, Mel, p. 112.

Alston, Walter, p. 150.

Andrews, Ivy, p. 281.

Ankenman, Pat, p. 278, 279.

Anton, LeRoy, p. 75, 81.

Avila, Bobby, p. 145.

Baker, Bill, p. 59, 69, 89, 93, 126.

Barrett, Bob, p. 27, 28.

Barrow, Ed, p. 10, 13-15, 17, 19, 21, 22, 24, 25, 29, 47, 52, 64, 73, 92, 107, 112, 113, 115, 135, 142, 161, 206-208, 266.

Barton, Vince, p. 41, 44, 50, 52, 58.

Basile, Joe, p. 99, 101.

Beggs, Joe, p. 78, 133, *134*, 135, 136.

Benton, Rube, p. 32-35.

Berly, Jack, p. 187.

Berra, Yogi, p. 122, 123.

Bithorn, Hiram, p. 78, 81, 85, 102.

Blackwell, Ewell, p. 135.

Blair, Lewis, p. 132, 136.

Blake, Sheriff, p. 43-45.

Block, Paul, p. 9-11.

Borowy, Hank, p. 24, 60, 109.

Boudreau, Lou, p. 145, 209.

Bouton, Jim, p. 123.

Boyle, Ralph, p. 68, 69, 79, 86, 88, 119

Bradley, Alva, p. 208, 209, 211.

Bragan, Bobby, p. 145.

Branch, Norm, p. 78, 93, 96.

Braun, F.J., p. 16.

Brennan, Don, p. 31-36, 40-44, 49, 52-55, 150, 155, 158, 163.

Breuer, Marvin, p. 132, 136, 157, 184.

Broaca, Johnnie, p. 42, 43, 45.

Brown, Bobby, p. 174.

Brown, Mordecai, p. 50.

Brown, Walter, p. 49, 51-53, 58, 115, 116, 119, 127, 128, 137, 140, 147.

Bush, Donie, p. 33-36, 205.

Byrne, Brendan, p. 290.

Caldwell, Earl, p. 187, 202.

Campbell, Bick, p. 253.

Cantrell, Guy, p. 27, 28.

Carey, Tom, p. 44, 45.

Carnegie, Ollie, p. 106.

Chambers, John, p. 262, 266.

Chandler, Albert (Happy), p. 262.

Chandler, Spud, p. 24, 68, 71, 107, 152, 175, 201, 202, 204, 215-217, 221, 224, 227, 252, 253, 270, 281, 287, 290.

Chapman, Ben, p. 209.

Chapman, Glenn, p. 252, 254.

Chartak, Mike, p. 153.

Cissell, Bill, p. 165, 250.

Cleveland Crybabies, p. 209-211.

Clymer, Bill, p. 14.

Cobb, Ty, p. 20, 64, 205, 206.

Cohen, Andy, p. 27-29.

Collins, Eddie, p. 116.

Collins, Joe, p. 174.

Combs, Earl, p. 14, 108, 113.

Conlan, John (Jocko), p. 185.

Cook, Earl, p. 238, 239, 242, 243.

Cooke, Dusty, p. 40, 41.

Cook, Jack, p. 74.

Cooper, Mort, p. 173, 262, 272, 273, 282.

Crabtree, Estel, p. 43.

Craft, Harry, p. 226, 234, 235, 238.

Cramer, Roger, p. 94.

Crawford, Sam, p. 64, 205.

Crelin, Wilbur, p. 17, 26, 49.

Cronin, Joe, p. 85, 172.

Crosetti, Frankie, p. 82, 142, 161.

Crouch, Jack, p. 261, 267.

Crouse, Bucky, p. 223, 236, 248, 250, 252.

Cuccinello, Tony, p. 150.

Cullenbine, Roy, p. 153, 161, 261.

Dahlgren, Babe, p. 116-118.

Danforth, Dave, p. 156.

Davis, Harry, p. 190.

Davis, Woodrow, p. 148, 175.

Day, Pea Ridge, p. 35.

Dean, Dopey, p. 95.

DeBarry, Hank, p. 81.

DeShong, Jimmie, p. 41, 43, 45.

Devens, Charlie, p. 41, 42, 50, 52, 53.

Devivieros, Bernie, p. 142.

DeWitt, William, p. 250.

Dickey, Bill, p. 24, 85, 108, 143, 161, 219-221.

DiMaggio, Joe, p. 24, 82, 112, 135, 138, 174, 192, 219, 220.

DiMaggio, Vince, p. 135.

Doerr, Bobby, p. 94.

Donald, Atley, p. 78, 106-110, 163, 169, 170, 183.

Downing, Al, p. 123.

Dressen, Charlie, p. 172, 208, 247.

Ducker, Jack, p. 170.

Duke, Marvin, p. 43, 50, 51, 53, 71, 199.

Durocher, Leo, p. 262.

Dwyer, Joe, p. 216.

Dykes, Jimmy, p. 145.

Ellenstein, Meyer, p. 101, 266.

Essick, Bill, p. 23, 25, 125, 142, 266.

Etten, Nick, p. 173.

Evans, Billy, p. 151.

Fallon, Jack, p. 78, 94, 128, 132, 133, 137, 148, 150, 157, 160, 170, 176, 185, 188, 192, 195, 199, 202, 203. 216, 226, 254, *255*, 275, 280, 290, *291*.

Farrell, Ed, p. 49, 58.

Feller, Bob, p. 112, 209-211.

Ferris, Don, p. 180, 181.

Fisher, Carl, p. 71, 72.

Fitzsimmons, Freddie, p. 220, 221.

Fletcher, Art, p. 14, 91.

Ford, Whitey, p. 24.

Fox, William, p. 101, 287.

Foxx, Jimmy, p. 94, 116, 190.

Gabler, Glen, p. 132, 167.

Gallagher, Joe, p. 75, 79, 85, 89, 202, 203.

Gamble, Lee, p. 234.

Ganzel, Babe, p. 32, 34.

Gavin, Michael, p. 43.

Gehrig, Lou, p. 24, 25, 82, 85, 95, 108, 117, 133, 172.

Gibson, Bob, p. 53, 58.

Gilbert, Wally, p. 45.

Gilder, Elam, p. 32.

Giles, Warren, p. 247.

Gleeson, Jimmy, p. *87*, 119, *120*, 121-123.

Glenn, Joe, p. 52, 53, 122.

Glossop, Al, p. 234, 238, 244.

Glynn, Jack, p. 79, 86, 88, 93, 94, 96, 97, 101, 115.

Goldberg, Hy, p. 132, 164, 239, 256, 279.

Gomez, Lefty, p. 217, 282.

Gordon, Joe, p. 79, *88*, 141-146, *291*.

Gray, Milton, p. 248, 250.

Greenberg, Hank, p. 261.

Grimes, Oscar, p. 161.
Grissom, Lee, p. 135, 191.
Grove, Lefty, p. 85, 156, 193.
Grube, Frank, p. 261, 270.

Harder, Mel, p. 162, 209, 210.
Hargrave, Pinky, p. 146, 150, 151, 155, 160, 165.
Hargreaves, Charlie, p. 26-28, 33-35, 44, 49.
Harper, Earl, p. 188.
Harrelson, Bud, p. 23.
Harris, Spencer, p. 32.
Harvin, Al, p. 26.
Hassett, Buddy, p. 161.
Hassett, John, p. 68.
Hauser, Joe, p. 32, 34.
Hayes, Frank, p. 162.
Heath, Jeff, p. 162.
Heffner, Don, p. 60, 68, 83.
Hemsley, Rollie, p. 209.
Henrich, Tommy, p. 109, 111-113, 138, 146, 147, 173, 192, 193.
Henry, Dutch, p. 34, 36, 44, 45.
Henshaw, Ray, p. 86.
Herr, Eddie, p. 119.
Hershberger, Willard, p. 79, 125-127.
Heusser, Ed, p. 282.
Heving, John, p. 69.
Higbe, Kirby, p. 191.
Hildebrand, Oral, p. 152.
Hill, Carmen, p. 32, 33.
Hill, Jess, p. 27, 28, 31, 33, 36, 49, 50, 51, 53, 58.
Hitchcock, Billy, p. 163.
Hoag, Myril, p. 40-42, 44.
Holly, Eddie, p. 14.
Holm, Billy, p. 78, 81, 95.
Holsclaw, Harry, p. 31, 33, 40.
Holt, Red, p. 121.
Hopp, Johnny, p. 150, 185, 192, 197.
Hornsby, Rogers, p. 50.
Howley, Dan, p. 111, 187, 236.
Hubbell, Carl, p. 182.

Hudson, Johnny, p. 93.
Huggins, Miller, p. 12, 14, 15, 17, 48.
Huston, Tillinghast, L'Hommedieu, p. 12.

Jablonowski, Pete, p. 34, 43, 46, 49.
Jackson, Travis, p. 74-75, 81, 130, 216, 236.
Jensen, Forrest, p. 31, 36, 40.
Johnson, Byron, p. 20, 21.
Johnson, Roy, p. 112.
Johnson, Walter, p. 10, 96.
Johnson, Walter Jr., p. 96.
Jones, Cleon, p. 23.
Joost, Eddie, p. 234, 235, 244.
Jordan, Jimmy, p. 261, 266, 270, 272, 278, 279.
Juelich, Red, p. 185, 192.

Kaufman, Tony, p. 44, 45.
Kelleher, Francis, p. 79, *80*, *88*, 138, 139.
Keller, Charlie, p. *84*, 192-197, *229*.
Kelly, Bill, p. 165.
Kelly, Mike, p. 17, 47, 137, 158, 159, 236, 238, 242, 244.
Kennedy, Ray, p. 49, 65, 73, 89, 92, 93, 110, 115, 127, 128, 136, 196, 208, 224.
Kies, Norman, p. 27, 40, 50, 69, 89.
King, Lynn, p. 260, 261, 267, 273.
Kleinhaus, Ted, p. 58, 60-62, 68, 70-72.
Klumpp, Elmer, p. 132, 137.
Kolp, Ray, p. 137.
Koosman, Jerry, p. 23.
Koy, Chief, p. 69, 93.
Kranepool, Ed, p. 23.
Krichell, Paul, p. 10, 24, 52, 83, 193, 250, 266.
Kuhn, Bowie, p. 290.

Landis, Kenesaw Mountain, p. 112.
Lane, Bill, p. 207, 208.
Lanier, Max, p. 262, 273, 282.
LaRocca, Jack, p. 48, 51, 53, 54, 58, 62, 68, 102, 111, 119.

Lazzeri, Tony, p. 64, 108, 124, 142, 143, 207, 208.
Lee, Hal, p. 81, 130, 132, 216.
Lindell, John, p. 185, 186.
Little World Series, p. 32-36, 64, 259-263, 266-273, *264-265*, 275-285.
Lohrman, Bill, p. 158, 252.
Lombardi, Ernie, p. 126.
Longacre, Ed, p. 79, 82.

Mack, Connie, p. 116, 162, 163, 173, 192.
Macon, Max, p. 262, 266, 269, 279, 280.
MacPhail, Larry, p. 145, 172, 208.
Madura, Frank, p. 127.
Makosky, Frank, p. 51, 58, 59, 62, 69, 128.
Mamaux, Al, p. 10, 15-17, 26, 27, 29-32, 35, 36, 40, 43, 45, 46.
Maranville, Rabbit, p. 151, 198, 199, 236.
Martin, Joe, p. 249, 252.
Martin, Pepper, p. 181.
Matheson, Bill, p. 79, 82, 96, 97, 106.
May, Merrill, p. 75, 79, 81, 89, 94, 97, 98, 119, 132, 136.
McCann, Gene, p. 10, 23, 83, 92, 160, 171, 189, 193, 250, 266.
McCarthy, Joe, p. 10, 24, 89, 91, 94, 108, 112, 116, 117, 129, 139, 143, 144, 160, 161, 163, 175, 190, 217, 221, 222, 224, 250, 251, 266.
McCarthy, John, p. 68, 69, 87.
McCormick, Frank, p. 234, 244.
McCormick, Mike, p. 147, 191, 204.
McGee, Bill, p. 261, 270, 277, 283, 284.
McGraw, John, p. 12, 198.
McGraw, Tug, p. 23.
McKechnie, Bill, p. 126.
McLaughlin, Justin, p. 189.
McQuinn, George, p. 79, *105*, 170-174.
Meyer, Bill, p. 47, 63, 64, 68, 142.
Midkiff, Dick, p. 85.
Miller, Bob, p. 58, 59.
Miner, George, p. 27, 28, 40, 49.

Mitchell, Joe, p. 75, 78, 96.
Moore, Lloyd (Whitey), p. 156, 203, 242.
Morrissey, Joe, p. 54.
Mowry, Joe, p. 32.
Muller, Fred, p. 53, 58.
Mulligan, Joe, p. 62, 124.
Murphy, Johnny, p. 24, 31, 40, 43, 152, 221.
Musial, Stan, p. 221.

Naktenis, Pete, p. 78, 85, 93, 95, 115.
Nee, Johnny, p. 23, 106.
Neun, Johnny, p. 27, 28, 35, 40, 42, 63, 64, 138, 171.
New Haven Colonials, p. 20.
New Haven Club, p. 19, 21.
Newkirk, Floyd, p. 50, 51.
Niggeling, John, p. 202, 203, 226, *243*, 255, 256, 268.
Night Baseball, p. 30, 137, 141.
Nunamaker, Les, p. 206.

Obojski, Robert, p. 177.
Olson, Marvin, p. 41, 49.
O'Neill, Steve, p. 180, 208.
Ott, Mel, p. 122, 123, 135, 136.
Outlaw, Jimmy, p. 234.
Overmire, Stubby, p. 261.
Owen, Marvin, p. 31, 35, 36.
Owens, Lem, p. 170, 171.

Page, Phil, p. 184, 192, 202, 203, 215, 226, *255*, 283, 284.
Parnham, Rube, p. 150, 183.
Pearce, Frank, p. 137.
Pearson, Monte, p. 152, 217, 282.
Pennock, Herb, p. 14, 47, 194.
Perkins, Cy, p. 14.
Perry, George, p. 266.
Petty, Jess, p. 32-34, 36.
Piechota, Al, p. 68, 69, 78, 82, 83, 86, 98, 102, 111, 128-130, 132, 136.
Pipp, Wally, p. 20.

Porter, Dick, p. 59, 61.

Potter, Nelson, p. 262, 266-270, 273, 277, 283.

Powell, Jake, p. 112.

Powers, Les, p. 83, 157, 249.

Puccinelli, George, p. 42-44, 83, 249, 252.

Raimondi, Bill, p. 68, 172.

Reese, Pee Wee, p. 220.

Reiser, Pete, p. 220.

Rhodes, Dusty, p. 129.

Rice, Grantland, p. 143, 144, 146.

Richardson, Nolen, p. 79, 224, 225, *276, 288.*

Rickey, Branch, p. 11, 259, 260, 271.

Rizzo, Johnny, p. 260, 266, 267, 270, 272, 284.

Rizzuto, Phil, p. 24, 161.

Robinson, Murray, p. 238.

Rolfe, Red, p. 24, 27, 28, 31, 33, 35, 36, 40, 41, 44, 82, 161, 196.

Roosevelt Stadium, p. 130, 136, 159.

Rosar, Buddy, p. 79, 160-163, *291.*

Ruffing, Red, p. 109, 217, 219, 282.

Ruppert, Jacob, p. *8,* 9, 11-13, 15-17, 19, 21, 22, 26, 29, 33, 47, 49, 52, 57, 64, 73, 82, 115-117, 152, 196, 208, 247, 259, 260, 266.

Russo, Marius, p. 78, 217, *218,* 219-222, *243.*

Ruth, Babe, p. 12, 13, 20, 47, 48, 59, 92, 108, 182, 194, 207.

Ryan, Rosy, p. 32, 33.

Saltzgaver, Jack, p. 35, 40, 41.

Scarsella, Les, p. 121, 126.

Schalk, Ray, p. 160, 236.

Schalk, Roy, p. 43, 44, 50-52, 58, 68, 69, 88.

Scoffic, Lou, p. 213, 225.

Seaver, Tom, p. 23.

Seeds, Bob, p. 79, *102, 178,* 179, 180-182, *276.*

Selkirk, George, p. 27, 28, 40-42, 45, 46, 50, 52, 82, 85.

Sewell, Joe, p. 14, 47.

Shaughnessy, Frank, p. 39, 40, 101, 148, 149, 252, 253.

Shawkey, Bob, p. 14, 15, 17, 48-55, 58-63, 116.

Shoffner, Milt, p. 27, 28.

Shotton, Burt, p. 262, 269, 270, 282, 283.

Siebert, Dick, p. 173, 261, 267-269, 272, 284.

Sisler, George, p. 118.

Sivess, Pete, p. 157, 254.

Skiff, Bill, p. 63, 64, 89, 160.

Slapnicka, Cy, p. 112.

Slaughter, Enos, p. 260, 266, 267, 272, 273, 277, 279, 280, 284.

Smith, Al, p. 209.

Solodare, Chuck, p. 165, 166.

Souchock, Steve, p. 173, 174.

Speaker, Tris, p. 10.

Spittler, Cecil, p. 58, 78, 128, 139.

Spring Training Schedule, pp. *76-79.*

Stanage, Oscar, p. 205.

Stein, Justin, p. 261, 266, 267, 270, 272, 279.

Stengel, Charles, p. 14, 23, 24, 113.

Steuer, Max, p. 11.

Stoneham, Horace, p. 74, 81.

Street, Gabby, p. 250.

Summers, Bill, p. 28, 35.

Tamulis, Vito, p. *90,* 188-191, 223, 224.

Terry, Bill, p. 118, 182.

Tobin, Jim, p. 89, 91, 95.

Toporcer, Specs, p. 43-46.

Trout, Dizzy, p. 261.

Trucks, Virgil, p. 261.

Tunney, Gene, p. 122.

Vandenberg, Hy, p. 165, 250, 255.

VanderMeer, Johnny, p. 135, 234-236, 240, 241.

Vitt, Oscar, p. 65, *66*, 67, 68, 74-75, *77*,
    78, 81-83, 85-86, 88-89, 91-92, 98, 106,
    111, 130, 154, 204-212, 215, 216, *288*.

Walker, Dixie, p. 26, 27, 31, 32, 36, 40,
    60, 68.
Walters, Bucky, p. 135.
Waner, Paul, p. 235.
Wanninger, Pee Wee, p. 95.
Weatherly, Roy, p. 161, 209.
Weaver, Jim, p. 31, 40-46, 50.
Webb, Jimmy (Skeeter), p. 261, 267.
Weiss, George, p. 19, 20-25, 39-41, 47-49,
    55, 57-60, 63, 65, 73, 89, 115, 132, 136,
    139, 140, 142, 146, 171, 182, 191, 193,
    204, 208, 247, 259, 266, 289.
Whiteman, George, p. 207.
Wicker, Kemp, p. 58, 70, 129, 130, *131*,
    132, 136, 139, 141, 147-149, 156, 159,
    165, 169, 175.
Wilburn, Wimpy, p. 165, 250, 251, 253,
    254.
Witek, Mickey, p. 79, 92, 93, 181.
Wright, Ab, p. 213, 215, 227, 248, 252,
    256.

Yocke, Bill, p. 78, 82, 124, 127, 128, 136,
    137.
Young, Norman (Babe), p. 135.

Ronald A. Mayer has been a baseball enthusiast all his life. He played high school, college, and semiprofessional ball, and coached little league for many years.

Mayer's other books include *Perfect!*, an account of all the perfect games in the major leagues through 1990; *Christy Mathewson*, a game-by-game profile of the Hall of Fame pitcher; and *The New Jersey Book of Lists*, co-authored with Gerald Tomlinson.

A native of New Jersey, Mayer received his B.A. degree from Montclair State College and his M.B.A. from Fairleigh Dickinson University. For 33 years he was employed by the Schering-Plough Corporation in Kenilworth. He resides in East Hanover with his wife, Arlene.